W9-BSW-017

#10366

**Mount Calvary
Lutheran Church
Library**

Mother Teresa's
SECRET
FIRE

Mother Teresa's
SECRET FIRE

The Encounter that Changed Her Life,
and How It Can Transform Your Own

Joseph Langford

Our Sunday Visitor Publishing Division
Our Sunday Visitor, Inc.
Huntington, Indiana 46750

Nihil Obstat: Rev. Michael Heintz, Ph.D.
Censor Librorum

Imprimatur: ✠ John M. D'Arcy
Bishop of Fort Wayne-South Bend
August 25, 2008

The *Nihil Obstat* and *Imprimatur* are official declarations that a book or pamphlet is free of doctrinal or moral error. No implication is contained therein that those who have granted the *Nihil Obstat* or *Imprimatur* agree with the contents, opinions, or statements expressed.

Mother Teresa's words © 2008 Missionaries of Charity c/o Mother Teresa Center, exclusive licensee throughout the world of the Missionaries of Charity for the works of Mother Teresa. Used with permission.

Every reasonable effort has been made to determine copyright holders of excerpted materials and to secure permissions as needed. If any copyrighted materials have been inadvertently used in this work without proper credit being given in one form or another, please notify Our Sunday Visitor in writing so that future printings of this work may be corrected accordingly.

Copyright © 2008 by Joseph Langford. Published 2008

15 14 13   4 5 6 7 8 9

All rights reserved. With the exception of short excerpts for critical reviews, no part of this work may be reproduced or transmitted in any form or by any means without permission in writing from the publisher. Write:

Our Sunday Visitor Publishing Division
Our Sunday Visitor, Inc.
200 Noll Plaza
Huntington, IN 46750

ISBN: 978-1-59276-309-2 (Inventory No. T407)
LCCN: 2007933561

Cover design: Tyler Ottinger.
Cover art: Tekee Tanwar/Getty Images; Marie Constantin.
Interior design: Sherri L. Hoffman.
Interior art: Magnum Photos;
Missionaries of Charity Fathers; Mother Teresa Center.

PRINTED IN THE UNITED STATES OF AMERICA

*"I came to bring fire to the earth,
and how I wish it were already kindled!"*

Luke 12:49
(NRSV)

———

For all those rich and poor,
empty in spirit, pummeled of heart,
who mark the hours
of long inner night —
a night this saint of the gutters traversed
and overcame
before you, and for you:

May these pages reflect
the light that overtook her
one September day,
plunging her, for love's sake,
into the dark
homes and hearts of the poor.

May her gentle, guiding light
born of the heart of the Almighty
be yours:
A light that flies not from darkness —
But ever towards it.

Contents

Foreword

The book you hold in your hands is itself the fruit of an encounter — one that took place years ago, as you will read, through the mediation of a photograph on the cover of a paperback book. As Providence would have it, that seemingly insignificant occurrence progressively involved Father Joseph Langford in Mother Teresa's life and work, to the point of founding with her the Missionaries of Charity Fathers, something for which I personally am particularly grateful. Throughout the years, he has prayed, reflected, and written on the charism — spirituality and mission — given to Mother Teresa for her religious family, striving to discover and articulate its depths and implications, something Mother Teresa herself did not do. This book can be said to be a synthesis of his work. It lays a groundwork for others to follow and build upon, for, as we discovered through her private letters contained in *Come Be My Light*,[†] Mother Teresa's charism, like her holiness, contains unsuspected profundity yet to be fully appreciated.

With his distinctive style and gift of eloquence, Father Joseph delves into the questions about Mother Teresa that shaped his own spiritual journey since that first encounter with her — and through

---

[†] *Mother Teresa: Come Be My Light*, edited and with commentary by Brian Kolodiejchuk, M.C. (New York: Doubleday, 2007).

her, with God — thirty-six years ago. In *Secret Fire*, he not only presents his reflections on what made Mother Teresa who she was and how we, too, can become who we are called to be, but provides meditations that have been a source of grace to many over the years.

In the last years of her life, Mother Teresa would exhort those she met, either individuals or groups, to take up the challenge to strive after holiness: "I want — I will — with God's grace — be — holy." May these pages enrich that striving and encourage you on your way.

FR. BRIAN KOLODIEJCHUK, M.C.
Postulator
Director, Mother Teresa Center
Editor, *Mother Teresa: Come Be My Light*

Fire in the Night

The light shines in the darkness, and the darkness has not overcome it.

—John 1:5

"In the world of today, Mother Teresa has become a sign of God's love. Through her, God has reminded the world of his intense love — his thirst — for mankind and his desire to be loved in return."[1]

— Fr. Brian Kolodiejchuk, M.C.

ONE

Why Mother Teresa?

It seemed as if she had always been there, on the horizon of our awareness, part of the way things should be. There was Mother Teresa, on the covers of our magazines and the back of our minds, touching hearts and mending lives, turning the world upside down without trying. From all around the globe we watched, as her labor of love drew both rich and poor, believer and skeptic, into the shelter of God's embrace.

We followed the unfolding of her life writ large across our newspapers. Her name had become a synonym for compassion and goodness, and she graced our daily lives, from conversations over coffee to sermons on Sunday. Her image added a note of goodness to the evening news, making a home for her not only in Calcutta, but in living rooms around the world. Effortlessly, almost without our noticing, she had made her way into our hearts. As the poor of the world clung to Mother Teresa's sari, and the rulers of nations showered her with accolades, we watched — and in some deepest part of us, we understood. We saw in people all over the globe, and experienced within ourselves, the attraction of her small, humble frame and her vast, resplendent work.

She had become a living icon, a symbol of things better and nobler, a reminder of how we and our world could be. Through the humble portal of her work for the poor, the immense goodness of God poured forth on us all. She became a reflection of God's glory in miniature, like the sun's full radiance dazzling off a tiny shard of glass.

God had sent her to soften the rude landscape of human suffering. She would accomplish this by "being his light" and radiating his love, illuminating the darkness that descends on the bearers of unrelenting hardship.

———

The day it was announced that Mother Teresa of Calcutta had won the Nobel Peace Prize, I had just arrived on campus at Southern Illinois University, where I was chaplain. Within minutes of the announcement, I received a call from Mother Teresa's Sisters in St. Louis, whom I had gotten to know during my chaplaincy. They were asking if I would come over to field questions from the newspaper and TV reporters who were gathering outside their convent. The reporters' comments revealed their understanding, and even delight, at Mother Teresa's nomination. They seemed genuinely intrigued that the prize winner had not been a president, scientist, or politician. For the first time, the Nobel Prize had been won by a diminutive, humble religious woman who worked obscurely in a third-world country. This disruption of the usual order had charmed the world and piqued their curiosity.

But as the days passed, while the world press lauded the Nobel Committee's choice, the professional religious I knew kept asking, "But why Mother Teresa? Aren't there others who do what she does, who serve the poor just as selflessly as she? Why such commotion over *her*?" An excellent question, I thought — and an important one.

The question brought to mind an episode from the life of St. Francis of Assisi. According to the thirteenth-century account, a certain pilgrim had been traversing the hills of Umbria in the hopes of meeting up with the young Francis. After weeks of searching, he finally found himself standing before a very ordinary looking man. Perplexed and disappointed, the young searcher looked intently at Francis and remarked, "Why is the whole world running after *you?*"

———

Indeed. Almost a thousand years later, we could ask the same question: Why was the whole world running after Mother Teresa? How do we explain the phenomenon of a Nobel Prize-winning, elderly Albanian nun, with no particular qualifications and no extraordinary talents? How do we account for her immense, seemingly universal impact? How do we explain the power of an attraction that only grew throughout her life, and continues still?

To answer the "why" of Mother Teresa's power of attraction, and to understand her relevance in our post-modern world, we need to examine both her and ourselves more deeply. We need to ask what it was in her that moved us so, and what it was in us that responded so readily. What hidden chords of soul was she touching? What was *God* touching in us, through her?

Understanding what she touched in us is significant, since it points to and constitutes our common ground with her. The unnamed place that she awakened in us reveals an interior terrain, a sacred inner ground that we share with her — placed within us by the One who fashioned us for himself.

Is the same divinity that claimed such unrestricted space in her heart, there beneath the surface of our soul as well? If so, why do we not advert to it, or attend to it as she? Perhaps because, in the main, we inhabit but the surface of ourselves. And so we can be surprised at times by the power of our response to deeper things, to sudden incursions of the divine, to unexpected touches of grace.

For many of us, discovering Mother Teresa, watching her or hearing her speak, became just such an incursion of the divine. She became a portal and guide to our neglected realms of spirit — and to meeting the God who awaits us there.

———

How do we account for the phenomenon of Mother Teresa, for the impact and attraction she wielded, even among the agnostic and unchurched? What was her secret? What made her who she was? What formed and inspired her? What hidden inner fire motivated her and drew her on, in the most squalid conditions, to become the saint she was?

And what of ourselves? Can we become for others a source of the same kind of goodness we saw in her? Can her inner fire yield a similar light and warmth in us?

Answering these questions is the purpose of this book.

———

Thankfully, Mother Teresa has left clear and abundant clues — clues that allow us not only to understand, but to share in the secret of her goodness, in the secret of her transformation from ordinary schoolteacher, to Nobel laureate, to saint. For those who would wish to emulate her, her life and teachings are replete — as we will see in these pages — with signs that point the way to finding her same happiness, her same fulfillment, and her same union with the Almighty.

The riches of Mother Teresa's example and teaching are more abundant than any single volume can hold (the documents used in her cause for sainthood comprise more than eighty volumes). While future volumes will explore other themes from her teaching, the scope of this book is limited to what Mother Teresa herself considered the core of her message.

This present volume is divided into three sections. The story of the inner fire that changed Mother Teresa's life is told in this first section, "Fire in the Night." The second section, "Illumination," introduces the festival of light issuing from this inner fire, a light that illumined the face of God for her — and through her, for so many. The final section, "Transformation," shows how her "consuming fire" within (Heb 12:29) changed a young and unsure Sister Teresa into Mother Teresa, and how it can transform us as well.

"Through the tender mercy of our God,
    ... the day shall dawn upon us from on high
to give light to those who sit in darkness and
    in the shadow of death."

— Luke 1:78-79

TWO

A Life Bathed in Light

After Mother Teresa's passing in 1997, a world that had come to admire her was hungry for details of her remarkable life. A multitude of books and articles appeared in those ensuing years, chronicling every aspect of her person and life, from her public accomplishments to the private mystery of her inner darkness. But as celebrated as she was in both life and death, after all these years Mother Teresa's central message, and the one great secret of her soul, remains almost entirely unknown.

What was deepest in her, what motivated and energized her, is still a mystery even to her most ardent admirers. But it was not her wish that this secret remain forever unknown. The answer to her mystery is there, like a golden thread, woven throughout the teachings she left for her religious family, particularly in the months leading up to her death. Scattered throughout Mother Teresa's letters and spiritual conferences, the full richness of her soul still awaits us.

Looking Back on an Extraordinary Life

Before exploring the secrets of this saint and Nobel Prize winner, let us step back a moment to review the highlights of her extraordinary life — as a refresher for those who may have forgotten the broad strokes of her life, and for the sake of a new generation that has not known Mother Teresa beyond name and renown.

Mother Teresa began life as *Gonxha Agnes Bojaxhiu*, the youngest of three children of an Albanian family, born August 26, 1910, in Skopje (in present-day Macedonia). In elementary school she developed a keen interest in the overseas missions, and by the age of twelve the future missionary had decided to devote her life to helping others. Later, at age eighteen, inspired by reports sent home from West Bengal by Jesuit missionaries, she applied to join the Sisters of Loreto, whom she had learned were doing mission work in India, and specifically in West Bengal.

She left home and entered the convent, and after completing her first stage of training with the Loreto Sisters in Rathfarnham, Ireland, took the religious name of Teresa (after her patron saint, Thérèse of Lisieux). Not long thereafter, the young Sister Teresa left Ireland and sailed for Calcutta, where she arrived in January 1929. She was assigned to the Loreto convent in Entally, in northeastern Calcutta, and began teaching geography in their middle school for girls. Her love for her new mission and the people of Bengal moved her to master the language, becoming so proficient that she was awarded the nickname "Bengali Teresa."

As the years went by, her desire to lift up the poorest moved her to venture into the slums on the other side of the convent wall. Having enlisted the help of her students, together they sought to bring to the poor what little aid and comfort they could. Her life went on this way, happily and productively by all accounts — divided between teaching class, mentoring her pupils, and reaching out to the poor — up until 1946, the eve of Indian independence.

"Come, Be My Light"[2]

On September 10, 1946, following her yearly custom, Mother Teresa left Calcutta for eight days of spiritual retreat — what was presumably to be a retreat like any other. At Howrah Station, she boarded the train that wound its way from steamy Calcutta and the broad, flat plains of the Ganges Delta, north into the verdant forests and cool nights of the Himalayan hills. Once again this year, Sister Teresa had left behind her work and her students to dedicate herself to prayer and reflection in the hill station of Darjeeling, where the Loreto Sisters had their retreat house, praying over what had taken place during the past semester, and preparing herself for the new school year to come.

Somewhere along the way, Mother Teresa had an extraordinary experience of God (explored more fully in the next chapters). In her characteristic humility, she would refer to this life-changing experience as simply "*a call within a call,*"[3] a call to leave Loreto and go into the slums. Only later would she reveal more of what transpired in her soul that September day, and of the extraordinary interior communications during the following year and a half, in which Jesus would commission her to "carry him" and "be his light" in the darkness of Calcutta's slums.

Returning to Calcutta shortly after her retreat, she consulted with her Jesuit spiritual director, sharing with him the notes she had made during her days of prayer. He advised her to communicate directly with the archbishop of Calcutta, asking for permission to leave her order and work alone, unaided but unfettered, in the streets of Calcutta.[4]

After long months of discernment and discussion, with letters back and forth, permission was suddenly given. Once she was free, Mother Teresa traveled to nearby Patna for a course in first aid and simple nursing. In December 1948, she returned again to Calcutta, dressed for the first time in the humble white cotton sari that would become her emblem. Alone, with only five rupees to her name (about $1 U.S.), she sought hospitality with the Little Sisters of the Poor, from whose convent she began going daily out into the slums.

She first returned to Moti Jhil, the vast slum she was used to seeing just outside her convent wall. Since she had been trained as a teacher, she began by starting a school for the children of the poor, using the ground as a blackboard, and a tree as roof and shelter. As rewards for attendance she gave out bars of hand soap, since her pupils' ragged clothing and unhygienic conditions were invitations to disease and early death.

In February 1949, a Bengali Catholic named Michael Gomes lent her a room in his house on Creek Lane. She moved in with a small suitcase and arranged a space for sleeping and working, with one packing case for a chair and another for a desk. As word spread of her one-woman outreach to the poor, people who had known her in Loreto began contributing to her new mission.

On March 19 of that year, one of Mother Teresa's former students, Subashini Das (who later took the religious name of Agnes, in honor of Mother Teresa's baptism saint), came to the home on Creek Lane and asked to join her. A few weeks later, another ex-student, Magdalena Gomes (Sister Gertrude), joined as well. By Easter, there were three women dressed alike in white blue-bordered saris, going together each morning to serve in Moti Jhil. By the time the group had grown to twelve, and no longer fit in their lent room, Mother Teresa and her little group were invited to take over an entire floor in the Gomes home.

Eventually, their slum school was moved from beneath a tree to a rented building. But she and her Sisters-to-be had encountered a new challenge. While on their way each day to Moti Jhil, they were coming across unexpected numbers of the dying — struggling for their last breath alone, penniless, and homeless in the alleyways of Calcutta:

> Mother Teresa's fledgling Missionaries of Charity had to pass the bodies of the destitute dying in the lanes and gutters of the city. A dirt-floored room was rented in Moti Jhil where a few dying men and women could be cleaned, fed and cared for until they recovered or passed on.

The city fathers of Calcutta, overwhelmed with immense human need and lack of resources, welcomed the work of these young Indian women and offered [them] a building. It was a hostel for pilgrims to the shrine of *Kali*, Hindu goddess of destruction and purification — two large halls opening on an inner courtyard.

City ambulances began to bring destitute men and women to the hostel. Because of its proximity to Kali's temple and the nearby *ghats* (cremation places), it was called *Kalighat*, a name applied to that section of Calcutta.

Already by the mid-1950s the Sisters in their blue-bordered white saris were a distinctive part of the great sprawling city. They trooped out in the morning, two by two, to feed homeless families, chiefly refugees, to a dozen slum schools, to the *Home for the Dying*, and to children's clinics in the worst slums.

In the Home for the Dying, Mother Teresa and her Sisters leaned over cadaverous men and women, feeding them slowly and gently. They lay side-by-side on a raised parapet, in separate wards, with a walkway in the center of the hall. Mother Teresa would go from patient to patient, sitting beside them on the parapet, giving them human comfort by holding their hands or stroking their heads.

"We cannot let a child of God die like an animal in the gutter," she declared. When asked how she could face this agony and serve these suffering people day after day, she answered, "To me, each one is Christ — Christ in a distressing disguise."[5]

The quantity of work and the number of her Sisters began to grow apace. She was invited to open new foundations in other parts of India, and soon extended her work to the rest of the world — beginning in Venezuela, in 1965. By the time of her death in 1997, her Missionaries of Charity had spread to more than 120 countries.

As she traveled to establish missions in other parts of the world, Mother Teresa soon discovered that the West was no less indigent, though its poverty better disguised, than what she had found in the Third World:

> In the developed world, in Europe and in the United States, the sisters had to deal with a different kind of need. Mother Teresa explained, "I found the poverty of the West so much more difficult to remove. When I pick up a person from the street, hungry, I give him a plate of rice, a piece of bread, I have satisfied, I have removed that hunger."
>
> In the West, she said, "there is not only hunger for food. I see a big hunger for love. That is the greatest hunger, to be loved."[6]

By the early 1970s, her work was being recognized and honored by religious and secular authorities alike. Most notably, she was awarded India's highest honor, the *Bharat Ratna* (the Jewel of India), as well as a host of accolades and honorary degrees from governments and institutions around the world — crowned by the Nobel Peace Prize, in 1979.

Mother Teresa went on to found five separate religious communities for the care of the poor. Along with the Sisters, founded in 1950, she began a male branch, the Missionaries of Charity Brothers, in 1966; then the Contemplative Sisters (dedicated to prayer and intercession for the poor), in 1976; the Contemplative Brothers, in 1979; and finally, as the child of her old age, the Missionaries of Charity Fathers, founded in 1984 to serve the inner pain and spiritual poverty of those served by her Sisters and Brothers.

In June 1983, while visiting her Sisters in Rome, she was hospitalized for a chronic and untreated heart condition. Over the next decade her health gradually but steadily weakened, though she would always rally and take up her exhausting schedule yet again. Finally, in

March 1997, her deteriorating condition forced her to resign as head of her order. A few short months later, on September 5, at 9:30 in the evening, Mother Teresa breathed her last — she had "gone home to God."

Not long after her passing, with the approval of Church authorities and at the insistence of faithful the world over, Mother Teresa began her journey on the path to sainthood, that last and ultimate stage from which to lift up the light she had carried all her life — no longer for the poor alone, but for us all.

—

Mount Calvary
Lutheran Church
Library

Mother Teresa's inner light drew our attention not only to her work for the poor, but to the city that had become part of her name, and part of a new vocabulary of compassion. She focused the eyes of the world on the open wound that was Calcutta in the 1950s — a sprawl of burgeoning slums and bustling sidewalks, seemingly forgotten by God and man. Calcutta was to be the divinely appointed backdrop for her work and her message, symbol of the wounds of the entire human family.

But Calcutta was likewise a symbol of the wounds of each human soul, of each of the least, the last, and the lost the world over — trampled upon and forgotten in modern society's rush towards a life free from suffering. But it is precisely there that Mother Teresa remained, rooted and anchored to the very places of pain we fled. Where there was no love, she put love. Where there was no hope, she sowed seeds of resurrection. She turned Calcutta, at least for those she was able to touch, into a true "City of Joy." Many saw — and many, from the beggar at her feet to the Nobel Committee half a world away, understood. The draw, the mystery, and the phenomenon of Mother Teresa and her mission had begun.

In Calcutta's night, a light was rising.

*The people who sat in darkness
have seen a great light, and for those who sat in
the region and shadow of death
light has dawned.*

— Matthew 4:16

THREE

Calcutta: Backdrop to an Epiphany

Calcutta sunrise. Even at this early hour, noisy, bustling, hot.

Humidity rides the air; from the shops of Chowringee to the hovels of Moti Jhil, it clings to the waking city like second skin. This is the hot breath of Kali — evil goddess who devours her husbands — for whom legend suggests the city was named.

Calcutta's sixteen million inhabitants begin to stir. Many wake to another day on the sidewalks, huddled under cardboard and tattered cloth. Out in the streets, Calcutta's traffic begins to move and swell, like a great sea overflowing its borders. Along the lanes and side streets, diesel fumes mix with sandalwood and the sweet smell of cooking fires, far away.

Crows caw noisily overhead, perched in trees and on housetops, arrogant and oblivious. Down on the sidewalk, men squat on the cracked cement smoking *bidis* and shooing flies, as they pore over the morning paper. Further up the road near Sealdah station, vendors display their wares piled high and spilling onto the footpath, circled by a moving sea of sandals and bare feet.

Along the sides of the road, rickshaw pullers run, swallowed up in smoke and traffic. Sun-bronzed and wizened they go, carrying the uniform-clad children of wealthy families to their private schools, while dodging walkers and hawkers and trams. Huge steel-sided buses ply the main roads, coughing and straining. They hurtle down the streets swollen to overflowing, with riders perched on the sides and hanging out windows and open doors. At each stop, they slow to a crawl, disgorge their passengers, and take off again spewing billows of smoke. Auto-rickshaws weave in and out of traffic, dodging and darting like insects, avoiding oncoming cars by inches and seconds.

Further out on the periphery, barefoot men push their handcarts, piled high and bound for market. They trudge on, amid clouds of mosquitoes, incessant horns, and the non-stop buffeting of passing trucks and speeding buses.

There, on the outskirts of the city, begin the slums that are Mother Teresa's Calcutta, notorious for their pavement dwellers, street children, scavengers, and disease. Though greatly improved in recent years, in Mother Teresa's time this area had become a cliché for the worst of human poverty. This would be Mother Teresa's domain for the rest of her days — her meeting place with God in the poor, and our meeting place with God in her.

———

To gain a better idea of what Mother Teresa faced when she stepped out of the convent with five rupees in her pocket, let us take a closer look at one of the more famous of Calcutta's slums, the ironically named "City of Joy," which once claimed one of the densest concentrations of humanity on the planet: two hundred thousand people per square mile:

> It was a place where there was not even one tree for three thousand inhabitants, without a single flower, a butterfly, a bird, apart from vultures and crows — it was a place where children did not even know what a bush, a forest, or a pond was, where the air was so laden with carbon dioxide and sulfur that pollution killed at least one member in every family; a place where men and beasts baked in a furnace for the eight months of summer until the monsoon transformed their alleyways and shacks

into lakes of mud and excrement; a place where leprosy, tuber-
culosis, dysentery and all the malnutrition diseases, until recently, reduced the average life expectancy to one of the lowest in
the world; a place where eighty-five hundred cows and buffalo
tied up to dung heaps provided milk infected with germs. Above
all, however, [it] was a place where the most extreme economic poverty ran rife. Nine out of ten of its inhabitants did not
have a single rupee per day with which to buy half a pound of
rice.... Considered a dangerous neighborhood with a terrible
reputation, the haunt of Untouchables, pariahs, social rejects, it
was a world apart, living apart from the world.[7]

Even amid such extreme poverty, Mother Teresa discovered in
the poor of Calcutta a nobility of character, a vitality of family ties
and cultural wealth, and an inventiveness and ingenuity that made
her genuinely proud. *"The poor are great people,"* she vigorously insisted. These were people she deeply admired, and of whom she was
undyingly fond. She insisted that the two-way exchange that passed
between her and the poor of Calcutta was forever tipped in her favor;
that she received much more than she gave, and was ever more
blessed than she was blessing.

Children sleeping under a portrait of Mother Teresa (Raghu Rai/Magnum
Photos)

Volunteers

After their day's work in the slums, Mother Teresa and her Sisters would return to north-central Calcutta. Here was Mother House, her headquarters, from which hundreds of Sisters would go forth each day to give comfort and care.

Once her mission began to be known outside of India, young people from far and near began offering to help with her work in Calcutta. From all over the world they came, young volunteers in Mother Teresa's army of love, giving a week or a month or more to help her Sisters serve the poorest of the poor.

Every morning the faces of these young foreigners could be seen moving along the swarming sidewalks, walking up Lower Circular Road on their way to morning Mass with Mother Teresa and her Missionaries of Charity. Later, after a breakfast of *chapattis* (Bengali flatbread) and home-brewed chai, they would set out for the Kalighat, with its narrow lanes and shop fronts festooned with flower garlands for the gods, on their way to the Home for the Dying. Here they would spend their days changing bandages, comforting the sick, and tending to the dying, alongside Mother Teresa's Sisters and Brothers.

After their initial struggles with the heat and the food and the difference of culture, these mostly First World youth would often find a new joy and sense of purpose stirring within — an experience often denied them by their affluent life abroad. As the days melted into weeks under Calcutta's merciless sun, they would slowly discover that while they were touching the poor of Calcutta, God himself was touching the less-accessible, less easily admitted poverty of their own souls. Changed from within, they would return home with new answers and a new peace. But they arrived with new questions as well; questions about the life-changing closeness to God they had experienced amid the squalor and hardships of Calcutta. Questions, too, about the smiling, sari-clad woman who had gently opened their hearts to God. Who was this Mother Teresa, and what made her special? What inner flame did she carry that had kindled their hearts, and brought light into their darkness?

In the Darkness, Light

But before investigating her light, some may ask: How could there be such luminosity in someone whose interior was buffeted by darkness?

Looking back over her life and the documents that have emerged since her death, it is clear that Mother Teresa's inner (and outer) world was a place in which the brilliance of God's light and the bleakness of man's darkness met and mingled — from which her victorious light only shone the brighter. What emerged from that inner struggle was a light in no way lessened by her bearing the cloak of humanity's pain, but a light all the more resplendent, and all the more approachable. The kind of divine light we saw in her was no more the restricted domain of mystics and sages, but a light entirely accessible to the poorest, beckoning to God's brightness all who share in the common human struggle.

In the wisdom of the divine plan, God sent Mother Teresa into the Calcuttas of this world — large and small, visible and hidden — so that precisely there, where our world (our inner world as well) appeared its darkest, the light he gave her might shine most brightly. Even more than to bring his comfort to the poor, God sent Mother Teresa to *be his light*. He invited her to pitch her tent in the blackest of places, not to build hospitals or high-rises, but that she might shine with his radiance.

Mother Teresa's darkness was neither deviation nor mistake. Rather than being a divine miscue, her journey through the night had a definite and deeper purpose in God's plan. Besides bringing her to share the dark struggle of Jesus on the cross, and the struggle of the poorest of the poor around the world, her darkness was intended as a light for the rest of us. Her night was a metaphor for the blackness of our "vale of tears," a cartographer's map etched on her soul to lead us through our own spiritual darkness into divine light. Paradoxically, her darkness became the vehicle for a much greater light, a light it could neither conquer nor contain, but only amplify, as it passed through her soul as through a prism.

A Message Meant for All

The energy and impetus for her new life came not only from her encounter on the train to Darjeeling, but from the *message* God had communicated to her there — a message revealing the immensity of his love for us, especially in our weakness and struggles. Throughout her life, Mother Teresa would cherish this message in her heart, and model it in all she did.

Mother Teresa shared her message with all who would hear — from Haiti's President Jean-Claude "Baby Doc" Duvalier, who had forgotten his own people starving outside his palace, to the rumpled man on L.A.'s skid row who had forgotten his own name. She knew that the greater our need, the greater our inner or outer poverty, the greater even our sin and moral failings, all the greater was God's yearning for us. For Mother Teresa, the impulse that led the Good Shepherd to leave the ninety-nine and go in search of a single lost sheep was no longer a mystery, for she had experienced it herself; the same divine impetus had taken possession of her life.

In the months following Mother Teresa's Nobel Prize, I offered to show the film portraying her work, *Something Beautiful for God* (later a book by the same name), to any group that was interested. I was invited to churches, civic organizations, schools, and gatherings of every sort — only to find the audience in tears by the end, so moved that they would queue up to offer me donations to send to Calcutta. I was witnessing not just the attraction of Mother Teresa, but the perplexity she caused, as people struggled with the new-found surge of generosity welling up inside them. Curiously, most of the audience seemed unable to find any deeper, more enduring response beyond tears and a hurried check.

Once I understood that people had difficulty extracting Mother Teresa's message simply from what they saw on screen, I began giving a talk after the film — trying to help them make sense of what they had seen, and deal with the intense feelings the film had stirred up in them. I told them what Mother Teresa herself would have said — that there was no need to go abroad, nor even across town, to imitate her or to do something significant with their lives. She would have pointed to the suffering in the hidden Calcuttas all around them — in their own homes and families and neighborhoods, in the blind man down the street or in the unforgiven relative, forgotten behind the walls of a nursing home. These were all Calcuttas-in-miniature, where Christ, hidden under his *"distressing disguise,"* awaits our *"hands to serve and hearts to love."* As Mother Teresa reminded every audience she addressed, whatever we do to the least of our brothers and sisters, we do it *to him* (cf. Mt 25:31-46).

Calcutta's extremes of physical poverty, and the inner pain it brought to the hearts of the poor, were largely foreign to Western audiences. It took a new level of understanding for people to transpose Mother Teresa's heroic charity in far-off Calcutta into small, seemingly un-heroic gestures of goodness and compassion in their own lives and limited surroundings. They were being challenged to alleviate the *same pain of spirit* they had seen on the screen, but hidden this time behind the manicured lawns and peaceable facade of their own neighborhood.

Only by explaining the applications of Mother Teresa's message to every life did my audiences begin to bridge the gap between Calcutta and home, between the material poverty of the third world and the spiritual poverty that was theirs. In the end, God was asking of them, and of us, the same kind of generosity lived by Mother Teresa — only lived in a different setting, and practiced in a different way.

Mother Teresa never asked or expected her hearers to contribute to her work by sending a check — instead, she would suggest that they "Come and see" the work of her Sisters, and learn to spend time with the poor and needy, to give of their heart and not just their pocketbook. Writing a check was easily done, and easily done with. It allows us to do "charity," while keeping at bay the inner tug that urges us to give more of ourselves and our time, rather than our possessions. This was the challenge people faced, as they discovered that the tug of conscience and heart Mother Teresa awakened both frightened and fascinated them at once.

Mother Teresa would point out that no matter how noble our intentions in giving monetarily, both God and neighbor needed more and better. God had not sent us a check in our need, but his Son. He gave of himself, without measure — as any of us can, anywhere we are, and whenever we choose. *We are the ones* called to help those around us, not Mother Teresa, not her Sisters in the far corners of the Third World, who have already done their part and more. We are the ones already there, living on the same street, in the same neighborhood, where so much hidden suffering and need go unheeded. We are the ones sent by God, anointed and equipped to give of ourselves to those he has placed around us. We need no special abilities or resources to do the work of love; we need *"only begin,"* even in the smallest ways. Mother Teresa knew that even the smallest seeds of charity could yield a rich and lasting harvest, had we but the courage to roll up our sleeves and begin. She would invite her audience to take some concrete step, no matter how small, to serve those around them, to put God's love and theirs into *"living action."*

In deference to the invitation of her friend, Pope John Paul II, Mother Teresa spent the greater part of her later years sharing this message with audiences worldwide, from kindergartens to the plenum of the United Nations. John Paul had asked her to proclaim God's love especially in those places where he could not go — places ravaged by war and hardship, and wherever political realities prevented him from visiting, such as the then Soviet bloc, and the vast expanse of the Muslim world.

If Mother Teresa's encounter and message were of such importance, why haven't we heard of them — or why have we heard so little? The main reason is that she chose to live out the grace of her encounter in her own life first, in silent service to the neediest, before sharing it with her Sisters or the world. Because of her long silence, not only the importance of her message but its very existence may come as a surprise, even to her admirers. This had been her great secret, from 1946 on. This was the inner flame that led her through her dark night of the soul, just as the column of fire that led Israel through the desert long ago.

Apart from the grace of Mother Teresa's encounter on the train, nothing adequately explains her. Nothing else can fully account for the life she led, or the extraordinary things she accomplished. Mother Teresa was more than merely a female Albert Schweitzer. She was above all a mystic, although a mystic with sleeves rolled up, whose spirit scaled the heights even while her body bent lovingly over the downtrodden and the dying. By exploring the secrets of her deep mysticism in the chapters to come, those who already knew Mother Teresa will know her better, and those who knew her only via the media will come to know her soul.

Her encounter and its message were, in the divine plan, more for us than for her. While this book is about the transformation Mother Teresa's encounter produced in her soul, more than anything else it is about *God* and about *the reader* — about what Mother Teresa learned about God and how he sees each one of us, how he longs for intimacy with us, and for the chance to remake our lives as he did hers. More than about God's message to Mother Teresa, this book is about God's message *through* her, to you who read these lines. It is surely her hope, from her place in the kingdom, that this message laid once gently on her soul, and retold in these pages, might touch and transform your life even as it did hers.

"The experience of 10th September is [something] so intimate. . . ."[8]

— Mother Teresa

FOUR

A Message Discovered

First Encounter

I can never forget August 17, 1972; it was the day Mother Teresa would change my life. I had gotten up that morning knowing nothing about her. I had never seen her face, never heard her name.

I had recently arrived in Rome to begin theological studies and, booklover that I am, found my way, almost immediately off the plane, to one of the large bookstores near St. Peter's Square. While browsing in the upstairs English section, my gaze fell on the cover of one particular book. Suddenly, my attention, and my whole being it seemed, was seized by the image looking back at me from this book. There, on the cover of this small paperback was the face of Mother Teresa — though at the time I had no idea who it was. Her countenance seemed somehow alive and engaging, almost three-dimensional. There was a goodness in her face, a kindness in her gaze, something appealing and deeply soul-soothing that was tugging at deep places in my spirit, places rarely touched. I felt as if she were looking through me, drawing me; and I found that I could not, I did not want to, resist.

Still shaken by what had taken place — more like a meeting with a living person than having stumbled across a book — I picked up the tiny volume, noticed its title (*Something Beautiful for God*, by Malcolm Muggeridge), paid for it, and made my way outside. I sat down at the bus stop, lost in thought, drinking in the goodness radiating from her countenance, reflected in page after page of photos depicting her work in the slums of Calcutta.

Who was this woman? How had she managed, in an instant, to touch the deepest part of me? How had she suddenly brought me to the end of a lifelong search, when I wasn't even aware that I was searching? How had her photo on the cover of a book brought me face-to-face with divinity, and stirred up in me a new hope in what was best in mankind, and in myself? If it took the rest of my life, I was determined to find out.

Such was my first encounter, mediated by a book, with the woman who had already changed so many lives, and was about to change my own.

Journey of Discovery

That first vicarious encounter launched me on a personal quest: I was determined to discover what it was that I had seen in her — and more, to learn what had made her who she was. How had Mother Teresa become Mother Teresa? My hope was that the goodness I saw in her might somehow be reproduced, in myself and others. I reasoned that if her secret was understood, those who admired her around the world might have a better chance of emulating her.

But to begin my quest I needed direction. I needed a starting point.

I began by approaching the Sisters and Brothers of the Missionaries of Charity stationed there in Rome. From them I learned that the key to understanding Mother Teresa lay in the two simple words she placed on the wall of her chapels around the world — Jesus' words from the cross: "I thirst" (Jn 19:28).

In each of her chapels I had visited in Rome, or seen in books depicting her work, there were always those same words written large beneath the cross. Carved in wood, painted on plaster, or cut from paper, the same mysterious words spoke silently of some great truth that had apparently been Mother Teresa's anchor and inspiration.

At the time, none of the biographies of Mother Teresa ventured to guess where, when, or why these words had entered her soul with such force; why she continued to place them so prominently for all to see; or what exactly they represented for her. While no one disputed their importance, their meaning in Mother Teresa's spirituality was not clear, even to the authors who lauded her most. Were these words part of some longstanding devotion? Did they come out of her early religious upbringing, or her training in Loreto? Or did they represent some personal, even mystical experience — since she was obviously a woman of deep prayer. Could it be that, unbeknown to all, she was not only a missionary but also a mystic?

I had already learned, both from reading and from the Sisters in Rome, that the inspiration for Mother Teresa's work with the poor had come from an extraordinary grace she received on a train ride to Darjeeling in 1946. But she explained that as simply God's call to leave her convent and to work in the slums — with no mention, no reference to the words she had placed on the wall, "I thirst." I began to wonder if more had happened that day on the train than she was letting on. At least it represented a place to begin my search.

As I started to ask questions about her grace of the train, I was told that Mother Teresa spoke of it very little and very reluctantly. Many years later, she would confide that she considered her experience of September 10 so intimate, and her own person of so little importance, that she preferred to talk around the subject rather than about it. Among the Missionaries of Charity, it was understood that the one thing you could not ask Mother Teresa was about the grace of the train. She would deflect the question, and speak only of a divine "command" to go into the slums to serve the poor. While true, this was but half the story, hiding under a mantle of silence the magnitude of what had transpired in her soul.

With few exceptions, her silence continued unabated throughout her early years. She was content to allow her wordless love for the poor, together with the silent words of Jesus placed on the chapel wall, to speak for her. Her most revealing comments would come only later, as the time of her passing drew near.

And so I found my first attempts to know Mother Teresa more deeply being thwarted by mystery, and this became both a challenge and a blessing. At the time, only two things were clear. First, that "something" extraordinary had happened on the train to Darjeeling, something that had changed her life. Second, that once she had left the convent and was free to do so, she placed the words "I thirst" next to the crucifix in Mother House. But there was still a veil of secrecy over what actually had happened on the train, and over the enigmatic origin of these words on the chapel wall.

As my association with Mother Teresa grew over the ensuing years, however, I was given the opportunity to delve more deeply into her letters and conferences, and was able to begin an ongoing conversation with her that would eventually reward my search, even beyond my hopes.

A Second Quest

During my studies in Rome, I had begun to volunteer at the homeless shelter run by Mother Teresa's Sisters near the Colosseum. During those years, and later after ordination, I was blessed with the opportunity to spend time with Mother Teresa during her frequent stops in Rome on her way from Calcutta to her various missions around the world. While I continued my quest to understand her inner fire, another quest was growing within me, even more unexpected than the first.

On one of her many visits to Rome (Ferdinando Scianna/Magnum Photos)

That first day in the bookstore, as I held *Something Beautiful for God*, I knew in my heart that I not only wanted to know all I could about Mother Teresa, but I also wanted to somehow dedicate my life to her work. While my first quest had proved difficult, the second was impossible. There was no branch of her religious order for priests, and in her advanced age she seemed in no position to start such a venture (her Sisters and Brothers had already been founded thirty years earlier). But as this desire would not disappear, my growing acquaintance with Mother Teresa reached a point where I was comfortable enough to mention the idea of beginning an order of priests devoted to her mission. Ironically, it would be this second, more improbable quest that would be realized first, well before my original endeavor to learn the secret of the words on the chapel wall.

After a long process of discussion and discernment, peppered with starts and stops, in the summer of 1983 Mother Teresa at last decided to undertake the foundation of a branch of her order for priests, to eventually be called the Missionaries of Charity Fathers. As I had come back to Rome after a series of assignments in the United States, once Mother Teresa said yes, we went together to the Vatican to seek permission and advice in establishing the new foundation.

After setting up our first house in a run-down area of New York's South Bronx, the first years were taken up not only with ministry in the streets and soup kitchens, but also in crafting the infrastructure of our fledgling community. In drafting our first constitutions, I wanted to present as full an understanding of Mother Teresa's grace as possible, as a model for our own — and so I hoped to include some more telling reference to, and explanation of, her experience on the train. To that end, I set out to gather as much information as possible about her trip to Darjeeling, in an attempt to understand, even in its external details, the events of September 10. What follows is an outline of the events as I could reconstruct them at the time.

The Train to Darjeeling: Another Reading

On the morning of September 10, 1946, Sister Teresa Bojaxhiu left Calcutta's Howrah Station, bound for Siliguri, in the northern plains of West Bengal. She would disembark in Siliguri and board what was affectionately called the "Toy Train," so nicknamed for its tiny dimensions, and from there continue on the last leg of her journey.

The tiny train's steam-powered engine climbed along a narrow, two-foot gauge track up to Darjeeling, snuggled five thousand feet high in the foothills of the Himalayas. We can surmise something of

Riding the Darjeeling Himalayan Railway on the "Toy Train" (Raghu Rai/Magnum Photos)

Mother Teresa's journey from an earlier account of a similar trip to Darjeeling, recorded by a visiting Englishman:

> [The fact that] here the meter gauge system ends and the two foot gauge of the Darjeeling-Himalayan railway begins, confirms what these things hint at. One steps into a railway carriage which might easily be mistaken for a toy.... With a noisy fuss, out of all proportion to its size, the engine gives a jerk and starts. Sometimes we cross our own track after completing the circuit of a cone, at others we zigzag backwards and forwards; but always we climb....[9]

"Inspiration Day"

As the train ascended into the clean, cool mountain air, Sister Teresa would have looked out her window onto lush, thickening forests. Trains were slow in that day, not because the engines were weak, but because the track was unreliable. A trip of several hours could turn into days, as late-summer heat could buckle rails and add hours to the journey. But, when the little train was moving, a passenger's mind could ride the rhythm of the train's progress and easily move into prayer.

Somewhere on this ordinary journey, in the heat, in the gathering shadows, in the noisy, crowded car, something extraordinary happened. At some unknown point along the way, there in the depths of Mother Teresa's soul, the heavens opened.

For decades, all she would tell her Sisters of that life-changing moment was that she had received a "call within a call," a divine mandate to leave the convent and to go out to serve the poor in the slums. But something incomparably greater and more momentous had transpired as well. We now know, thanks to early hints in her letters and conversations, and her own later admissions, that she had been graced with an overwhelming experience of God — an experience of such power and depth, of such intense *"light and love,"* as she would later describe it, that by the time her train pulled into the station at Darjeeling, she was no longer the same. Though no one knew it at the time, Sister Teresa had just become *Mother* Teresa.

For the still young nun, barely thirty-six years old, another journey was beginning — an inner journey with her God that would turn every aspect of her life upside down. The grace of the train would not only transform her relationship to God, but to everyone and everything around her. Within eight short days, the grace of this moment would carry her and her newfound inner fire back down the same mountainside, and into a new life. From the heights of the Himalayas she would bring a profoundly new sense of her God back into the sweltering, pestilent slums of Calcutta — and onto a world stage, bearing in her heart a light and love beyond her, and our, imagining.

From then on, Mother Teresa would simply refer to September 10 as *"Inspiration Day,"* an experience she considered so intimate and ineffable that she resisted speaking of it, save in the most general terms. Her silence would prevail until the last few years of her life, when she at last was moved to lift the veil covering this sacred moment.

The Message of Divine Thirst

Reflecting on her writings, and on my conversations with her Sisters in Rome and now in the Bronx, I had begun to conclude that Mother Teresa had been entrusted with a *message* — in addition to her divine encounter that day, and as the result of it: a message that in some way echoed Jesus' words "I thirst," placed in every chapel.

But what message could there be in these words that could be so important to her? What deeper meaning could they hold? Mother Teresa had already hinted at their core meaning in her *Original Rule Explanation*, written a few short years after the experience of September 10. In explaining the mystery of Jesus' thirst, she writes that *"He, the Creator of the universe, asked for the love of His creatures."* He thirsted not for water, but for us and for our love.

For Mother Teresa, already at the beginning of her mission in the early 1950s, the message behind Jesus' cry of thirst was clear, inviting, and urgent. As she told her early followers, these words reveal much more than the dying Jesus' desire for water. Towards the end of his time on the cross, as the need for water increased due to loss of blood, Jesus' physical thirst reached its apex, and became symbol of an *inner thirst that far surpassed it.* At this deeper level, Jesus' words speak eloquently, even passionately, of God's "thirst" for man, of his thirst to *"love and be loved."* [10] In Jesus crucified and thirsting, God was revealing his *"infinite longing"* [11] for his children, a longing just as keen as any man's thirst for water in the desert heat.

Putting It All Together

As I worked on our constitutions in the Bronx, I began to ask myself if there might be a connection between Mother Teresa's experience on the train and Jesus' words "I thirst." Could they both be part of the same grace? Could it be that Mother Teresa's encounter on the train was, at its core, an *encounter with Jesus' thirst*? If that were the case, the words on the wall would simply be her way of telling us, without training the spotlight on herself, yet in a way we would not forget, the essence of what had happened that grace-filled day on the train.

As I prayed and thought over it in those months, I became more persuaded that the grace of the train had been, at least in part, Mother Teresa's own overpowering experience of Jesus' thirst. The only thing left to complete my quest was to seek her confirmation.

On her next visit to New York, in early 1984, I finally had both reason and opportunity to ask her about the experience of the train. A few days into her visit, when I was alone with her in the front garden outside our house in the Bronx, I told her of what had been my long search to better understand her "inspiration," and my desire to describe it accurately in our community's constitutions. I explained to her that, for me, the only thing that made sense of her placing "I thirst" in her chapels, was that it grew out of *her own experience of the thirst of Jesus* — and most importantly, that her encounter with the divine thirst had been the heart and essence of September 10. If this were true, I did not want to leave it out of our constitutions; but if it were not, I did not want to continue being in error.

I waited in silence for an answer. She lowered her head for a moment, then looked up and said, *"Yes, it is true."* Then after a pause, she added, *"And one day you must tell the others. . . ."*

At last I had the confirmation I was seeking, and the answer to the questions sown in my soul years before in a Roman bookstore. Here, finally, was the core of Mother Teresa's secret. In the end, it had not been some dry command to "work for the poor" that had made Mother Teresa who she was. What had forged Mother Teresa's soul and fueled her work had been an intimate encounter with the divine thirst — for her, for the poor, and for us all.

More than a confirmation, her words that day were a mandate. This was not to be the end of my quest, nor of delving into the words on the chapel wall. It was, instead, another beginning. I had to somehow "tell the others." And while I felt entirely inadequate to the task, I needed to find some way to share her words, not only with her Sisters, but with a wider public.

In the most indirect and humble of ways, not unlike the Virgin Mary, Mother Teresa had wished to exalt the goodness of the God she had met on the train, and the divine message that, after changing her life, held the power to change our own. She had always known, as I later realized, that her message was meant for us all — for the neediest and furthest away first of all. And the message of Jesus' thirst, of his longing to love us, silently conveyed in her works of love as much as by her few and gentle words, was bearing fruit all around her and all around the world. Already, in the time I had known her, I had seen with my own eyes how her unspoken message could touch, and heal, and change lives.

Thankfully, in the ensuing years, perhaps as she saw the growing impact of her message, Mother Teresa became less insistent on passing over her grace in silence. What had been confided in whispered tones outside our house in the Bronx, she would begin to confirm — gradually and obliquely at first, but then ever more clearly, in her conferences and general letters. One of her handwritten letters, in particular, would help launch the writing of this volume.

"I am a little pencil in the hand of a writing God who is sending a love letter to the world."[12]

— Mother Teresa

FIVE

In Her Own Words

Mother Teresa's Handwritten Presentation

Sometime in 1986, not long after receiving Mother Teresa's confirmation and the mandate to "tell the others," I began to work on presenting the insights I had gleaned from her over the years, especially the one great secret of her soul: the mystery of Jesus' thirst. After discussing this project with her on various occasions, and pointing out the great good her message could do for so many struggling with their own inward "Calcutta," she not only gave the project her blessing, but put pen to paper and wrote the presentation reproduced below.

Through twenty years of starting and stopping, these lines she wrote have kept both author and manuscript on track. Providentially, the long march from her handwritten presentation in 1986 to a completed manuscript years later allowed Mother Teresa to express her insights on the thirst of God more clearly and fully in the interim, right up until her death, and allowed access to the invaluable personal documents that came to light after her passing.

A page from Mother Teresa's handwritten presentation (courtesy of the author)

Besides lending these pages a validation only she could bestow, the importance of her presentation is simply in the fact that she offered to write it at all. If there was much of her soul recorded in her private letters that she had hoped to keep hidden (which, fortunately for us, did not occur, inspiring as these are), this presentation, and the divine message it introduces, represents that which she expressly *did* want known. In the end, this is what she had wanted to "tell the others."

Her Message Launched

Mother Teresa's understanding of the thirst of God was entirely simple, yet deep, powerful, and engaging. She learned that God not only accepts us with all our misery, but that he longs for us, "thirsts" for us, with all the intensity of his divine heart, no matter who we are or what we have done.

But how can God "thirst" for us if there is no lack in God? While thirst can imply lack, it also has another sense. In Mother Teresa's lexicon, thirst signifies deep, intense *desire*. Rather than indicating lack, the symbol of divine thirst points to the mystery of God's *freely chosen longing for man*. Simply put, though nothing in God needs us, everything in God wants us — deeply and intensely, as he shows throughout Scripture.

Mother Teresa's insights reveal something important, even essential, in the depths of God's being. Mother Teresa insists that the thirst of Christ reveals something not only about Jesus, but about God himself. Jesus' thirst points us toward a great mystery in the very bosom of the Godhead — what Mother Teresa describes as *"the depths of God's infinite longing to love and be loved."* [13] As ardent a statement as this is, her insights are confirmed by no less a source than the Fathers of the Church. The great St. Augustine would write that "God thirsts to be thirsted for by man" (see Appendix Three for a collection of patristic quotes on the divine thirst). In our own day,

Pope Benedict XVI would affirm that "Christ's thirst is an *entrance-way to the mystery of God*." [14]

The mystery of God's thirst for us was the one great light Mother Teresa held high in the night, hers and ours. This was the banner she raised for the poor and suffering of Calcutta and beyond. It was as *witness to this message* that Jesus commissioned her, soon after the experience of the train, to *"Be My light"* [15] — and this she would energetically do, in season and out of season. She would spend her whole life proclaiming the light of divine love — even when her words fell silent, her hands spoke more eloquently still.

The "Varanasi Letter"

It took many years for Mother Teresa to feel less uneasy in speaking about her experience of the train — a grace she at first felt unworthy to bear, and unable to express. Though she had at times made passing references to September 10, it was not until the 1990s that she began to speak more clearly and openly of the *"light and love"* [16] she had received on the train.

I personally had the chance to witness her gradual change of heart, late in 1992, just five years before her death. Mother Teresa was eighty-three at the time, and had already suffered numerous bouts with heart disease. During my stay in Calcutta that year, I had gone one afternoon with another member of our community, to visit with Mother Teresa in Mother House. While we were with her in the parlor, the conversation unexpectedly turned to September 10, to her experience on the train, and to the importance of the message she had received that day.

To our surprise, she began to speak animatedly of Jesus' thirst, of what she had experienced and understood that day, and of how life-changing it could be. She kept coming back to how different the lives of her Sisters and her poor would be if only they drew closer to, and took more seriously, the reality of Jesus' thirst. Encouraged by our enthusiasm and primed by our questions, she went on speaking for the better part of an hour — about the beauty of this message, about the power of her encounter to heal and transform, and how all of us could share in this grace.

Though we may never know what prompted Mother Teresa's unprecedented outpouring that afternoon, she may have felt interiorly freed to do so by Pope John Paul II's Lenten letter, released just prior to our conversation with her.[17] For the first time, the thirst of Jesus had been mentioned in a Church document, and in Mother Teresa's same terms and language. She had been deeply moved by the letter, and spoke of it repeatedly. Touched and grateful for this implicit affirmation of her insights, and for helping her to lift up the light of the divine longing, she immediately wrote to John Paul to thank him. This exchange, and the fresh enthusiasm that John Paul's letter had generated in her, had been the larger context behind what we had just heard her so uncharacteristically, yet so eagerly, share.

When she had finished speaking, Father Gary and I both urged her to share what she had said with her entire order, perhaps in one of her general letters, recording this for posterity. Despite her initial misgivings, she agreed to go upstairs and write down what she remembered. Since she had been speaking spontaneously, the writing turned out to be more difficult than she had foreseen. But with the help of a few memory jogs (she asked that I jot down the main points of her conversation as best I could), over the coming weeks she was able to complete the task.

Her conversation that Calcutta afternoon became the seed for her "Varanasi Letter," the end result of her efforts at recording her conversation. The letter was so named after the city on the Ganges

where she visited on March 25, 1993, the feast of the Annunciation
to Mary — the date she wished to affix to this letter that, for the first
time, would speak openly of her experience and her message. Her
insistence on that date for her letter would honor the original "message" announcing the fullness of divine love given in Jesus, revealed
to Mary by the angel Gabriel on this day.

After Mother Teresa's arrival in Rome some weeks later, she
continued going over her letter, editing and revising the text until
she was satisfied. Though she attempted repeatedly to write it out
longhand, the arthritic pain in her hands did not allow her to finish.
She ended up handing her still marked-up draft to her Sisters, to be
typed and duplicated. Its more salient passages are reproduced
below.

Mother Teresa's "Varanasi Letter" (Excerpts)

*"My children, you don't have to be different for Jesus
to love you. . . ."*

MOTHER TERESA

———

25 March 1993
Varanasi, India

My dearest Children ~

Jesus wants me to tell you again, how much is the love He
has for each one of you — beyond all that you can imagine. I
worry some of you still have not really met Jesus — one to one
— you and Jesus alone. We may spend time in chapel — but
have you seen with the eyes of your soul how He looks at you
with love? Do you really know the living Jesus — not from

---

books, but from being with Him in your heart? Have you heard the loving words He speaks to you?

Ask for the grace, He is longing to give it. Never give up this daily intimate contact with Jesus as a real living person — not just an idea.

How can we last even one day living our life without hearing Jesus say "I love you" — impossible. Our soul needs that as much as the body needs to breathe the air. If not, prayer is dead — meditation is only thinking. Jesus wants you each to hear Him — speaking in the silence of your heart.

Be careful of all that can block that personal being in touch with the living Jesus. The hurts of life, and sometimes your own mistakes — [may] make you feel it is impossible that Jesus really loves you, is really clinging to you. This is a danger for all of you. And so sad, because it is completely opposite of what Jesus is really wanting, waiting to tell you.

Not only He loves you, even more — He longs for you. He misses you when you don't come close. He thirsts for you. He loves you always, even when you don't feel worthy. Even if you are not accepted by others, even by yourself sometimes — He is the one who always accepts you.

My children, you don't have to be different for Jesus to love you. Only believe — You are precious to Him. Bring all you are suffering to His feet — only open your heart to be loved by Him as you are. He will do the rest.

You all know in your mind that Jesus loves you — but in this letter Mother wants to touch your heart instead. Jesus wants to stir up our hearts, so not to lose our early love....

Why is Mother saying these things? After reading [John Paul II's] letter on "I Thirst," I was struck so much — I cannot tell you what I felt. His letter made me realize more than ever how beautiful is our vocation. How great is God's love for us in choosing [us] to satiate that thirst of Jesus, for love, for souls — giving us our special place in the Church. At the same time we are reminding the world of his thirst, something that was being forgotten.

———

I wrote to Holy Father to thank him. [His] letter is a sign ... to go more into what is this great thirst of Jesus for each one. It is also a sign for Mother, that the time has come for me to speak openly of the gift God gave Sept. 10th — to explain fully as I can what means for me the thirst of Jesus.

For me, Jesus' thirst is something so intimate — so I have felt shy until now to speak to you of Sept. 10th — I wanted to do as Our Lady who "kept all these things in her heart." [Jesus'] words on the wall of every MC chapel, they are not from the past only, but alive here and now, spoken to you. Do you believe it? If so, you will hear, you will feel His presence. Let it become as intimate for each of you, just as for Mother — this is the greatest joy you could give me.

Jesus Himself must be the one to say to you "I Thirst." Hear your own name. Not just once. Every day. If you listen with your heart, you will hear, you will understand.

Why does Jesus say "I Thirst"? What does it mean? Something so hard to explain in words — if you remember anything from Mother's letter, remember this — "I Thirst" is something much deeper than just Jesus saying "I love you." Until you know deep inside that Jesus thirsts for you — you can't begin to know who He wants to be for you. Or who He wants you to be for Him.

Before it was Our Lady pleading with Mother; now it is Mother in her name pleading with you — listen to Jesus' thirst.

How to approach the thirst of Jesus? Only one secret — the closer you come to Jesus, the better you will know His thirst. "Repent and believe," Jesus tells us. What are we to repent? Our indifference, our hardness of heart. What are we to believe? Jesus thirsts even now, in your heart and in the poor — He knows your weakness, He wants only your love, wants only the chance to love you. He is not bound by time. Whenever we come close to Him — we become partners of Our Lady, St. John, Magdalen. Hear Him. Hear your own name. Make my joy and yours complete.

Let us pray,

God bless you,

M. Teresa MC

The Grace of Jubilee

Three years after penning her "Varanasi Letter," in another confluence of grace and circumstance, Mother Teresa again began sharing the secrets of her soul, on the thirst of Jesus and her experience of the train. The turning point came in January of that year, as her Sisters were preparing to celebrate the fiftieth anniversary (1946-1996) of her Inspiration Day.

I had traveled from our priests' community (whose headquarters had recently moved from the Bronx to Tijuana, Mexico) to join Mother Teresa and her Sisters in Washington, DC. From there I was to return with her for a visit to our priests and seminarians in Tijuana. The day after I arrived in Washington, her Sisters held a special

Mass in anticipation of the golden jubilee of September 10. Immediately after the festivities, we left for the airport for the flight to San Diego, and on to Tijuana.

I had the chance to sit next to Mother Teresa for the first part of the flight. Shortly after takeoff, she began gazing out the window, lost in thought. From time to time, she would make comments — quiet remarks, almost asides — that told me she was reminiscing, absorbed in another time and place. It became clear that she was recalling, in some detail, the experience of September 10, fifty years earlier. I was struck not only by what she was revealing, but by how unusual it was for her to be commenting like this on memories so intimate.

As that jubilee year of 1996 went on, and she visited her Sisters around the world, each community in turn celebrated the fiftieth anniversary of Inspiration Day. Each celebration became another occasion for her to reminisce, to bring those deep waters to the surface again, preparing the veritable flood of references to September 10 that would fill her letters throughout the following year, 1997 — the last year of her life.

———

We have begun, in these chapters, to uncover the rest of the story, the unknown story of Mother Teresa. This was what happened on the train, this was what made her who she was, and most importantly for us, this was the message she wanted written down and shared — inviting us into the same "light and love" she discovered long ago.

The light Mother Teresa received, the transforming light of God's thirst for us, was the very light that gave her victory over her darkness — and not only hers, but over the bleak darkness of Calcutta. This was the light she hoped would touch our lives and transform our darkness as well. And this is the light whose beauty and power we will begin to explore in Section Two.

SECTION TWO

Illumination

"The strong grace of Divine Light and Love . . . received on the train journey to Darjeeling on 10th September, 1946, is where the M.C. [the worldwide work of charity] begins — in the depths of God's infinite longing to love and to be loved."[18]

— Mother Teresa

"They don't know Me — so they don't want Me. . . ."[19]

— Jesus to Mother Teresa (1947)

"You are the light of the world."
              — Matthew 5:14

"Come, be My light...."[20]
      — Jesus to Mother Teresa (1947)

SIX

In the Darkness, Light

St. Teresa?

Mother Teresa's holiness — seldom discussed in accounts of her life — is the passkey to understanding the very qualities we most admire in her. Her sanctity is the ultimate source of the light she shone on the world. Without understanding the role of personal holiness, a holiness open to us all, one can only conclude that Mother Teresa had been born that way, a rare kind of prodigy, like an Einstein or Mozart of the spiritual realm, rather than a model inviting imitation, drawing us on.

But what the commentators tended to overlook, the poor and the simple had already sensed. They could feel the presence of God in Mother Teresa; they intuited her holiness, and were drawn to it. As her work progressed, a growing groundswell of recognition and respect — even in the press — pointed to the presence of God in her. By the time she won the Nobel Prize, *Time* magazine had already proclaimed Mother Teresa a "living saint" on its front cover. On the other side of the world, the poor of Calcutta, sleeping under bits of paper and cloth, lit candles to the divinity they saw in her, honored in makeshift shrines by the roadside.

People praying at an altar for Mother Teresa (Raghu Rai/Magnum Photos)

Saints, however, are so rare in our experience, and so often relegated to the past, that we no longer realize what sainthood means, nor what the saints might have to do with our lives. And so, before examining Mother Teresa's light, we first need to understand the source of her light, the *state* of "being light" that Jesus called her to, which is sanctity.

God's purpose in sending the saints lies well beyond our usual supposition that the saints are merely distant moral beacons, standard-bearers to which the rest of humanity can never quite measure up. The mystery of the saints is something deeper and far more attractive — more than austere asceticism and images on holy cards, stained-glass windows, or statues. In sending us saints, God indicates his yearning, and his ability, to participate fully in our world. The saints reflect the beauty of God and his plan for us, a beauty they make concrete and tangible — and inviting. In the words of Thomas Merton, a saint is "a window through which God's mercy shines on the world. And for this reason, he strives to be holy in order that the goodness of God may never be obscured by any selfish act."

The saints illumine us with the Creator's own light, granting us a glimpse of who both he and we truly are. They are a mirror of our God-given dignity, of what we were created to be, and of what we can yet become.

Primordial Light

The story of Mother Teresa, and of all the saints, does not begin with their conversion, nor even with their birth. The real history of the saints reaches back to the beginning of all things, as described in the book of Genesis, when, on the first day of creation, God said, "*Let there be light*" (Gen 1:3). This first step in creation does not refer to the light of the sun, which was not created until the fourth day, but to *God's own light* — a divine light destined to dispel the darkness and bring order out of chaos, from before the dawn of time until time is no more. Before there was anything else, there was light, as the atmosphere and foundation of all.

Adam and Eve were created to inhabit and embody that first light, as the crown of God's creation. According to Jewish tradition, after the Fall, God left a trace of original glory on the body of Adam and Eve. At the tip of their hands and feet, God left slivers of flesh dipped in light, translucent tokens of that first light that is still our dignity and destiny. Something as humble as fingernails would be God's reminder to us of the transparency that once was ours, and of the light from which, and for which, we were made.

The saints still serve this same evocative and ultimately practical purpose. They are that small sliver of humanity, dipped in God, that still shines with his light. Their lives serve to beckon us back, to call us to our senses and our source, as God called out to Adam after the Fall, "*Where are you?*" (Gen 3:9). Despite the variety of their lives, their backgrounds, and their stories, the saints all embody this one sweeping truth: that with the coming of Christ as New Adam, the prophesied times of restoration are here. In him, and in those transformed by him, the glory of the first Adam is once again restored. But the saints are not only heralds of this promised restoration; they are its living proof. They reflect here and now, for every generation and culture — mirrored in the joy, the innocence, and the goodness suffusing their countenance — the luminous faces of our first parents, coming forth fresh from the hand of God.

But there is something more. The saints show us not only how good *we* can be, but more importantly, they show us how supremely good *God* is. The saints are the living reflections of God's goodness in our midst. In their role as mirrors of God, each saint is unique, for God's goodness and beauty are infinitely rich. Like precious stones in a great mosaic, each saint reveals some facet, some special attribute of God's boundless being, some unique hue of the divine splendor.

The saints not only reflect God's light, they also echo his voice, calling humanity back into the divine embrace. The saints are God's reminders, his memos to mankind, re-enacting the message and the beauty of the gospel before the eyes of each era. Like the ancient prophets before them, the saints reverberate with that particular Word of God most necessary to each age.

What Word of God was Mother Teresa's life echoing? Why did he send her, rather than another, into our night? To fathom God's purpose in sending her, we need to know more of Mother Teresa's interior life — to see her not only from the outside, through the lens of her accomplishments, but illumined by her own sense of purpose, to allow her to point us toward the unseen north star of her soul.

Though all the saints are in some way "light-bearers," witnessing to the light would become the focus of Mother Teresa's entire vocation. Jesus sent her to "be his light" in the darkness of a Calcutta night that transcended geography. Mother Teresa's Calcutta was everywhere, symbol of a night that invades and lies in wait in every heart.

Mother Teresa was not called to share her light from "above," nor from afar — unlike some contemporary proponents of a prosperity gospel, she was not one to stand above the fray, dispensing wisdom from a peaceful and pampered life. Instead, she accepted to be plunged body and soul into the lowest depths of our night, illuminating that night *from within*, forging a path through our inner darkness into light. The fact that she confronted the night in her own soul first, as her personal letters reveal, does not diminish her spiritual credentials; rather, it augments her credibility. Her dark night makes her not just a teacher but a guide — an escort and companion for our own labored journey into light.

Bowed by Darkness, or Beacon of Light?

But before we move on to explore the secrets of Mother Teresa's interior life, we first need to be sure not to misconstrue her "darkness" — a darkness God allowed her to experience as a share in the inner night of Calcutta's poorest of the poor. Mother Teresa was wounded with the inner wounds of her people; she bled with them and died with them. God was calling her to share the heavy, if forgotten, *inner* burdens of the poor, not only their material deprivation. She was to be fixed to the hidden inward cross of the poor, and to be riven by the same interior anguish that Jesus himself had undergone.

But as painful as her darkness was, *theirs* was the true night, the darkness that eats away at faith. In Mother Teresa's time, millions of Calcutta's street population drew their dying breath under the dusty feet of passersby, after having spent an entire existence deprived of any human evidence of a loving God. This was a tragedy not of God's making, but man's — yet one that burdened not man's heart, but God's. This was the ultimate sense of Mother Teresa's dark night, borne in the name of her God, and her poor.

But what of reports that suggested that Mother Teresa had undergone a crisis of faith, or worse, that her smile and her devotion to God and neighbor were little more than hypocrisy? Emphatically, Mother Teresa's dark night was not a "crisis of faith," nor did it represent a wavering on her part. Far from being a loss of faith, her letters reveal instead her hard-fought *victory* of faith, the triumph of faith's light that shines even in the darkness, for "the darkness has not overcome it" (Jn 1:5).

The same letters that recount her darkness at the *feeling* level (not at the level of faith) testify, too, to her unshakeable belief, even when she no longer sensed God's presence. Her letters reveal a supreme, even heroic exercise of faith at its zenith, free of dependence on circumstance or feelings. She consistently *chose* to believe, refusing to turn away from a brilliance once beheld, simply because clouds had covered her inner sky. No matter how long the hours of her night, never once did she suspect that the sun existed no more. Even in the deepest night of her inner Calcutta, she kept her course towards the Day Star, and never lost her way.

The passages that speak of her darkness recount as well her deep yearning for God through it all. Her constant longing itself witnesses to the solidity of her faith, for no one continues to long for the return of a loved one who no longer exists.

Mother Teresa's trial of faith is not without precedent in Christian tradition, nor without parallels in Scripture. Recall Jesus' challenge to the Canaanite woman, who, after begging that he cure her daughter, was seemingly rebuffed in the harshest terms. In both cases, Jesus used what appeared to be rejection in order to *draw out the fullness of their faith*, precisely by challenging that faith to the maximum. Jesus gave each one the chance to surmount his challenges one by one, and to stand triumphant as a model for the rest of us. His appreciation of the Canaanite woman could have been addressed just as easily, two thousand years later, to Mother Teresa: "O woman, great is your faith!" (Mt 15:28).

Sharing the Darkness of the Poor

As difficult and painful as her dark night became, Mother Teresa never allowed herself to become "lost" in her darkness. She never rebelled against it, nor against the God who laid it on her shoulders, nor against the poor of Calcutta with whom and for whom she bore it. On the contrary, she gradually came to understand its deeper meaning, and even to willingly embrace it for the sake of her God — who had borne that same agony for her sake, in Gethsemane.

Even while tending to the physical and material needs of the poor, feeding the hungry and clothing the naked, Mother Teresa's primary focus was their *"salvation and sanctification,"*[21] their inner advancement toward divine union, as their highest dignity and long-term vocation. She was not sent simply to work for material betterment, a point even her admirers often miss. Calcutta's poorest, living and dying on the streets, enjoyed neither sufficient material goods nor the goodness of their fellow man. Since they were left with nothing and no one to mirror to them the face of God, Mother Teresa was sent to *show* them in his name, in concrete works of love, how beloved of God they were. For love's sake, she herself would bear a portion of their interior pain. She would give of herself, in this life and the next, to *"light the light of those in darkness on earth."*[22] The more the truth of her victorious faith is known, the more she will be an inspiration to those who are learning to find their peace, to make their contribution, and to cling to their God, as she did, in the night.

Lessons in the Night

For all who "have eyes to see," there is a great light hidden here. Beyond the obvious light of Mother Teresa's charity, there in the heart of her night lies a deeper light still.

But how can light be born of darkness? This question is critical, for it is key to the process and the history of divine transformation. First, there is the creation story, in which the Almighty transformed the dark void into substance and light. There is the second creation story, where Adam and Eve are cast from a luminous Eden into a world of darkness and temptation. The Redeemer, light of the world, is heralded by a night star at his birth. The Nicene Creed sings of him as "light from light, true God from true God." Finally, in the Resurrection, the darkness of death is conquered by his brilliance emerging from the tomb.

Darkness need not be the opposite, the enemy of light. When seeded with God's grace, darkness becomes its catalyst. Night becomes the womb to the day. It is the *power of love*, of God's own nature as love, that works this alchemy. When embraced for others, when transformed by love, darkness indeed *becomes* light.

Paradoxically, by embracing her darkness for the sake of the poor, Mother Teresa fulfilled her call — in her welcomed darkness she *became* God's light. Her sacrifice shone with a light that transcends our logic. As St. Paul comments on the archetypal mystery of divine light clothed in human darkness, shining forth from Jesus' passion and death,

> For Jews demand signs and Greeks seek wisdom, but we preach Christ crucified, a stumbling block to Jews and folly to Gentiles,

but to those who are called, both Jews and Greeks, Christ the power of God and the wisdom of God. (1 Cor 1:22-24)

This crucified light, so utterly "other" that it seems to us darkness and scandal, is the refulgence of God's *self-emptying* love (Phil 2:6-8). Divine love wraps itself in our pain and darkness, as Mother Teresa would say, "*without counting the cost.*" God's very nature as love plunges him headlong into our neediness and, unbelievably, even into our sin. In St. Paul's bold words: "For our sake he made him to be sin who knew no sin (2 Cor 5:21).

Mother Teresa would follow Jesus' lead. She, who from childhood knew no darkness, would accept to "become darkness" for the sake of the poor. She gathered into her soul and flooded with love the very blackness that denied God's existence, drowning the darkness in light.

The importance of Mother Teresa's example, even for those who bear much milder Calcuttas, is in showing *how far faith and love can reach* in this life — even in the night, even buffeted by pain, with every wind against it. Her victory in the night is proof that the exercise of faith and love is ultimately our free choice, never beholden to circumstance, a decision accessible at all times. God makes it always possible to move beyond preoccupation with our own pain, and to reach out to assuage the pain of others. Rather than isolating us, we can choose to make of life's burdens a sacred bridge into the pain of others.

Light on Our Horizon

There is more to Mother Teresa's wisdom than the otherworldly, however. As global events unfold, we can already see a growing timeliness and relevance to her teaching, one that even her followers would not have foreseen — but that surely did not escape the foresight of the God who sent her.

Increasingly, the importance of Mother Teresa's message will come from having modeled an effective, even elegant, way to live, to work, and to overcome in the face of the most daunting and overwhelming odds. Mother Teresa not only survived, but she also managed to become a saint and Nobel laureate amidst the material and spiritual challenges of civil-war Calcutta (sundered, bloodied, and impoverished by clashes between Hindus and Muslims). This chaos was the backdrop for her experiments in faith and love, a confluence of adversities that surely surpassed our own, yet giving rise to a resilient faith that can still inspire our own.

While the challenges of her life may seem to have little to do with us, in coming years this may no longer be the case. The specter of severe change looms over us on many fronts — the environment, hunger, global debt, climate change, diminishing oil reserves, and health challenges and pandemics that may stretch our ability to cope.

If in the future even some of the deprivations that Mother Teresa faced in Calcutta become ours, might the life of this woman, who navigated the problems of Calcutta with such grace, hold lessons for us all — for our spiritual and emotional viability, whatever may come? Might she yet be a mentor to future generations, teaching us that circumstances need not dictate the tenor and purpose of our life, but instead, by remaining God-anchored and proactive, that we can turn even the worst circumstances to advantage?

But even if none of the gloom gathering on our horizon comes to pass, we will still need grace and courage to face the fact that our present tenor of life cannot continue indefinitely. In years to come, we all will know unforeseen suffering; we all will taste deprivation, in health if not in finance. Whatever our present circumstances, a share of personal tragedy will one day touch us all. The normal course of life will bring, along with blessings, disease to our children, accidents to loved ones, responsibility for bed-ridden relatives or a cancer-ridden spouse, loss of employment or loss of relationship, sudden reversals of fortune, or the untimely death of those we cherish. We will all need to find other sources of happiness, purpose, and fulfillment, beyond possessions and ease and protecting the status quo. In the end, the very process of our aging will itself frame the geography of our personal Calcutta.

Who will teach us to deal with such trials when they come? What solutions will there be for us, besides escape or despair, the hollow promises of a prosperity gospel, or the cosmic secrets of "attracting abundance"? Mother Teresa's secret was quite another — more robust, reliable, and real. It was born of the *most* powerful force in the universe — the only One to have faced death, and overcome it forever.

Over the darkness of our inevitable night, her light shines — no longer only as "saint," but as model and teacher, thanks to her own graced path through the night. She has shown us what the human spirit can accomplish, clinging to God, no matter the odds. As the years go by, her challenges will seem less foreign, and her solutions more meaningful, even vital. Our common human plight has become our bond with her, and our invitation to enroll in her school of the heart.

Turning the Darkness to Light

We are each called and equipped by God not only to *survive* our personal Calcutta, but to *serve* there — to contribute to those around us whose individual Calcuttas intersect our own, just as Mother Teresa did, if on a different scale. If she could face the worst of human suffering in such immense proportions — and do so despite bearing her own pain — then there must be a way that we can do the same in the lesser Calcutta that is ours. We must never forget, distracted by the demi-problems of our routine existence, *just how important our one life is in the plan of God*, and the great amount of good we can yet contribute.

How important can our one small, unspectacular life be? Consider this: the good that each of us can accomplish, even with limited resources and restricted reach, *not even a Mother Teresa could achieve*. The family, friends, and coworkers whom we alone can touch, with our unique and unrepeatable mix of gifts and qualities, not even Mother Teresa could reach. No one else on the planet, and no one else in history, possesses the same network of acquaintances and the same combination of talents and gifts as each one of us does — as *you* do.

There is no need, then, to travel to far-off lands to contribute to Mother Teresa's mission, or to follow her example. Wherever we are, with whatever talents and relationships God has entrusted us, we are each called not to do *what* a Mother Teresa did, but to do *as* she did — to love as she loved in the Calcutta of our own life.

Mother Teresa's Secret

The inner fire that saw Mother Teresa through the night will be her contribution for generations to come. Here is the wisdom of a Nobel Prize laureate and a saint. Here is her recipe for happiness in the midst of want; for living for others despite one's own needs; for hoping in the face of setbacks; for peace within, while conflict and struggle reign without; for giving our time and our love, even while our own health and supports are wrenched away. Mother Teresa has taught us the divine alchemy that turns our personal hardships into compassion for others; our lack of material goods into wealth of spirit; and, should it come to that, the loss of our standard of living into the chance to become what ease and abundance would never have allowed us to be.

Mother Teresa's lessons will prepare us, as no political plan or economic program could, to live through our trials with grace, and to turn them into blessing for others. If this simple, humanly un-extraordinary woman could have filled Calcutta's slums with such love and energy and ingenuity, then we can learn to do the same in our life, no matter what may come.

"Try to deepen your understanding of these two words, 'Thirst of God.'"[23]

— Mother Teresa

SEVEN

"I Thirst":
A Window on the Heart of God

The Good News Retold

Who of us would not have been overwhelmed by such an experience as Mother Teresa had on that September day in 1946 — having encountered a God who not only accepts us, but who actually *longs* for us, even as we sleep, and even when we wander.

Mother Teresa encountered a God who yearns for us — exactly as we are, even the worst among us; a God who wishes to draw us into his embrace, regardless of past failings or present weakness. She came to understand a cornerstone of God's mercies, of his way of dealing with us, in realizing that we each need more love than we deserve.[24] Has God not indeed shown us his greatest love precisely when we deserved it least, from the tree of Eden to the tree of Calvary, and beyond?

But lest we make the mistake of seeing God's unconditional longing as a license for laxity or complacency, there is another corollary key to Mother Teresa's understanding of God's plan. His longing for us is not the end of the story. The same God who loves us as we are also loves us too much to *leave us* as we are. This is why he urged Mother Teresa to labor not only for the salvation of the poor, but for their full sanctification — that is, for their complete *transformation*; for nothing less than the fullness of their potential and dignity in God. Salvation is the beginning, but there is always more this side of heaven, and God's thirst for us will always draw us on to a still deeper union with him. Rather than being the domain of the few, holiness — the free gift of ultimate transformation worked by divine love, and the final goal of the divine thirst — is open to one and all. In fact, the needier we are, and the farther away, the more God strives to draw us into his kingdom, where the "first will be last, and the last first" (Mk 10:31).

The Good News of the gospel is laced throughout Mother Teresa's message — tidings that may seem radically new, unheard of, hard to believe, especially for those who have yet to personally encounter God's love. Her message may indeed be radical, but it is far from new. The mystery of the divine longing has always been there, hidden in the books of the Old Testament, and woven throughout every page of the New.

If this is so, then why have we not heard it before? Perhaps because we tend to hold to ideas about God that reflect our own suppositions and fears, more than God's self-revelation. We reduce God to our own dimensions, ascribing to him our own reactions and responses, especially our own petty and conditional kind of love, and so end up believing in a God cast in our own image and likeness.

But the true God, the living God, is entirely "other." Precisely from this radical otherness derives the inscrutable and transcendent nature of divine love — for which our limited human love is but a distant metaphor. God's love is much more than our human love simply multiplied and expanded. God's love for us will ever be mystery: unfathomable, awesome, entirely beyond human expectation.

Precisely because God's love is something "no eye has seen, nor ear heard, nor the heart of man conceived" (1 Cor 2:9), Mother Teresa meditated on it continuously, and encouraged us to do the same, to continue plumbing this mystery more deeply. To this end she invites us: *"Try to deepen your understanding of these two words, 'Thirst of God.' "*[25]

Seeing Through Her Eyes

If we accept Mother Teresa's invitation to contemplate the same light she beheld on the train, we need to try to see that light, first of all, through her eyes, through the lens of her own soul, before making that light our own. And so our first step on our journey into the light is to ask what the mystery of Jesus' thirst meant to *her*. What is there about God that Mother Teresa came to know and experience, but that (perhaps) eludes us still? What divine depths still await us, unknown, beckoning us into God's embrace?

Let us begin to answer these questions by exploring some of Mother Teresa's insights into the divine thirst.

———

First of all, what does the thirst of Jesus tell us about God? The symbol of thirst is neither complicated nor hard to understand: As the burning desert yearns for water, so God yearns for our love. As a thirsty man longs for water, so God longs for each of us. As a thirsty man seeks after water, so God seeks after us. As a thirsty man thinks only of water, so God thinks constantly of us: "Even the hairs of your head are all numbered" (Lk 12:7). As a thirsty man will give anything in exchange for water, so God gladly gives all he has, and all he is, in exchange for us: his divinity for our humanity, his holiness for our sin, his paradise in exchange for our pain.

For Mother Teresa, the mystery of God's thirst, revealed in Jesus, is at the center of all, and the key to all. God's yearning to "love and be loved" is the supreme force that inspires and directs all his works, from Creation, to Calvary, to the present day.

Jesus' words "I thirst" echo down throughout history. In these two words are reflected all that God has said and done from the beginning, and all he would wish to say to each of us. All of God's words to humanity are a reverberation of this one humble phrase. In fact, all of Scripture is a commentary on the divine thirst, and in turn, the divine thirst sheds light on all of Scripture, on all of Revelation, on all that is.

Why the Symbol of Thirst?

Since it would be impossible to give an adequate sense of the infinite longing in the heart of God in mere words, or theological descriptions, God chose to communicate this mystery in metaphor — that of a burning, relentless, divine "thirst."

Mother Teresa was given a symbol to lift up before the poor that was entirely simple, yet many-faceted; simple enough to touch the hearts of the poor, yet deep enough to engage the intellect of scholars. The Holy Spirit portrays God's longing in the most accessible language possible — that of *human experience.*

As descendants of a nomadic desert people, constantly in search of water, the Israelites of Jesus' time would have easily understood thirst as metaphor. So, too, would the poor of Calcutta, who had to scavenge for every drop of clean water they could find. Thirst is a metaphor that does not depend on culture, nor on erudition; a language capable of expressing the deepest truths without relying on technical, theological terms, nor on expressions that change from one era to the next, but solely on the universal human experience of thirst, and its attendant inner longing.

To discover what the mystery of Jesus' thirst meant to Mother Teresa, we can do no better than to read her own words. The following brief overview (see Appendix Two for a fuller presentation of her quotes on "I thirst") is drawn from Mother Teresa's writings and conferences, spanning the period from the earliest days of her mission until the months prior to her death:

> *Jesus is God therefore His love, His thirst is infinite. . . . [We are called to] quench this infinite thirst of a God made Man. . . . The Sisters . . . ceaselessly quench the thirsting God by their love and of the love of the souls they bring to Him.* (Mother Teresa: Come Be My Light, p. 41)

> *I long for God. I long to love Him with every drop of life in me.* (Mother Teresa: Come Be My Light, p. 203)

> *What is the reason for our existence? We are here to satiate the thirst of Jesus, to proclaim the love of Christ — the thirst of Jesus — for souls by the holiness of our lives. . . . We are here to satiate the thirst of Jesus . . . that is why we must be holy.* (Mother Teresa's Instructions to the M.C. Sisters [January 1980])

> *"I thirst" — we are so busy to think about all that. The words, "I thirst" — do they echo in our souls? . . . Today, let us try to go over that word, "I thirst."* (Mother Teresa's Instructions to the M.C. Sisters [February 1980])

> *Right today and everyday He is thirsting for my love. He is longing for me, in my soul.* (Mother Teresa's Instructions to the M.C. Sisters [December 7, 1982])

> *It is very important for us to know that Jesus is thirsting for our love, for the love of the whole world. . . . Ask yourself. Have I heard Jesus*

directly say this word to me personally? Did I ever hear that word personally? "I thirst." "I want your love" ... *If not, examine yourself: why could I not hear?* (Mother Teresa's Instructions to the M.C. Sisters [December 1, 1983])

He longs for you. He thirsts for you. ... *My children, once you have experienced the thirst, the love of Jesus for you, you will never need, you will never thirst for these things which can only lead you away from Jesus, the true and living Fountain. Only the thirst of Jesus, feeling it, hearing it, answering it with all your heart will keep your love* ... *alive. The closer you come to Jesus the better you will know His thirst.* (Mother Teresa's Letters to the M.C. Sisters [July 29, 1993])

Grow in that intimate love, and you will understand not only "I thirst," but everything. Humanly speaking we cannot understand "love one another as I have loved you;" "Be ye holy as I am holy." But it all comes under "I thirst." The fruit of faith is the understanding of "I thirst." ... *Get rid of sin quickly so we can hear Jesus say, "I thirst for your love." The most important thing is that we must encounter the thirst of Jesus, but the encounter with Jesus' thirst is a grace.* (Mother Teresa's Instructions to the M.C. Sisters [February 1994])

What is that word, "I thirst," to you personally? What connection do you make in your life? (Mother Teresa's Instructions to the M.C. Sisters [August 8, 1994])

The strong grace of Divine Light and Love that Mother received on the train journey to Darjeeling on 10th September 1946 is where the MC begins — in the depths of God's infinite longing to love and to be loved *[emphasis added].* (Mother Teresa's Letters to the M.C. Sisters [April 24, 1996])

Why Calcutta?

In the case of Mother Teresa, however, studying her words is just the first step in uncovering her understanding of the divine thirst. We must remember that, given the nature of her mission, her works were her most eloquent language, since her deeds spoke just as convincingly of God's longing as anything she might say. She was a divine messenger, like the prophets of old, sent not only to speak God's message but to *act it out*, since it is precisely through deeds that God's message is made visible — no longer mere theory, but "made flesh."

Mother Teresa's double mission was to communicate the divine longing through both deeds and words, as part of God's plan for this incredulous age. As Paul VI observed, "Modern man listens more

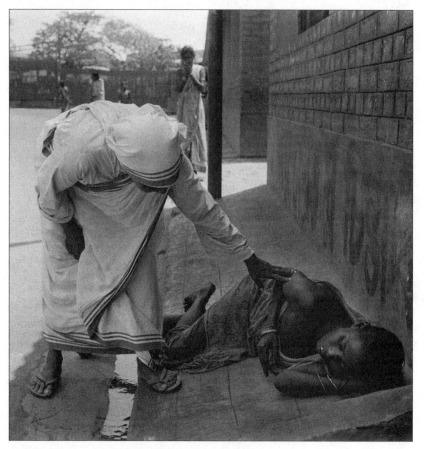

Comforting the sick (Raghu Rai/Magnum Photos)

willingly to witnesses than to teachers, and if he does listen to teachers, it is *because* they are witnesses."[26] Faced with the external darkness surrounding the poor, and the internal darkness assailing the
rich as well, Mother Teresa understood that the light of her words
was not enough, that more than ever in this era, "God wants to *show*
us who he is, not just tell us."[27]

Proclaiming God's thirst solely in words, simply saying it is so,
could never validate such a message, especially to the poor dying
on the streets of Calcutta. But it was precisely to the poorest that
she was sent — to the outcastes, the lepers, the hungry and naked,
the *"throw-aways of society,"* as Mother Teresa called them. These
were the ones for whom God most urgently longed. And these
were the ones who needed his love most — yet had least reason to
believe in it.

Since nothing in their surroundings spoke of God or his love to
Calcutta's poor, Mother Teresa was sent to show them that love, to
reflect his invisible presence, to speak of him through the eloquent
silences of her charity. In the words of St. Augustine, "Whoever has
seen charity, *has seen the Trinity.*"[28] For this reason, Mother Teresa
would seek no other pulpit than the hovels of the poor, and no other
sermon than her works of love, performed for the unloved, in God's
name.

The Hidden Calcuttas of the West

As the years went on, Mother Teresa felt moved to begin bringing
the light of God's love beyond the realm of physical pain and material poverty. God was showing her, through her travels in the developed world, that *wherever there is humanity, there is pain,* be it in
slums or prisons or palaces — and that wherever there is pain, there
is Jesus, fixed to the cross of our wounds of body or soul, thirsting for
us, thirsting within us.

In 1960, Mother Teresa was invited to the United States to address a national women's gathering — to be held, of all places, in Las Vegas. This visit would mark her first venture outside the borders of Third World poverty, and her first opportunity to share her message in the affluent West.

Like Calcutta, Las Vegas was not just another city — it was an icon. But unlike Calcutta, Las Vegas (at least the Las Vegas the world imagines), with its casinos and night life, was an icon of opulence and dissipation, poor with a very different poverty. To emphasize the universal scope of her message, God was sending Mother Teresa to the other extreme, to the opposite end of the economic spectrum. He was sending her to "be his light" in an anti-Calcutta; not a slum in any classic sense, but in many ways a slum of the spirit. Here, and throughout the developed world, Mother Teresa would confront an entirely different poverty, a proud but soul-stripping poverty that knew not its nakedness.

It was after this inaugural trip to the West that she began to be as deeply moved by First World inner poverty as by Third World material want. She began to understand that *every* place and person bears a miniature Calcutta within. The streets of Calcutta lead to every man's door, and the very pain, the very ruin of our Calcutta of the heart witnesses to the glory that once was and ought to be. From then onward, encouraged by her friend John Paul II, she increasingly brought her message wherever she was invited. At this mature stage in her mission, the light of her message was reaching not only to the slums of the world, but beyond, to the threshold of every hurting heart.

———

Mother Teresa's great contribution has been the gift of resplendent light entrusted to her on the train, a light mirrored for the rest of us in her words and deeds of love.

An intimate moment with Pope John Paul II, Calcutta, 1986 (Raghu Rai/Magnum Photos)

She has brought our attention to the divine words "I thirst," to this unique portal into the light, this providential means to "[know] the gift of God, and who it is that is saying to [us], 'Give me a drink'" (Jn 4:10). In the cry of thirst uttered by the Son of God on Calvary, and raised up in our day by Mother Teresa, we have been given a lens to behold both God and all creation more deeply and anew. Her vision takes us into the depths of the Trinity in one direction, and the depths of human nature in the other. As I had the opportunity to comment in a homily in Mother House, in Calcutta, on the anniversary of Inspiration Day, September 10, 1997, just five days after her passing:

Because of Mother Teresa and her message, because of this secret fire entrusted to her, countless generations will come to know God better. Through this encounter, received on the train to Darjeeling, lived in the slums of Calcutta, and shared with us all, she has given the world her greatest gift — for in a new and unique way, she has opened for us a window on the heart of God.

"They don't know Me — so they don't want Me...." [29]
— Jesus to Mother Teresa

EIGHT

A Legacy of Light: Part I

A Mosaic of Light

The same light of Jesus' thirst shines in yet another way, reflected in the person of the one sent to "be his light" — in Mother Teresa herself.

We saw this same light, reflected like sunlight through a prism, in her goodness and gentleness and charity. In all she did, Mother Teresa made visible the hidden mystery of God's longing. Her every word and gesture cried out to us in his name, "*I thirst for you. . . .*"

Because she so faithfully reflected the light she beheld, simply by observing Mother Teresa we can gather important insights into her experience of God — into those divine qualities that touched and transformed her most, and which she in turn most brightly mirrored.

———

The ten points that follow reflect the key facets of the divine thirst, as Mother Teresa understood it. These points are garnered from her writings, from conversations with her, and from observing her at close quarters, as she went about mirroring the light she carried within. In pondering this mosaic of light, reflected in the various qualities and aspects of her own life, we can come closer to beholding the light and love of her inner fire.

We begin this journey of discovery as Mother Teresa did that September day — with her same sincerity and goodwill, with open mind and supple heart. And just as she that day, we begin from zero — we, too, like the rest of humanity, have lived our lives entirely unaware of God's longing for us.

But before approaching this light — in order that we be more than casual observers or indifferent — it is crucial to realize that God's longing holds more than only beauty, more than consolation, more even than light for our darkness. The divine thirst is also tinged with pain — the pain of our ignorance, of our rejection and indifference, of the pain of our sin. Mother Teresa called this Jesus' *"painful thirst."*[30] Unknown, unanswered, and unsatiated, God's longing for wayward humanity took on a poignancy and an urgency that overwhelmed her heart. As she writes to her Sisters:

> *My children, you do not know the terrible pain there is in my heart for not being able to fully answer the terrible thirst Jesus asked me to satiate through the Society [i.e., her Missionaries of Charity] — through each one of you. If I am feeling like this, I wonder what the Heart of Jesus must feel? Is it not at this time again, as He did on September 10th — is He not looking at each one of us: "I chose you and called you to be an MC to satiate My painful thirst; and where are you?"*[31]

A Vision of Light in Darkness

Mother Teresa's sense of the pain that suffused an otherwise consoling message dates back to the beginnings of her mission, to the time immediately following her grace of September 10. During the last months of 1946, she began receiving almost daily interior communications, which would last well into 1947, in which Jesus explained to her in detail the nature of her mission to the poor. At the conclusion of these extraordinary revelations, she was shown a symbolic vision, a series of three tableaus, summarizing all that had been revealed to her in the preceding months.

In the first of the three scenes, Mother Teresa was shown the painful plight of the poor — but also the still greater *inner* poverty hidden beneath their material need. She saw a large crowd of the "poorest of the poor," reaching out to her as she stood in their midst. They were calling for her to rescue them, to bring them to the One who alone could save them — to bring them to Jesus.

In the second scene, the same crowd was there, with great sorrow and suffering in their faces. And this time, Mary, the Mother of Jesus, was also there among them, mystically present at this modern Calvary — just as she had been two thousand years ago. In the vision, Mother Teresa was kneeling at Mary's side, and though she could not see the Blessed Mother's face, she heard her say: "*Take care of them — they are mine — Bring them to Jesus — carry Jesus to them — Fear not.*" [32]

In the third and final scene, Mother Teresa was shown the same crowd, though this time she could see that they were covered in darkness. There, in the midst of this sea of anguish, was Jesus on the cross — with the only light coming down from above, shining on, and from, the mystery of the cross. The poor were unaware of Jesus' presence with them in their pain, sharing their suffering, and turning it into seeds of resurrection. Mother Teresa heard him say to her from the cross: "*I have asked you. They have asked you, and she, My Mother, has asked you. Will you refuse to do this for Me — to take care of them, to bring them to Me?*" [33]

In the months before her vision, Jesus had explained to Mother Teresa his reason, the *driving purpose*, for sending her to the poor, summed up in his touching lament: "*They don't know Me — so they don't want Me....*" [34] This was the cause of his "painful thirst"; and the motive for her mission to pierce their darkness with the light of his longing.

But she was sent not only to the poor of Calcutta, and not only to pierce the darkness of material want. She was sent also to us — to

A painting of Mother Teresa's vision of 1947 (Cristina Cruz-Parra/Missionaries of Charity Fathers, Mexico City)

a modern culture of which, for different reasons but with the same effect, Jesus could also say, *"They don't know Me — so they don't want Me. . . ."* He sent Mother Teresa to proclaim his thirst to this generation so that, in an age grown cold, to a world living under the same blanket of darkness and unredeemed pain portrayed in her vision, she might remind us of God's yearning, and so reawaken our own.

May her God-given light lead us to "know him and to want him," to want the God who wants us, thirsting for us from a tree.

———

1. Infinite Longing

The first light to come from Mother Teresa's experience on the train touches on the central message of Jesus' thirst — the "infinite longing in the heart of God" for us, his children.

In the deepest part of our soul we all yearn to be loved — but most especially by the God who is the source of all love. What more consoling news can there be, then, than to know we are loved beyond all we could hope or imagine, with a love infinite in magnitude and intensity, beyond all measuring or conceiving? This mystery is so great that it requires effort on our part to approach it, since we have no concept of what an "infinite love" might be.

We have no analogies for infinity, nothing to compare it to, and so our best recourse in the quest to understand God's love are analogies that are within our grasp, such as "thirst" — human metaphors that help point us towards the divine reality. Those analogies that convey something of the intensity and immensity of God's love, like thirst and longing, help us draw closer to the divine abyss.

St. Catherine of Siena, the great mystic and Doctor of the Church, shared many of Mother Teresa's intuitions regarding the divine thirst. She speaks of the crucified Jesus as "slain with such fire of love... as seems insatiable. Yet still he thirsts, as if saying: 'I have greater ardor and desire and thirst for your salvation than I am able to show you, [even] with my Passion.'"[35] From her own mystical experience, Catherine could only describe the God she had encountered with her own analogies: as "*pazzo d'amore; ebbro d'amore*" — as "crazed with love, drunk with love."[36]

If we derive anything from the *ardor* of divine love described in Scripture, in the Song of Songs, in the spousal language of the Old Testament, or in the role of Jesus as Bridegroom of Israel, it is that in some inconceivable way, God not only loves us, but he is also *in love* with us. This profound mystery lies at the core of Mother Teresa's discovery. There is a definite *eros* in God's love for us, which must be correctly understood (as we shall see) but not discarded, lest we reduce divine love to mere benevolence. His love revealed in Scripture, even in the Old Testament, is a "passionate" love,[37] a love Mother Teresa fully understood, appreciated, and made bold to proclaim:

> *That boy and girl who fall in love with each another, that love is "I thirst." You have to experience it. Same thing — we come to that conviction. . . . His love is thirst.*[38]
>
> *When we look at Jesus during His humiliating Passion & death we ask — why all this? for what purpose. . . . No one, not even Jesus could have gone through all that humiliating suffering if He was not in love.*[39]

This ardent love is not only the domain of the Son, who shares our humanity; its source is the Father. It is staggering to realize that the Father loves all of mankind with the same love, with the same magnitude and the same intensity, with which he loves his divine Son. Mother Teresa understood that it is God's nature to love this way, to love us with the entirety of his being, and that he cannot love us any less. For this reason she so often came back to the word "infinite," to clarify the nature of his thirst. *"Jesus is God therefore His love, His thirst is infinite. . . . [We are called to] quench this infinite thirst of a God made Man."*[40]

If we were to take all the love in every heart of everyone on earth, and add to it all the love of all those who ever existed throughout history, then add the love of all the saints in heaven, and all the angels, cherubim and seraphim, and pour all that love into *one* heart, and direct all that love on ourselves, it would still fall infinitely short of the love God is pouring out on each one of us, right now. Because God is infinite, *his love is not divided*, with each of us receiving but a portion. We each receive the totality, the fullness of divine love, twenty-four hours a day, every day of our lives.

A Pencil in God's Hand

Mother Teresa was so conscious of her mission to communicate the "light and love" she had received, that she *defined herself in terms of her message*, describing herself as *"a pencil in God's hand, that He might write His love letter to the world."*[41] In service to that message, she never shied away from using the most ardent language to describe the intimacy to which Jesus' thirst invites us, a language that fills the pages of Scripture itself:

For the LORD delights in you,
    and your land shall be married.
For as a young man marries a virgin,
    so shall your sons marry you,
and as the bridegroom rejoices over the bride,
    so shall your God rejoice over you. (Is 62:4-5)

Mother Teresa understood that the only way to approach God's thirst for us is to *open to it*, without insisting on understanding or being worthy. As theologian Karl Rahner observed, "Some things are understood not by grasping, but by allowing oneself to be grasped." Such a love can never be earned, nor fully understood, for it remains wholly beyond us, but at the same time wholly *for* us. It is a love that can always be believed in and welcomed into our heart, entirely free, and ever close at hand.

2. GOD'S DELIGHT

In all our life, no one will ever love us as God does — nor love us with a love so undeterred by our imperfections. In the heart of God, Mother Teresa encountered a love not inspired by condescension or pity, nor much less by obligation, but a love that *delights* in us, that finds joy in loving us. Scripture affirms that God indeed rejoices over his creation:

"You shall no more be termed Forsaken,
    and your land shall no more be termed Desolate,
but you shall be called My delight . . .
for the LORD delights in you." (Is 62:4)

"[God] will rejoice over you with gladness,
    he will renew you in his love;
he will exult over you. . . ." (Zeph 3:17)

Such exuberance points to a God who not only loves us, but *likes* us, enjoys us, and delights to be with us: "I was . . . delighting in the sons of men" (Prov 8:30, 31). We please God just by existing; like parents who thoroughly delight in their children, long before they are old enough to do anything "worthy" of their delight.

Does the artist not delight in his handiwork? Does God's very thirst for us not indicate his delight? His message to Jesus, and through him to us, is unchanging, from Old Testament to New:

> "Behold my servant, whom I uphold,
>   my chosen, in whom my soul delights." (Is 42:1)

> "You are my beloved . . . with you I am well pleased." (Lk 3:22)

To all who approached her, Mother Teresa mirrored and mediated the experience of God's delight in us. Almost universally, those who met her would remark on this sense of basking in her delight, of finding such welcome and attention, such interest and obvious delight in her look and smile and warmth of touch. Even when surrounded by a crowd, people invariably felt as if they alone existed for her in all the world, as if Mother Teresa had nothing else to do but attend to them, and no other desire than to be with them. Her eyes would light up whenever someone approached, making them feel like a long-lost relative finally come home. She would help them to sit down, and hold their hand while she listened to them intently. When anyone was in her presence, time seemed to stop. It was as if she, and by extension the God who sent her, neither had nor wanted anyplace else to pour their love.

Love Transforms

God's thirst for us is not dependent on who or how we are. His love is not about us, and does not depend on us — it is rather about *him*, about a God whose *nature* it is to love. Because God is free in loving us, he is likewise free to delight in us. Since only his freely given love makes us lovable, it is our willing acceptance of that love, our accept-

Missionaries of Charity Sisters welcoming Mother Teresa (Raghu Rai/Magnum Photos)

ance of his delight, that transforms us and makes us "grace-ful," and beautiful, and loving in turn.

Even where there is no beauty in us, God's love works its divine alchemy, rendering even the least of us beautiful. Look at Mother Teresa herself. There was an aura about her, a radiance and beauty beyond worldly attractiveness. She possessed the unmistakable bearing and exuberance of one who lived in a *state of being loved*. The love-light that shone in her made people see beyond the lines in her face; they noticed only the inner beauty that suffused her countenance, a beauty born of knowing herself so thoroughly loved. Just as people delighted in beholding Mother Teresa despite the lines on her features or her human limitations, even so can God delight in us — even as we are, as he pours into us the love that makes us lovable, even beautiful. God's delight makes us delightful; but it works its sacred alchemy only if we choose to believe it, and are open to receive it.

Meeting God's unqualified acceptance of us banishes our fears and renders our defenses needless, allowing them to fall away one by one. God's loving gaze, the same we glimpsed reflected in Mother Teresa's eyes, frees us to journey to our depths, and to make peace with those parts of ourselves we had feared admitting. We become more sincere, more vulnerable and open, and more tender in turn. The more we are in touch with God's pleasure in loving us, the more we ourselves become pleasing.[42] As Mother Teresa reminds us, in words reminiscent of her own inner journey, our task is to *believe unswervingly in God's delight*, and to remember it in times of trouble:

> *You are precious to Him. He loves you, and He loves you so tenderly that He carved you on the palm of His hand. When your heart feels restless, when your heart feels hurt, when your heart feels like breaking, remember, I am precious to Him, He loves me. He has called me by my name. I am His.*[43]

Being in Mother Teresa's presence gave the poor of Calcutta, and those of us who watched from afar, a glimmer of what awaits us in the kingdom, in that ocean of delight that is the Father's heart. She has granted us a foreshadowing of what it will be like to rest in the Father's loving gaze, and to spend our eternity in his cherishing.

3. PRESENCE

The God who delights in us does not do so from a distance. His longing for union with us, and his yearning to be with us, *draws him to us* constantly. God's thirst draws him closer to us than we can imagine, closer than we are to ourselves. The God who was so powerfully present to Mother Teresa on the train is just as present to us, twenty four hours a day. The same Heavenly Father who lives turned towards his Son (cf. Jn 1:1-2) also lives ever turned towards and focused on each one of us, his children.

Mother Teresa's own desire to live *with* the poor, in imitation of her Lord, led her to dwell in their midst and to share their poverty — just as did the God of Israel, who instead of staying aloof on the heights of Sinai, chose to dwell under a tent in the company of his people. Likewise, Jesus our Emmanuel, who, instead of saving us from afar, came to pitch his tent among us, wrapped not only in the desert dust, but in our very flesh.

We witnessed God's yearning to be with us, and to love us face-to-face, reflected in Mother Teresa. Beyond whatever material assistance she gave to the poor, she made it a point to, first of all, sit, listen, and comfort. She would spend time simply being present with the poor, face-to-face and heart-to-heart with those who had no one — knowing that no amount of blankets or bricks could warm the human heart. No government program could give the gift of presence — only individual hearts. Only the human heart can communicate the heart of God.

As Mother Teresa gave the entirety of her attention to each one, so God attends to every breath we take, and every movement of our inmost heart, with the fullness of his being. His presence to us is never just a portion of himself — as if the billions of people on the planet only had claim to their tiny portion of the Godhead. God is present to each of us with the *totality of his being*. No part of the Godhead is ever absent, or distracted, from any of us — so much so that even "the hairs of your head are all numbered" (Lk 12:7).

God's entire being attends to every faintest whisper of our soul — just as a mother who listens in the night for the breathing of her newborn. We each have, as it were, a personal channel connecting us to God, our own individual frequency to which he is tuned day and night. Even when we are not speaking to or thinking of him, God is listening to us. Such is the attentive presence of the God who thirsts for his children.

4. REACHING OUT IN MERCY

How often, in struggling with our weakness and failures, have we not felt alone and ashamed, unworthy of God, tempted to flee from his presence as Adam and Eve after the Fall? After tasting this inner bitterness and pain wrought by our own hands, by our own sin, have we not feared being abandoned by Love?

But this is not the God revealed in Scripture, nor the God mirrored for us by Mother Teresa. She reflected a God whose thirst moves him to reach out to us, to bring us back when we are lost; a God who is always seeking after us, always drawing us to himself.

All who sought out Mother Teresa during her life, whether rich or poor, brought with them a deep yearning to be accepted, to be wanted, despite their failings. Whether it was a leper with gnarled limbs, an old man abandoned and dying in a Calcutta sewer, or a troubled princess drawn to Mother Teresa without knowing why — all came with the same pain, and seeking the same reassurance. In our darkest moments, in our own dark night of the soul, we all yearn to know that *Love has not left us.* We long to be assured that God does not flee from our faults, that he does not demand we first scale some moral Olympus before we can win back his favor. This is the unfortunate image of a severe God, laid on the stooped shoulders of too many of his children.

But the God of Israel is another:

Israel has committed "adultery" and has broken the covenant; God should judge and repudiate her. It is precisely at this point that God is revealed to be God and not man: "How can I give you up, O Ephraim! How can I hand you over, O Israel! ... My heart recoils within me, my compassion grows warm and tender. I will not execute my fierce anger, I will not again destroy Ephraim; for I am God and not man, the Holy One in your midst" (Hos 11:8-9). God's passionate love for his people — for humanity — is at the same time a forgiving love.[44]

Mother Teresa's very act of presence, choosing to live in the worst of Calcutta's slums, and doing so in God's name, is a sign to us that God will never leave us alone to fight our battles, helpless as leaves in a hurricane; he will always be our "God-with-us," who gladly leaves the ninety-nine to rescue the lost and the fallen, and carry them in his arms.

Unconditional Longing

Mother Teresa taught that God's thirst for us was unconditional and unchanging, even when we find ourselves lost in the struggle with sin. Far from diminishing God's yearning for us, our brokenness unleashes in him yet deeper wellsprings of tenderness and mercy. God's mercy is more than passive acceptance of us, more too than ready pardon should we return. God's thirst for us is a relentless, never-regretted resolve to be with us *in our wandering* — to seek us out and bring us back, and once we have returned, to shower us with blessings greater than those we had lost.

In each moment of our wandering, God is already there awaiting us, along the very path of our betrayal. The gospel account of the Samaritan woman (Jn 4:7-42) tells the story of an adulteress who comes, burdened with disgrace, to draw water at the village well. She deliberately comes at high noon, long after the other women have drawn water and long since returned home. She is met there, precisely at the place that recalls her isolation and shame, by a Jesus who is already awaiting her, and who gently begins to draw her into dialogue; and then, gradually, into grace and restoration.

The same theme is reiterated and recast in every possible setting throughout the gospel — from the parable of the lost sheep, sought after and carried back in the arms of the shepherd (Lk 15:3-7), to that of the lost coin (Lk 15:8-10), to the parable of the lost (prodigal) son, who returns home only to find a fatted calf and joyous feasting, a ring for his finger and sandals for his feet, and the heart's festival of an exultant father (Lk 15:11-32).

In his extreme of mercy, God takes on himself not only our sin, but all its attendant pain and shame. We need only cast this divine mercy in human terms to better understand its true radicality. What dentist takes on the pain of his patients? Or what judge, no matter how merciful, would take on the sentence of the accused? But God never shies away from the consequences of his thirst for us, no matter the price, even unto "death, even death on a cross" (Phil 2:8). Far from ignoring or even causing human suffering, God plunges himself directly into it. He fills our pain with his love, weds it to himself, experiences it head-on in all its cruelty, and bursts its chains from within — turning all into resurrection. God transforms our pain and dying not only into a *new* life (i.e., our previous life restored), but a qualitatively different life, a sharing in *his own* life as free gift.

Mother Teresa invites us to believe in a God who never tires of seeking us out and forgiving us. To the poor of Calcutta, she communicated this experience of *being sought* in God's name — even as she had been sought out on the train to Darjeeling. She spent her life seeking out the poor and the lonely, walking in the footsteps of the Good Shepherd, salving wounds of body and soul. She showed us that whenever we wander, there is a gentle shepherd, a hound of heaven, already pursuing us. Knocking at the door of our heart, he calls us back in a refrain that has echoed down the ages since the Garden: "Where are you?" (Gen 3:9).

But is there a hidden flaw in God's mercy? Does his benevolence inadvertently become license to sin? Does his acceptance and thirst for us, no matter how we are, diminish the seriousness and consequences of human evil, or lessen our need of conversion? Certainly not. God's mercy has but one purpose — it is an ever-open doorway to the possibility of a changed and different life; an invitation to new beginnings, free and clear, beyond the weight of past wrongs. The Father's generous mercy, as he awaits each prodigal along his or her very road of undoing — sending his Son to the furthest end of that road, wrapped in our sin on Calvary — is anything but license.

More than anything else, God's loving mercy calls forth our own repentant love in return. In contemplating this mercy given unto folly, Mother Teresa's namesake, St. Thérèse of Lisieux, proclaimed: "Even if my conscience were burdened with all the sins possible to commit, I would still throw myself without hesitation into God's arms."

———

Mother Teresa discovered that God delights in authoring new life, especially where it had been lost: "Behold, I make all things *new*" (Rev 21:5). Once we have returned to him, God not only forgives us, but he also makes our last state even more blessed than the first. In the end, our forgiven condition is yet more blessed than was our original innocence — just as the paradise that awaits us is unspeakably greater than Eden's paradise lost. In contemplating such unexpected, undeserved goodness, the Church would exult over Adam's fall as *Felix Culpa* — "Happy Fault!" God's heart has not changed since the Garden; he still longs to transform our failings into blessing and new life, to make of our past sins a new beginning, to turn all our failures into "Happy Fault."

As St. Thérèse proclaimed, indeed, *"All is grace."* Even our pain and trials carry the seeds of hidden blessings, blessings far greater than the trials that veil them. Mother Teresa insisted that, in the last analysis, there are no problems, only gifts, since without exception, "in everything God works for good" (Rom 8:28). Mother Teresa saw for herself that God's eleventh-hour blessings far overshadow the trials from which they come, emerging as a butterfly from a long-forgotten cocoon.

How consoling it is to know that we need not beg God to bless, to forgive, or to lift us up after a fall. "Fear not, little flock, for it is your Father's good *pleasure* to give you the kingdom" (Lk 12:32).

Finally, more than sentiment, the mercy born of God's thirst is true *power*. God has placed all his creative power and energy at the service of his mercy. Our God is a master craftsman so skilled that, when his beloved child brings him the pieces of the crystal vase he had fashioned and given as a gift, broken though the child's own negligence, he cannot resist not only repairing it, but making it *even more beautiful* than it was before. This is the extent, the reach, and the power of his mercy.

5. FAITHFUL LOVE

After one of her Sisters had earned some reprimand and been corrected by Mother Teresa, she would immediately shower the Sister in question with marks of affection, and rather than remove her from her post, she would often give her a higher position than she had before. Though at times her Sisters were puzzled by this, wasn't Mother Teresa modeling the same *faithfulness* accorded us by God himself? Is this not how God treats us after we fall and fail — with fresh marks of love, and new gifts of grace, greater than what we had lost?

God's faithfulness, exalted in the psalms and prophets, is the inescapable consequence of his thirst for us. God's fidelity is *his thirst for us acted out* in real time — as he immerses himself in the details of our life, and pursues us with his love. The divine faithfulness is his longing for us applied in the here and now, even when our present is made up of weakness and sin. In fact, the Scriptures show us a God whose faithfulness is most powerfully roused when confronted with its opposite — with our *un*-faithfulness. Mother Teresa reflected this divine fidelity in her non-judgmental concern for the "unfaithful," even for criminals and subjects of public scandal (curiously, something that won her criticism even among those who profess the same merciful Redeemer). As Scripture says, we may be unfaithful, but God will always remain faithful; we may deny him, but he *cannot* deny himself (2 Tim 2:13). He cannot deny his nature as unconditional love, nor his eternal dream for each one of us.

What does this divine faithfulness mean in practical terms? It is God's unshakeable commitment to continue loving us, and to bring his dreams for us to fruition, a commitment from which he will not be turned away. It means that no amount of evil we could commit could make God love us any less than he has from all eternity. And no amount of good we could do, no amount of virtue we could attain, could make him love us *any more than he already does* right now. Witness God's dealings with David after his adultery with Bathsheba and the murder of her husband, Uriah. Not only does God still trust and entrust him with the kingship of Israel, but a thousand years later, the Son of God himself will proudly bear the title "Son of David."

Witness, too, God's faithful dealings with Israel throughout its history — and the promise centuries later in the New Testament, that the chosen people of the Old will once again return to their position of favor (cf. Rom 11:25-28). All this is proof that for Israel, as for us, his Israel in miniature, "the gifts and the call of God are irrevocable" (Rom 11:29). Once again, God's love for us is *not about us, but about him*; it is not given as reward for good behavior, nor withdrawn in punishment when we stray.

Our unevangelized supposition is that our bad behavior causes God to love us less. Or worse, that his offended love turns to hostility and rejection. But God does not hate. The only thing God "hates" is sin (never the sinner); and that, too, is entirely out of love — as a grieving mother "hates" the cancer eating away at her dying child.

Does our behavior lose its importance if God loves us always and anyhow? Do our good or bad actions make any real difference, for him or for us? We can illustrate the relationship between God's faithful love and our free choices, with the example of a house in the middle of a field warmed by the noonday sun. A small child living in that house might think, when his parents open the shutters to let in the sun, that it is his parents who are in control, that they are the ones somehow turning up the volume of the sun — or that by closing all the shutters, they are turning down the brightness of the sun. But the truth is that the sun shines equally, neither augmented nor diminished by what takes place beneath it.

In the same way, God loves us equally and always, independently of our behavior. Whether we behave ill or well, God's love and blessings continue to be poured out on our world: "Your Father who is in heaven . . . makes his sun rise on the evil and on the good [alike]" (Mt 5:45). God's love is not conditional, as is human love. Just as the sun's nature is to shine and not to vary, so it is God's nature to love completely and infinitely, and not to vary. "It is because *he is so unutterably good* that he loves all persons, good and evil. . . . He loves the loveless, the unloving, the unlovable. He acts, he doesn't react. He initiates love. He is love without [human cause or] motive."[45] Loving is what God does, all the time. Without this eternal and unconditional outflow of love, in fact, God would cease to be God.

What takes place when we freely choose evil? We close the shutters of our soul, as it were, so that the rays of the divine sun — constantly shining down on us — cannot enter. We end up closing ourselves up against God and his love, filling our souls with a self-made darkness. God has not rejected us; rather it is we, who, by abusing the gift of our freedom, have deliberately withdrawn from him, moving ourselves beyond the pale of his love, and closing ourselves off from his blessings. In taking up the armor of sin and selfishness as protection for our egos, we end up shielding ourselves, barricading ourselves against God's love; for he will not, he cannot, give us his love by force. On the other hand, when we freely seek the good, we throw open the shutters of our soul, allowing in the full warmth of the divine sun.

Mother Teresa mirrored this kind of divine faithfulness with friend and foe alike. In the early days of her work in the Home for the Dying, the head priest of the Kali Temple, situated on the same grounds as her shelter, stirred up the people of the area against her, leading them in public protests outside Kalighat. No matter the slurs and stones thrown at her as she walked to the Home for the Dying in those days, she continued, faithful and undeterred — with no thought to whether the poor she was serving, or the people of the neighborhood, deserved or ever thanked her for her efforts.

Some months later, it was discovered that the same head priest, who had so vociferously opposed her work with the dying, was himself dying of leprosy. He was put out in the street by his own family and shunned as unclean by his fellow priests. As soon as Mother Teresa heard about it, she went out looking for him. She found him and took him in, and began tending to him herself, without a word of reproach.

Such is the beauty of God's faithfulness in action, "made flesh" in Mother Teresa's life.

———

In the following chapter we will continue our overview of the "light and love" Mother Teresa beheld on the train, as we examine the five remaining elements of her graced mosaic.

"When He [Jesus] asked for water, the soldier gave Him vinegar to drink . . . but His thirst was for love, for souls. . . ."

"The fruit of faith is the understanding of 'I thirst' . . . ." [46]

— Mother Teresa

NINE

A Legacy of Light: Part II

Mother Teresa's faith convictions, rooted in Scripture and illumined by her experience of September 10, formed her attitudes, guided her choices, and molded her into the person she became. These same convictions can be a doorway for us as well, allowing us to behold more fully the face of our God, drawing us into a new relationship with him, and into a new way of living under his light.

What was "new" for Mother Teresa that September day is, in fact, not new at all. The core of Mother Teresa's message is drawn entirely from Scripture[†] — it is purely gospel; but it is the gospel taken at its word, without half measures or dilutions. Her light is nothing but the light of Christ — a Christ whom (too often) we do not really know, and whom we may not have personally met at any deeper, more transforming level. As she writes in her letter of 1993, cited above:

> *I worry some of you still have not really met Jesus — one to one — you and Jesus alone. We may spend time in chapel — but have you seen*

[†] For a more thorough treatment of the scriptural riches of Mother Teresa's message, see Appendix One.

with the eyes of your soul how He looks at you with love? Do you really know the living Jesus — not from books, but from being with Him in your heart? Have you heard the loving words He speaks to you?[47]

But meet him we must — in the intimacy of our hearts while we live, or in the skies at his return, when it will be too late to change:

When the Son of Man comes in his glory, and all the angels with him, then he will sit on his glorious throne. . . . Then the King will say to those at his right hand, "Come, O blessed of my Father, inherit the kingdom prepared for you from the foundation of the world; for I was hungry and you gave me food, I was thirsty and you gave me drink. . . . Truly I say to you, as you did it to one of the least of these my brethren, you did it to me." (Mt 25:31, 34-35, 40)

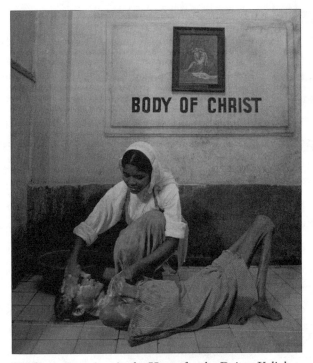

Tending to a patient in the Home for the Dying, Kalighat, Calcutta (Raghu Rai/Magnum Photos)

More than being about the afterlife, this passage is about the here and now. It shows that wherever love is needed, wherever there is suffering, Jesus is already there, uniting himself to every smallest expression of human need, and awaiting our gift of compassion.

Whenever Mother Teresa spoke in public, she loved to repeat the last line of this gospel passage, counting off the words "You-did-it-to-Me" on her five fingers. She wanted to remind us that our lives on earth are an *uninterrupted series of encounters with the Son of God*, hidden in mystery, under what she called the *"distressing disguise"* of human pain and poverty — a mystery that Jesus presents as the one theme of our "final exam" on the Last Day. There we will not be asked if we did "mighty works" in his name (Mt 7:22), but *if we loved*, even as the Father, who "makes his sun rise on the evil and on the good, and sends rain on the just and on the unjust" (Mt 5:45).

Mother Teresa wanted us to awaken from our sleep, to see the light of Christ's presence hidden under the veil of human darkness and pain. She urged us not to ignore Jesus' unseen presence wherever our fellow human beings suffer in body or soul.

This was not only true of Christ's presence in the sufferings of others, but equally in our own. In times of trial, she hoped we would not lament the absence of a Christ ever-present, concealed within the shackles that bind us, yoked to our predicament and our pain. What Mother Teresa called Jesus' *"distressing disguise"*[48] is actually the face of everyman. The fact that the crucified-risen Son of God has united himself to every manifestation of human suffering points to a God who is always at our side, bent to lift the burden of our struggles *from within*, united with us fully, his unchanging love wedded to our changing conditions, even to our pain, each day.

Encounter

Our lives are not complete until we have consciously met the God who awaits us, beneath the surface of our rushed existence. We each need our own September 10, our own conscious meeting with the God who (in the elegant words of Indian poet Rabindranath Tagore) "comes, comes, ever comes." It is not enough to merely learn, as from a distance, from Mother Teresa's light. We need our own personal epiphany, our ongoing encounter with the light of God and the God of light — renewed daily, always beckoning, ever filling us. Mother Teresa's example shows that by cultivating this encounter, we can successfully navigate the challenges of our Calcutta and, as she, leave a legacy of light and goodness along our path.

Those light-bearers who have gone as pilgrims before us, ordinary people like Sister Teresa, the Loreto schoolteacher, are proof that we *can* encounter the divine, proof that this grace is not reserved for a restricted elite, for Moses or Elijah or a few chosen disciples two thousand years ago. This encounter is accessible to all, and always.

Reflecting God

It stands to reason that those who knew Jesus more intimately also saw the God he reveals, reflected in him, more clearly: "He who has seen me has seen the Father" (Jn 14:9). This intimate circle includes not only his first disciples, but also in our day, the saints. With a two-thousand-year buffer separating us from Jesus of Nazareth, the insights of those closest to him, of those most transformed by Jesus, help us to better understand him and draw nearer to his light.

Though far from being on a par with Revelation, the insights of the saints add clarity and detail to the concentrated light of Revelation. Their teachings both illumine God's word and draw us closer to knowing the Father.

"Be transformed by the *renewal of your mind*" (Rom 12:2), St. Paul exhorts. Mother Teresa's journey on the train to Darjeeling invites us to undertake our own transformational journey, renewing our image of God with the same divine light accorded to her.

As we continue "trying on" the light of Mother Teresa's convictions, we may be surprised at how well they "fit" the human soul. Just as Mother Teresa after September 10, thanks to our encounter with God's radiance, we, too, can begin relating to God, and to life itself, in an entirely new way. Let us pick up our journey where we left off, joining Mother Teresa on her pilgrimage into the light.

6. DIVINE HUMILITY — THE MYSTERY OF GOD'S SELF-EMPTYING

Inevitably, after meeting Mother Teresa people would be struck by the remarkable humility of this living icon, this friend of presidents and princesses. I, too, was struck by her profound sense of self-effacement, and had many opportunities to witness it in action. Once, after celebrating morning Mass for her Sisters in Calcutta, she came to sit with me while I had breakfast, as she often did. On this particular occasion I watched, not quite believing my eyes, as this Nobel laureate picked up the orange next to my plate and began peeling it. She carefully separated the sections and handed them to me, one by one, to eat. She did this without the least affectation, and without saying a word. I learned that she had often done this for her Sisters as well.

Mother Teresa was grounded in a serene humility that left its fragrance on everything she did. Here was a world figure who chose for her room the worst place in the building, abutting the common latrine — and jealously kept for herself the job of cleaning them. With her, this kind of self-effacement was normal — humility was not an effort for Mother Teresa, but a way of life.

Perhaps we can understand humility in someone who, like Mother Teresa, shares our common human lot. But how can we explain humility *in God*? Humility is usually defined as the recognition of our nothingness, the acknowledgement of faults, and the effort not to appear more than we are. But if God has no faults, and if he is truly infinite, how can he be humble?

Humility, however, is not only a negative, not only the absence of something (pride). Understood properly, humility is a positive quality essential to the act of loving; it is the "humus" inseparable from love, both a condition for and a component of all true loving. Humility is the hidden ground of love that we do not immediately perceive. The opposite of love is not hatred, but pride, the source of all hatred. Therefore, there can be *no love without humility* — since love and pride cannot coexist. Humility is the matrix of love, the unseen wellspring of all self-giving, human and divine. Only to the extent that we are humble, are we free enough from self to love and give.

If God loves, he must necessarily be humble. In fact, in the letter to the Philippians (Phil 2:6ff.), St. Paul lifts the veil on a God whose *very nature* is self-emptying, who "emptied himself, taking the form of a servant." God not only has love, as we humans do, God is love. Love defines him, and he defines genuine love.

But if we affirm that God is love, we also need to say that, in some real way, God *is humility*. And if we go on to take the next step and say that God is *infinite* love, we must also be ready to take a yet bolder step and affirm that in a certain sense God is *infinite humility*.[49] Here the mind reels. Yet, as we look to the gospel and all that the Son of God does there, we find the expressions of this divine humility everywhere.

Why choose this kind of abasement, a scandal to his own people? Why be born in a stable, while the high priest who awaits the Messiah's birth lives in a palace? The only possible reason is that the God whom Jesus came to reveal is himself a being of humility: "In Jesus, we see God showing himself to be eternally and mysteriously a servant of humility, even in the very depth of his glory."[50]

This explains the incomprehensible choices Jesus makes — the extremes of humility (and even humiliation) that he embraces, from birth to death. The Son of the Most High begins life in a cave, cradled between beasts of burden, and ends his life on a cross, nailed between thieves.

But how do we reconcile God's humility with his power? Though God is indeed all-powerful, his power is not opposed to his self-emptying, but at its service. The pinnacle and the true nature of his power are revealed in the all-powerlessness of Calvary. God's love in Jesus crucified *is* the summit of divine power — for only a God who is extraordinarily powerful can efface himself so extraordinarily. Even a casual reading of the gospel shows that the God revealed in Jesus, especially in Jesus crucified, is a God of unlimited self-effacement.[51]

———

In his extreme of humility, the Son of God not only clothed himself in our flesh, but in our sin: "For our sake he made him to be sin who knew no sin" (2 Cor 5:21). God thirsts not only for our love, but for all of us, even for our sins.

We see this *humble* thirst for us demonstrated in a famous episode from the life of St. Jerome — Father of the Church and the first to translate the Bible into the language of the day.

After many years spent in Jerusalem translating the Word of God, Jerome finished his grand project just days before Christmas. To celebrate his accomplishment, Jerome decided to spend Christmas Eve in nearby Bethlehem, praying in one of the many grottoes that dot the countryside. According to the ancient account, sometime around midnight Jesus appeared to him, saying, "Jerome, what will you give me for my birthday?"

Immediately and enthusiastically, Jerome declared, "Lord, I give you my translation of your word." But instead of congratulating him, Jesus simply replied: "No, Jerome that is not what I want."

Jerome was speechless. Then he began to complain and remonstrate with Jesus, asking why he had let him go on for forty years, far from home, laboring at something other than what God most wanted from him. But Jesus remained silent. Jerome started suggesting other ways of honoring Jesus' birthday — fasting, becoming a hermit, giving his possessions to the poor. To each of these Jesus replied, "No, Jerome. That is not what I want most."

Finally, Jerome protested, "Then you tell me, Lord. Tell me what would give you most joy on your birthday, and you shall have it."

"Do you promise, Jerome?"

"Yes, Lord, anything at all."

Jesus replied, *"Give me your sins. . . ."*

———

"Give me your sins." In his limitless humility, more than any service we can render him, the Lord considers it a *gift* that we "allow" him to take away our sins. Why? Precisely because he thirsts for us, because he longs for union with us, and the only obstacle to that union is our sin — which in his eyes, then, becomes the most precious gift we can offer. This is the God revealed in Jesus, the God Mother Teresa met — an infinitely humble God who thirsts for us, and even for our sins.

7. THE DIVINE TENDERNESS

In observing Mother Teresa, it was obvious how keenly she felt the suffering of the poor and identified with their distress. She not only accepted a share in their deprivations, she sought it out. She took on voluntary fasting and other self-imposed penances so as to share more closely in the pain and lot of the poor. She slept on a hard prison bed, with no fan, her tiny room sweltering in Calcutta's oven-like heat. Her little room was both sleeping space and office, with no more than a table and a stool for furnishing. If such was the lot of the poor, who had neither fans nor a fancy desk, it would be her lot as well. This kind of tenderness of heart, this chosen vulnerability before the sufferings of others, was another attribute of the thirst of God that Mother Teresa had discovered, and reflected, and whose deep roots fill the pages of Scripture.

Already the Old Testament celebrates this divine tenderness, giving Yahweh the title *Av Rahamim* (Tender Father).[52] Then, as the New Testament opens, Zachariah rejoices in the "tender mercy of our God" (Lk 1:78), a meekness of heart (cf. Mt 11:29) that Jesus will reveal, on behalf of the "Tender Father," throughout his life.

———

How can we say God is "tender," if he is above human emotions, even the most noble? Though Scripture portrays God as grieved, moved to the depths, vulnerable to our sufferings, and affected by our behavior towards him — especially our lack of love — can this be taken literally?

Here we stand on the edge of mystery. While holding to God's utter transcendence, we must not back away from the way he himself has chosen to describe his divinity. God desires and decides to show himself — through the prophets, and all the more radically in Jesus — as vulnerable, tender, and sensitive to our suffering, to our rebellion, and especially to our love or lack of love; with all that this implies for the understanding of his interiority and divinity.

Does God, or better, *can* God be moved by our human suffering, or "grieve" over our sin? If we are speaking of the way we humans suffer and are moved, in our finite, fallen human nature, then clearly this is not the case with God. But safeguarding that distinction, there is still a profound truth beyond the powerful, even passionate figures of speech employed in God's self-revelation.

While the idea of God's tenderness and vulnerability may strain our comprehension, it remains in some way an essential part of his character, and an inescapable aspect of his being — if we are to take his word seriously. Our God is not the god of the Greek philosophers, the *Unmoved Mover*, remote and indifferent atop Olympus. In some mysterious way, there is not only *agape*, sacrificial love, in God, but a divine *eros*, a love that is "moved" before the sight or the plight of the beloved. In the words of Pope Benedict XVI, in God's revelation, and especially in the crucifixion of Jesus, "eros and agape, far from being opposed, enlighten each other."[53] In a way that transcends our understanding, God is indeed "moved" by the state of mankind, moved to the very depths of his "womb of tenderness." As Pope Benedict affirms:

> God's love is also *eros*....The prophet Hosea expresses this divine passion with daring images....[54]

Though this insight may be radical and challenging, it is by no means new. Both the language of Scripture and the teachings of the Fathers point to the mystery of God's tenderness in the face of our suffering and sin, of God's freely chosen vulnerability before his children. In the words of Origen:

> What is this passion that Christ first suffered for us? It is the passion of love. But the Father himself, the God of the universe, who is full of forbearance, mercy, and pity, does he not also suffer in some way? The Father himself is not impervious! ... He [too] *suffers a passion of love.*[55]

The great patristic scholar Henri de Lubac comments on this passage: "Surprising and admirable text! [Origen] affirms that, in his love for man, the Impassible [God] has suffered a *passion of mercy.*"[56]

How can this be, in an almighty God? There is something essential to the nature of love — and therefore to the nature of God — that makes the lover *vulnerable to the one loved*, not out of need or lack, but out of free and sovereign choice. A mother does not "need" her newborn child in any essential way, but by her freely chosen love she *makes* herself vulnerable to the child, to his needs, to his pain, to his love.

Love and vulnerability, love and sensitivity, go hand in hand. The more a person loves, the more he or she becomes sensitive to the response of the beloved (or to its lack). A stranger or an enemy may insult us, but they leave our heart untouched. Yet the smallest gesture, a mere look from someone deeply loved, can touch or wound us to the core.

So it is with God. If the degree of love determines the degree of sensitivity, and if God's love for us is infinite — then in a certain sense (and here again the mind stumbles) God is *infinitely sensitive* to our love. His divine eros, his divine "sensitivity," is not only beyond our own, but beyond our imagining. Here is the ultimate mystery hidden beneath, and revealed by Jesus' cry of thirst. Here is the rationale for believing that an infinite God can yearn for us, sinners that we are, even "unto death . . . death on a cross" (Phil 2:8).

God is moved not only by the overall tenor of our lives, but by every single movement of our heart. Our smallest return of his love has more impact and importance with God than we will ever know. Mother Teresa taught insistently the importance and significance of our poor human love to the heart of God — that God not only welcomes our love but *yearns* to be loved by us. He wants us to love him in the same way that he loves us — that is, *to thirst for him*, even as he thirsts for us. In the words of St. Augustine, "*Deus sitit sitiri*" ("God thirsts to be thirsted for").[57] With all his being, God longs to be longed for, by each one of us, without exception. Such is the tenderness and sensitivity of the heart of our God.

8. Intimacy and Union

No one I know enjoyed weddings more than Mother Teresa. She who saved every grain of rice so that nothing would be wasted, happily "wasted" whatever it cost for her orphan girls to have a proper trousseau on their wedding day.

For Mother Teresa, the intimacy of human marriage was a reflection of the union God wished to forge with all mankind, and with each individual soul. While the gods of other religions wished to be feared, served, or simply worshiped, the God of Israel longed to relate to his people *in love*, to the point of making love his central command, the core of his Covenant, and the first hint of how serious was his thirst for our return of love: "You shall love the LORD your God with all your heart, and with all your soul, and with all your might" (Dt 6:5).

Since we are created in the image of God, our human longing for intimacy is a reflection of God's own nature, and a sharing in the divine impetus to love and be loved. Time after time, the prophets turn to this motif in describing the inner life of Yahweh, and the intimacy he desires with his people:

> Ezekiel, speaking of God's relationship with the people of Israel, is not afraid to use strong and passionate language (cf. 16:1-22). These biblical texts indicate that *eros* is part of God's very Heart: the Almighty awaits the "yes" of his creatures as a young bridegroom that of his bride.[58]

Because we are fashioned in his image, there is a stirring in the human soul that longs for union with God, and for communion with one another. The longing to merge in love, as Father and Son in eternal union, is written in our very nature. No one needs to teach an infant to embrace his parents. No one ever needed to show another culture how to hold and hug their loved ones to themselves. The innate, spontaneous drive to embrace those we love points to the full merging and eternal union with the Godhead for which we were created, and which is symbolized in every human embrace.

This mystery of God's thirst for union, lived out in the Trinity's eternal embrace, is written in the depths of all being. Not only humanity, but all creation exists *for communion*. Every entity is drawn to, and exists for, another. From the heart of God to the heart of man, from the spiral of the galaxies drawing their countless stars in a single dance to the entwined double helix of DNA, the Trinitarian mystery of communion is reflected and played out in all that is.

The kind of intimacy God offers us, even here on earth, not only approaches our highest experience of human intimacy, but surpasses it. No matter how close human spouses may come, they can never truly dwell one within the other, inseparable, their souls forever merged. While the soul was created for, and longs for, this ultimate kind of union, it is only symbolized and prepared for in marriage. The true inter-dwelling of lover and beloved takes place only in our relationship with God: "You ... in me ... and I in you" (Jn 17:21).

After all, we never truly *feel* the love of another human being — we only experience our own love for them. Only God's love is capable of penetrating and being perceived directly by the human soul — and, not uncommonly, even to the point of overwhelming the senses. The common experience of the saints is that our union with God, even here on earth, knows no bounds — save those we ourselves set. The great Spanish mystics Teresa of Ávila and John of the Cross paint as close a picture as can be of the full panorama of blessedness and bliss that awaits us in God, in the full inter-dwelling of Creator and creature, even in this life. As the Mystical Doctor proclaims in his *Spiritual Canticle*:

> O you soul, then, most beautiful of creatures, who so long to know the place where your Beloved is, that you may seek Him, and be united to Him, you know now that you are yourself that very tabernacle where He dwells, the secret chamber of His retreat where He is hidden. Rejoice, therefore, and exult, because all your good and all your hope is so near you as to be within you; or, to speak more accurately, that you can not be without it, "for lo, the kingdom of God is within you." So says the Bridegroom Himself, and His servant, St. Paul, adds: "You are the temple of the living God." What joy for the soul to

learn that God never abandons it, even in mortal sin; how much less in a state of grace![59]

Those who have discovered this blessedness, as have Mother Teresa and the saints, gladly give up not only selfishness and sin, but every other lesser good, to possess this "pearl of great price." Like the merchant of fine pearls in the gospel story (Mt 13:45-46), so overjoyed at his good fortune that he never thinks of the cost, the saints experience their sacrifices not as deprivation, but as a small price for such an immense reward. The saints have been the truest and the greatest lovers in human history, those who have gone furthest in the pursuit of love, all the way to its divine Source — and they have marked out a path for us, living to the full the divine union for which we all exist.

In the end, it is our union with God that makes life not only bearable in the night of our Calcutta, but beautiful. As Mother Teresa attests, "The more you are intimately in love with Him, the more you are specially attached to Him, the more He is really that intimate love in your heart — it is really something beautiful."[60]

9. DIGNITY AND DIVINITY

Of all the myriad sufferings that Mother Teresa tended to in the poor, the common denominator she discovered in all of them was the *loss of human dignity* — since the poor found themselves so often among those she termed society's *"throw-aways."* Together with their loss of human dignity there was the added loss of *divine* dignity, as the poor and the outcaste never knew what it was to be treated as God's children, as temples of the living God, *"created for greater things, to love and be loved,"* [61] as Mother Teresa would say. She wrote in one of her letters:

Poverty doesn't only consist of being hungry for bread, but rather it is a tremendous hunger for human dignity. *We need to love and to be somebody for someone else. This is where we make our mistake and shove people aside. Not only have we denied the poor a piece of bread, but by thinking that they have no worth and leaving them abandoned in the streets, we have denied them the human dignity that is right-fully theirs as children of God. The world today is hungry not only for bread but hungry for love, hungry to be wanted, to be loved.* [62]

Because of her grace of the train, Mother Teresa had experienced the profound esteem in which God himself holds us; as Scripture affirms, "You have made him little less than the angels, and you have crowned him with glory and honor" (Ps 8:5).

Mother Teresa wanted her Sisters to make it a special point to reflect to the poor the fullness of their God-given dignity. She insisted that our greatest sense of worth comes from *being wanted*, from knowing that there is someone who longs for us and wants our love, that we are that important to another human being. And so she strove in every way, in look and voice and touch, to show the poor that they were precious to God, that they were wanted by the One who mattered most. What dignity is ours when we realize how much, and by whom, we are wanted — that we are yearned for by the Almighty himself, and that we are each that important to the living God.

Despite what our failures and inadequacies may suggest, our God-given dignity is *innate* and cannot be lost, neither at our own hand, nor taken away by society, nor by the abuse of others, for it is immutable. No meandering on our part, nor any humiliation directed at us, can destroy our divine endowment — though we may lose our ability to enjoy and draw from our dignity until we repent and return, as did the prodigal son. But, just as the prodigal son, come what may, our God-given dignity remains; for just as St. Paul writes of the blessings reserved for Israel despite their infidelities, "the gifts and call of God are irrevocable" (Rom 11:29).

Consider the example of a finely handcrafted silver dish. No matter how roughly it is treated, *it remains forever silver*. Someone may see it left in the garbage, abandoned and tarnished, and pass it by. But a jeweler who happens to pass by, and recognizes it as silver, knows that its true value is still there, intact. He retrieves it eagerly, knowing that with a buffing he can restore its original brilliance. We are all like that silver dish. What God has given, we or others can neglect, deny, or abuse — but never destroy.

Mother Teresa showed us the restorative power of seeing the God-given dignity in others, wherever that dignity may have been lost, and reflecting it back to them with our own gaze. Disinterested love reveals our dignity to us anew, and frees us to reclaim it. The poor and the rejected rediscover not only their own human dignity, but the loving gaze of the Father, reflected in the eyes of those who have learned to love as genuinely as she.

There are countless examples of the restorative power of love in Mother Teresa's work. In Calcutta, many children who began life literally thrown away, cast aside as infants on a rubbish heap by parents who could not afford, or did not want, to keep them, have been rescued by Mother Teresa and her Sisters. Loved back into life, smiled on and caressed, told and retold of their goodness, they were gradually prepared in body and spirit for adoption by a waiting and loving family. Today those same children are graduating from universities, having children of their own, and passing on the miracle of restorative love that had given them new life and dignity out of the ash heap of the slums.

———

Human dignity is not bestowed en masse, however. There is no "generic" human dignity. Mother Teresa not only loved the poor, but loved them *individually, uniquely.* She insisted that *"every person in the world is unique;"*[63] and helped all who met her experience that uniqueness, to feel that they were each special and irreplaceable, in her eyes and God's.

This very uniqueness lends an added dimension to our dignity — the fact that, even in its universality, it is a dignity that is *ours alone.* No one else can ever take our place; no one else has, nor will ever

have, the same personality, the same combination of gifts and blessings, that God has prepared for each one of us.

Since our dignity is individual and unique, God's longing for us
is likewise individual and unique. Does Jesus not tell us that the
Good Shepherd leaves the ninety-nine to go in search of the one, single lost sheep? If God's yearning for us is individual, it means that no
one else on earth, no one else in all of history, can ever take *our place
in his heart*. No one else can satisfy God's thirst for love in the way
that each of us can. No one else can satisfy God's thirst for me — just
as no amount of coffee can satisfy our thirst for tea.

This is our dignity and uniqueness in the heart of God.

10. FATHERHOOD

Mother Teresa's close relationship to her own father, whom she
lost while she was still young, made her painfully aware of the deep
soul-wound in the lives of the poor caused by the *absence of the father*.
This is true especially in the Third World, where so many fathers are
forced to leave home and family in search of work.

But it was not only in the Third World that Mother Teresa found
the father-wound, this loss of the father. As she visited the more-
developed nations, she was saddened to see not only the increasing
absence of the father, but also the *distortion of the father's image*.
Unlike fathers in poorer countries who were deprived of meaningful work, fathers in the First World were being deprived *by* their work
— deprived of giving the time and energy and attention their children deserved. Due to the demands and stress of around-the-clock
careers, many First World fathers were either absent from the home
or emotionally distant, or even abusive, when present.

One of the deeper consequences of the father-wound is the dam-
age done to the image of *God* as Father. This negative image could
not be further from the image of the God whom Jesus had revealed,
and Mother Teresa had met. She had come to know God as Father
not only from her catechism, but through personal communion with

him — through a life lived as a child held in the Father's embrace, and carried in his arms. For her, as for all Jesus' disciples, to adore the God of Israel meant "no longer covering the eyes and face with one's hands, but surrendering with boundless trust into the powerful and tender hands of One who is forever *Abba*, 'Papa.'"[64]

Though Mother Teresa referred sparingly to the Father by his title, the countless references to God in her writings were, in fact, about the Father. All that she had discovered in Jesus, all the "light and love" he had given her on the train — all of it came ultimately from "the One who had sent him" (cf. Jn 13:20), from the Father. Everything Jesus said and did reveals the Father, and leads us back to the Father. By her vision of faith, Mother Teresa followed the mystery of Jesus and his thirst on the cross, all the way into the bosom of God the Father:

> *How much are we truly seeking to satiate the thirst of God, our loving Father in heaven, for our holiness — the thirst which Jesus expressed on the Cross when He cried out "I Thirst."* [65]

Mother Teresa hoped to demonstrate the tenderness of God the Father to a whole sector of society who had no way of knowing him. Through her works of charity, she manifested to the poor not only her own human heart, and not only the heart of Jesus, but she also modeled for them the *heart of the heavenly Father*. If it was the heart of Jesus that we saw reflected in Mother Teresa, then we were also, and ultimately, seeing the heart of the Father who sent him. In seeing Mother Teresa (or any of the saints), we have not only seen something of Christ, but something of the One whose image he is, the gentle Father of us all.

———

Does the authority associated with human fatherhood reside in God the Father as well? The answer is both yes and no. God the

Father is indeed the source of "all authority in heaven and on earth" (Mt 28:18), but not so much as the One who commands but rather as the *One who authors*. It is the Father who conceives and brings everything into being — all life, and every blessing, and every good thing under heaven. What is fatherhood, if not this overflow of creative love? As the author of all — as the initiative-taking, all-creative, inventive Father — God uses his power and authority *only to bless*: only to love, to give, to rescue, to forgive.

Precisely in his role as Father, God has been preparing his blessings for us from before our birth, like an earthly father preparing gifts for his children long before Christmas. But what is unique about the heavenly Father's gifts is that they cannot be undone — not by events, nor by the plotting of enemies, nor by our own sin once repented. The Father's power to author is such that the vicissitudes of history and the vagaries of human freedom cannot succeed at derailing his dream for us.

Precisely because of the Father's ultimate authority, no one has the same power to affirm as he: "And God saw everything that he had made, and behold, it was very good" (Gen 1:31). The Father is ever declaring each of us "good" — echoing his message about Jesus at the Jordan: "This is my beloved Son, with whom I am well pleased" (Mt 3:17). To rest in his presence in prayer — as did Jesus, who spent entire nights in communion with the Father — is the ultimate source of affirmation and inner healing. As Mother Teresa reminds us: "*When you feel lonely, when you feel unwanted, when you feel sick and forgotten, remember you are precious to the Father.*"[66]

Our Image of God

Our image of God as Father dictates and forms who we are — just as Jesus himself was formed by the image of the Father, taught to him in the Scriptures and beheld in the intimacy of prayer. We become like the God we image, so that healing our image of the Father ultimately heals our image of ourselves. The importance of Jesus' revelation of the Father, especially in his cry of thirst made in the Father's name, is in presenting a God who is far "more loving, more forgiving, more cherishing than Abraham, Isaac, or Jacob could have dreamed."[67]

> In Jesus, God cries out to us his thirst.... Our whole understanding of God, and of God's involvement with the world, is completely changed.[68]

Whether or not she was conscious of it, Mother Teresa spent her life healing our image of God. She allowed people to vicariously experience the same gentle face of God communicated to her on the train. For those who still feared him, she helped recast our image of the Almighty in tones of tenderness.

She mirrored the gospel's vision of the Father as the prodigally generous source of all abundance — the One who gives, and keeps giving, even beyond our capacity to understand or receive. Witness the glory and abundance of his creation, the untold billions of galaxies that we will never know, nor ever traverse, strung across a universe we can observe only from distances that stagger the imagination. As the doted-on children of a great and benevolent king, God our Father has placed more gifts and goodness, more power and protection, at our disposal than we will ever need, or ever know.

———

Before closing this overview, I invite the reader to go back over these chapters and spend time savoring, and ruminating over, the divine thirst as Mother Teresa understood it. If we return to ponder her light-laden vision, often and deeply enough, we will eventually make this vision our own.

Once this light is familiar enough to be an anchor and source of comfort for us, as it was for her, then we can begin to follow that light *into the presence* of the One whose light she beheld. These seeds of light, shining forth from the heart of God, will always lead us back to the divine heart from which they come.

Meditating more deeply on the light of God's goodness can help focus that light on our own soul. This divine light will begin to transform us, just as a magnifying glass focuses the sunlight on a dry leaf, and sets it ablaze. As the burning leaf holds the secret of its fire, so does the soul of every saint. So did Mother Teresa, and so can we.

"What is that word, 'I thirst,' to you personally? What connection do you make in your life? ..." [69]

— Mother Teresa

TEN

Meditation: Entering the Light

In the preceding chapters, we have surveyed the unsuspected depths of divine light contained in Jesus' words "I thirst," spoken long ago on the cross, and taken up again in our day by Mother Teresa — depths of light that illumine the face of God. As Pope Benedict XVI observes:

> Look at Christ pierced on the Cross! He is the unsurpassing revelation of God's love, a love in which *eros* and *agape*, far from being opposed, enlighten each other. On the Cross, it is God himself who begs the love of his creature: He is thirsty for the love of every one of us.[70]

Mother Teresa's transformation began by *living under this light*, and letting it draw her deeper into its divine Source, day after day, like a moth to a benevolent flame. As she did, we also need to spend time under this light, meditating and absorbing it — precisely as Mother Teresa did in the weeks of prayer following her grace of the train.

It is not enough to meditate on God's thirst for "us" in the anonymous generic, however. The essential point, the grace that Mother Teresa communicated to the poor, is that God thirsts *for me* — for the reality of who I am, right here and now. The light Mother Teresa beheld, and the words Jesus spoke from the cross, contain much more than speculative truth. While there is much for theologians to reflect on, none of it would have interested Mother Teresa if it could not be applied to individual human lives.

The reason that all transformation begins with meditation, with "renewal of the mind" (cf. Rom 12:2), is that the mind is *the doorway to the heart*. By illumining the mind, this divine light allows us to distinguish the true face of God, and gradually draws us into his presence. There before him, as our reality as "sons of men" (Lam 3:33) opens to his reality as God, the Almighty begins to communicate divine "light and love" to the soul. In beholding the true face of God in Jesus, as did St. John on Calvary, and as did Mother Teresa on the train, we begin to hear the echo of his words, addressed to us each: "*I thirst.*"

The Power of the Word

Because of the anointing of the Spirit on the Word of God, the divine word has an infinite creative power — specifically, the *power to produce what it expresses*: "And God said, '*Let there be light*'; *and there was light*" (Gen 1:3). Jesus' cry from the cross is no exception — his word of thirst is spoken to us *in power*. The same divine word that transformed Mother Teresa has the unchanging power to transform us. Prayerfully reflecting on this word intimately connects us to the One who still speaks that word — and produces in us the purpose for which it was spoken long ago.

Unlike human words that once spoken fall away, God's word stands forever, as fresh and new as the day it was first uttered.

Every Word of God reverberates through all history. The God who created all things by his word continues to create new life in us, to communicate his love and power, in the same way — by his living word.

Each Word of God is imbued with the same divine *reality* it reveals; and so God's word is not to be read once and passed over, but ruminated on and savored, as a honeybee returning to the same flower. This is what Mother Teresa did as she meditated on the beauty of God's longing, expressed in Jesus' cry of thirst on the cross, and followed its light into the divine embrace. As one rereads old love letters and is touched anew by the ever-present love that inspired them, so Mother Teresa pondered Jesus' cry of thirst newly each day, throughout the years and decades following her grace of the train — and continued to be illumined, drawn, and transformed by his word until the day she died.

For all those drawn to Mother Teresa's spirituality, God will continue to communicate the same light and love she received, and to do so by means of his words of longing, "*I thirst.*"

Guided Meditation

The following meditation is meant to assist us in entering into our own inner journey, following the path marked out by Mother Teresa. This simple presentation of her message has changed lives around the globe — from slums to suburbs, from prisons to hospitals and rehab centers, and beyond. Those who have lived far from God, and far from others, have found new hope in a message that still carries the same power it had when Mother Teresa lived, and when Jesus first proclaimed it on Calvary.

This meditation is designed to bring us face-to-face with the mystery of God's longing for each one of us, here, in the present moment. It is recommended to take time with this exercise before proceeding to the following chapters, and to return to this meditation from time to time while continuing with the remainder of the book — and, hopefully, with the remainder of one's life.

GUIDED MEDITATION

"I Thirst for You"

The divine words, *"I thirst,"* first spoken on Calvary, still echo throughout every time and place. God still speaks them in the empty space, the dark and lonely place in every human heart.

> *"Jesus is thirsting for us right now. . . . Do we listen to Him saying, 'I thirst for your love?'. . . Do we really hear Him . . . He is saying it right now."*[71]
>
> — Mother Teresa

———

"Behold, I stand at the door and knock" (Rev 3:20).

It is true. I stand at the door of your heart, day and night. Even when you are not listening, even when you doubt it could be me, I am there. I await even the smallest sign of your response, even the slightest hint of invitation that will allow me to enter.

I want you to know that whenever you invite me, I come. Always, without fail. Silent and unseen I come, but with infinite power and love, bringing the many gifts of my Father. I come with my mercy, with my desire to forgive and heal you, and with a love for you beyond your comprehension — a love every bit as great as the love I myself have received from the Father. *"As the Father has loved me, so have I loved you"* (Jn 15:9). I come longing to console you and give you strength, to lift you up and bind your wounds. I bring you my light, to dispel your darkness and all your doubts. I come with my power, that I might carry you and all of your burdens; with my grace, to touch your heart and transform your life; and my peace I give to still your soul.

I know you through and through. I know everything about you. The very hairs of your head I have numbered. Nothing in your life is unimportant to me. I have followed you through the years, and I have always loved you, even in your wanderings. I know every one of your problems; I know your needs, your fears, and your worries. I hear your every whispered prayer, always. Even when it seems I am silent, I am ever at work in your life to bless you and protect you.

Every movement of your heart I follow, and your every thought. I know all your pain, your struggles and trials, your failures and heartaches. And yes, I know all your sins. But I tell you again that I love you, and not for what you have or haven't done. I love you for you; I love you because you are. I love you for the beauty and dignity my Father gave you, creating you in his own image. It is a dignity you have forgotten, a beauty you have tarnished by ego and sin. But I love you as you are, infinitely, completely, without reserve; and I have shed my blood to win you back. If you only ask me with faith, my grace will touch all that needs changing in your life, and I will give you the strength to free yourself from sin and from all that binds and burdens you, and from all that takes you away from me.

I know what is in your heart. I know your loneliness and all your hurts: the rejections, the judgments, the humiliations. I carried it all before you. And I carried it all *for* you so that you might share my strength and my victory. I know especially your need for love, how you thirst to be accepted and appreciated, loved and cherished. But how often have you thirsted in vain, seeking that love outside of me — I who am its Source — striving to fill the emptiness inside you with passing pleasures, and often with the even greater emptiness of sin. Do you thirst for love? *"If any one thirst, let him come to me . . ."* (Jn 7:37). I will satisfy your desire for love beyond your dreams. Do you thirst to be appreciated and cherished? I cherish you more than you can imagine, to the point leaving heaven for you, and of dying on a cross to make you one with me.

Don't you realize that your thirst for love is a thirst for me, I who *am* Love? I am myself the answer to your deepest desires.

I THIRST FOR YOU . . . Yes, that is the only way to describe my love for you: I thirst to love you and to be loved by you — that is how precious you are to me.

- Come to me, and I will fill your heart and heal your wounds. I will make you a new creation, and give you peace in all your trials.
- You must never doubt my mercy, my acceptance of you, my desire to forgive, my longing to bless you and live my life in you.
- If you feel unimportant in the eyes of the world, that matters not at all. For me, there is no one more important than you.
- Open to me, come to me, thirst for me, give me your life — and I will prove to you how important you are to my heart.

Don't you realize that my Father already has a perfect plan to transform your life, beginning from this moment? Trust in me. Ask me every day to enter and take charge of your life — and I will. I promise you before my Father in heaven that I will work miracles in your life. Why would I do this? Because I thirst for you. All I ask is that you entrust yourself to me completely. I will do all the rest.

Even now I behold the place my Father has prepared for you in my kingdom. Remember that you are a pilgrim in this life, on a journey home. The things of this world can never satisfy you, nor bring the peace you seek. All that you have sought outside of me has only left you more empty, so do not cling to material things. Above all, do not run from me when you fall. Come to me without delay. When you give me your sins, you give me the joy of being your Savior. There is nothing I cannot forgive and heal. So come now, and unburden your soul.

No matter how far you may wander, no matter how often you forget me, no matter how many crosses you may bear in this life, there is one thing I want you to always remember, one thing that will never change: *I thirst for you* — just as you are. You don't need to change to believe in my love, for it will be your belief in my love that will change you. You forget me, and yet I am seeking you every moment of the day, standing at the door of your heart and knocking. Do you find this hard to believe? Then look at the cross — look at my heart that was pierced for you. Have you not understood my cross? Then listen again to the words I spoke there, for they tell you clearly why I endured all this for you: "*I thirst*" (Jn 19:28). Yes, I thirst for you — as the rest of the psalm-verse I was reciting says of me: "*I looked for pity, but there was none*" (Ps 69:20). All your life I have been looking for your love — I have never stopped seeking to love you and to be loved by you. You have tried many other things in your search for happiness. Why not try opening your heart to me, right now, more than you ever have before?

Whenever you do open the door of your heart, whenever you come close enough, you will hear me say to you again and again, not in mere human words but in spirit:

No matter what you have done, I love you for your own sake. Come to me with your misery and your sins, with your troubles and needs, and with all your longing to be loved. I stand at the door of your heart and knock. Open to me, for I thirst for you.

Guided Meditation: "I Thirst for You"

———

"Jesus is God, therefore His love, His Thirst, is infinite. He the Creator of the universe, asked for the love of His creatures." [72]

"He thirsts for our love...." [73]

"These words: 'I thirst' — do they echo in our souls?" [74]

"Today Jesus had His arms extended to embrace you. Today Jesus' Heart was opened to receive you. Were you there?" [75]

Mother Teresa

(Please note: This meditation is also provided in Appendix Four for the convenience of the reader.)

SECTION THREE

Transformation

"We are so close to Him, does His presence change us?" [76]

— Mother Teresa

"Yesterday is gone; tomorrow has not yet come. We have only today. Let us begin." [77]

— Mother Teresa

ELEVEN

The Power to Change

In Section One, we learned of the secret inner fire that changed Mother Teresa's life. Section Two went on to examine the "light and love" emanating from that divine flame — a light that illumined the face of God for her, and even through her darkness drew her to the love it revealed.

In this first part of Section Three, we will examine how this light and love[†] transformed Mother Teresa from the inside out, despite her own weakness and despite the immense challenges she faced, and did so by its own divine power.

Having traced Mother Teresa's personal path of transformation, in the second part of Section Three we will discuss how any of us can share this transformative, divinizing grace, regardless of past or present weakness. This final section offers all the necessary tools, the same tools used by Mother Teresa, to open the door to this encounter — an encounter for which (at least in Mother Teresa's mind, and arguably in God's) we were all created.

[†] Or better, the light *of* love; the light that illumines and reveals love; the light that comes from love and leads back to love.

The Power of Grace

We turn now to look at how Mother Teresa became the person she was, and how the process of her transformation, born of her encounter on the train to Darjeeling, holds the same life-changing promise for us. She was always convinced of this — that the same light which led through her own darkness would, of its own power, illumine and transform all those who opened themselves to it.

When we think of emulating Mother Teresa, we should not focus on how far we are from the goal of goodness and godliness that she represents. Rather, we should remember that Mother Teresa's transformation was not due to some inborn human attributes. They were due, almost entirely, to the power of the grace she received — a grace that she constantly invited her Sisters, and the rest of us, to share in.

The fact that Mother Teresa was not born the same person she became, not already imbued with the qualities for which she would became famous, means that the rest of us, too, have hope to change and improve. No matter our present foibles or lack of human qualities, we can all hope to arrive at deeper intimacy with God and deeper care for our neighbor; to live more generously and whole-heartedly, even in the midst of our own trials, and to make a difference with our life; to leave a legacy.

———

According to the Loreto Sisters who knew her during her training, Mother Teresa had always been generous with God, but had not been particularly remarkable. What was special about the young Sister Teresa, humanly speaking, was that nothing was special; there was nothing *merely human* in her to account for her later transformation.

The key to her metamorphosis was not human effort, but her encounter with the thirst of God. It was the mystery of this grace, at work over time, that transformed Mother Teresa — and even if she cooperated wholeheartedly, it remained a grace, God's free gift. The thirst of Jesus, which she clung to throughout her dark night, like Jacob clinging to the angel (cf. Gen 32:24), is what produced the great blessings we saw in Mother Teresa.

Her Arduous Path

No matter what challenges and difficulties seem to bar our path to reaching the heights, we need to recall that Mother Teresa's path was surely no easier than ours. She, too, had to face her share of obstacles, and to overcome the same kind of inner resistance we experience. This is borne out in her journal, where she recorded the interior conversations with Jesus that followed her grace of the train:

My own Jesus — what You ask it is beyond me [. . .] I am unworthy — I am sinful — I am weak — Go, Jesus and find a more worthy soul, a more generous one.[78]

I am so afraid. — This fear shows me how much I love myself. — I am afraid of the suffering that will come — through leading that Indian life [of the poor], clothing like them, eating like them, sleeping like them — living with them and never having anything my way. How much comfort has taken possession of my heart.[79]

You are I know the most incapable person — weak and sinful, but just because you are that — I want to use you for My glory. Will thou refuse?[80]

It is only with time, as she continues returning in prayer to the divine source of her September grace, allowing its power to gradually set her free, that she can finally respond when again asked by the divine voice:

Will you refuse to do this for Me — to take care of them, to bring them to Me? I answered — You know, Jesus, I am ready to go at a moment's notice.[81]

As the grace that had freed and empowered her "yes" continued to deepen, Mother Teresa would look back in wonder at God's penchant for bestowing his gifts on the little and the weak. She looked forward to putting into action the growing desires she found in her soul, especially the desire to satiate the immense thirst of Jesus for the poor and the suffering. In a letter to the archbishop of Calcutta, whose permission she needed to begin her work outside the convent, she, who at first drew back, now speaks of her desire to go into the slums without delay:

Why has all this come to me — the most unworthy of His creatures — I do not know — and I have tried so often, to persuade Our Lord to go and seek another soul, a more generous — a stronger one, but He seems to take pleasure in [. . .] my weakness. — These desires to satiate the longing of Our Lord for [the] souls of the poor [. . .] goes on increasing with every Mass and Holy Communion. All my prayers, and the whole day in a word — are full of this desire. Please do not delay longer.[82]

Midlife Grace

These passages show us a Mother Teresa not unlike the rest of us, as we struggle to answer the promptings of grace that nudge us beyond ourselves. Unfortunately, when faced with new challenges our first response is often negative, as we listen instead to the voice that insists we cannot change.

As she, when faced with God's unexpected invitations, we find ourselves held back by fear, fatigue, tepidity, and a reluctance to take on new challenges. And we pull back. Mother Teresa shows us, though, that despite our struggles it is never too late to change, to grow, to say yes to the God who calls — if only we trust more in him than we mistrust ourselves: "*Give yourself fully to God. He will use you to accomplish great things, on the condition that you believe much more in his love than in your own weakness.*" [83]

Remember that her September encounter was a mid-life grace for Mother Teresa, *a mid-life call*. When she first stepped out alone into the slums, leaving behind her familiar existence, she was almost forty years old. Later, she would launch a pioneering network of AIDS shelters at the age of seventy. And by the time our community of priests was approved, she was already eighty-two. She is proof that it is never too late for God to transform us, never too late to launch us on a new plan, to use us for the good.

In the parable of the workers of the eleventh hour (Mt 20:6, 14), those who began work at the end of the day received the same wage as those who worked since dawn. For God, it is never too late to begin the work of our divinization; each day is always a new beginning, always full of hope. This is the principle Mother Teresa learned, and she encourages us to remember this: "*Yesterday is gone; tomorrow has not yet come. We have only today. Let us begin.*" It is never too late to change, never too late to be more than we are, to live a better and more fruitful life than we have until now.

Malcolm Muggeridge, the BBC commentator whose 1971 book *Something Beautiful for God* introduced Mother Teresa to the world, tells the story of her beginning the Home for the Dying in Calcutta, despite having done nothing like it before. Years later she reflected that had she "*not picked up that first person dying on the street,*" had she not risked beginning something entirely new in mid-life, she "*would not have picked up the thousands later on.*" [84]

Mother Teresa's success was the result of an ongoing series of *small but courageous beginnings.* She is proof that God is always starting fresh with us, and always has been, from the Garden of Eden until now. Even when we deviate from his original plan, rather than being the end, he makes it instead the beginning of a new plan, and a new path, often more beautiful than the first.

Surprised by Grace

If Mother Teresa stepped out of her convent into the slums with no special skills, with less than a dollar in her pocket, and with no help, her life is proof that despite our limitations, nothing need prevent us from accepting the invitation of grace. Nothing is lacking to us, for God's grace is (by its very nature) *sufficient* (cf. 2 Cor 12:9). Mother Teresa needed none of the usual requirements for success — neither the latest in technology, nor financial support, nor special talent and influence to achieve the highest goals — and neither do we. Mother Teresa accomplished what she did without any of this world's "essentials," without beauty, wealth, genius, or privilege. She had nothing but God — in whose hands she left her weakness and her worry. Her life shows *how much God can do in us*, once we give him free rein.

Keep in mind that Mother Teresa's call came entirely unexpectedly, when she was on her way to doing something else — as so often we are when God calls. Grace took an ordinary person, seemingly set on her life path, and placed her on a new and unimagined course, weaving her past history and her present gifts into a new future. Mother Teresa's personal transformation and her accomplishments on the world stage *all came after mid-life*. This holds promise for the rest of us, who, as the years go by, may come to question our worth and our legacy.

If Mother Teresa could be surprised by grace, we can as well. We, too, can discover unexpected opportunities hidden in our present routine and circumstances, even in our trials. We, too, can find grace and transformation in our personal Calcutta and our inner nights, awaiting us at every turn.

The Power of Conviction

But, even while insisting on Mother Teresa's human ordinariness, it is important not to underestimate the more-than-ordinary perseverance with which she held to grace — for God will do nothing without our cooperation — and her generosity in keeping the seed of grace watered and flourishing.

Time and again I have asked myself how Mother Teresa did what she did, how she managed to go on with meager food and little sleep, often answering letters until after midnight, yet being the first in chapel at 5:00 a.m. She bore the weariness of constant travel, as she visited her missions across the globe, and faced the persistent expectations of a world that could not get enough of her. There were relentless demands on her time, her attention, and her energy wherever she went — from the poor, the press, well-wishers, and coworkers; from visitors, government officials, and VIPs who came calling wherever she visited; from constant crowds, in airports and train stations; and last but not least, from her own Sisters.

I remember a scene played out time and again during my years in Rome. On arriving at the Sisters' convent near the Colosseum, I would find people lined up out the convent door and into the small adjacent park. This meant one thing — that Mother Teresa was in town. The press had not reported it yet, but somehow word had spread. There would soon be a queue of visitors of every description: the homeless in rags and countesses in furs; monsignors from the Vatican; staff from the mayor's office; and passersby who asked what all the fuss was, and after hearing that Mother Teresa was there, decided to stay. They were all hoping to have a moment with her; and she would receive them all, one by one, hour after hour, and all with the same interest and attention.

She spent the same long hours in airports, while people crowded around to ask for prayers, or a signature, or simply a word. As always, no matter her fatigue or failing health, each would go away feeling not only blessed, but cherished. The smile on her face, the glimmer in her eye, and the warmth of her touch told them that Mother Teresa had been delighted to be in their presence.

How did she do it, day after day for an entire life, remaining upbeat and optimistic in the worst of conditions? In the hurry and hustle of her demanding life, Mother Teresa's *convictions of faith* were her secret to unlocking, day after day, the light and love of the train. Mother Teresa's daily faith-encounter with the *"depths of God's infinite longing to love and be loved"* went on forming her image of God. She came away from Darjeeling equipped with a set of new (in their magnitude, if not in content) and unshakeable convictions — about God's goodness, about how he sees us, and how precious we are in his eyes. These convictions would produce a set of new attitudes, a new way of seeing the world around her, and a new way of living — all of which helped form her into the Mother Teresa we knew.

Envisioning God and our relationship to him aright is not just a question of theology; it is a question of life — God's life, in ours. Mother Teresa's insights born of the train, the faith-convictions explored in Section Two, were the light that shone in her night, that illumined her challenges and recast her Calcutta in tones of hope, throwing open the doors of her soul to the presence and power of the God she could not feel and could not see — but could always touch, in her soul and in the poor.

These simple but solid faith convictions made all the difference; they governed who she became and what she accomplished. And these convictions, which connect us to the same God and the same divine power, are open to us all.

We don't need to have come to these convictions by ourselves, through our own study and prayer independent of Mother Teresa, in order to benefit from their power in our lives. No matter their provenance, our faith convictions matter; they begin changing and forming our inner world as soon as we adopt them. They craft our attitudes, our choices, our sense of self and of God — and, most importantly, they open us onto the *reality of the God they describe.* Through the direct access to God opened by her belief, Jesus' thirst remained a constant reality in Mother Teresa's life, one that filled and fueled her without fail, until nigh her ninetieth year.

As we begin to share Mother Teresa's convictions, just as she, we will begin to see in an entirely new light. Whatever we thought we knew before — about God or about ourselves — will emerge from this experience changed and expanded, like a butterfly from its chrysalis. Our inner world of attitudes, emotions, and choices will gradually realign itself with this vision of faith in small but significant inner shifts.

For Mother Teresa, the cycle of transformative grace begun on the train would continue throughout the rest of her life — taking her from encounter to belief, and from belief to renewed encounter. Fortunately, *it is of little importance at which point we enter this cycle of grace*: whether it begins, as for Mother Teresa, with an encounter that engenders new belief, or whether it begins by "trying on" her beliefs which, when taken to prayer, engender an encounter. In the end, the God we meet, and the transformative result, are the same.

Love Beyond Feeling

Mother Teresa's personal correspondence shows that she was not carried through her challenges by waves of consolation. The darkness and dryness that we all carry, she carried as well. This brings us to an important point concerning the process of transformation — that we do not need to feel God's presence, *we do not require sensible consolation*, to begin the journey of change, or to enter into intimacy with God.

In Mother Teresa's case, though the feeling component of her encounter on the train was certainly overpowering, it was in no way lasting. The emotional component, the fervor and consolation of that September day, served to open her heart and etch that encounter and its message in her memory. But it was not emotion that changed or sustained her. What changed, formed, and sustained Mother Teresa was not emotion, but a deep, daily faith-contact with the mystery of God's thirst — a divine reality that is by its very nature beyond the grasp of feelings.

The transforming power of divine love is accessed simply by *believing in it* and *opening to it*, even in interior dryness. Even though our faith convictions may be rooted in a past event (the grace of the train, the great events recorded in Scripture, or those moments when we have experienced the divine close at hand), these convictions point us towards, and *put us in touch with*, the same original gift — always present in the now, springing ever fresh from the heart of God.

No one can reproduce what Mother Teresa felt that day on the train — nor could she, even twenty-four hours later. But what she could do, and did faithfully, was to access anew *the grace* (not the feelings) of that day, opening herself afresh to God's longing for her in each moment. And what the light of these convictions opened her to, they open for us as well, as often as we desire. God's yearning for us does not change from one day to the next, nor from one decade to the next, nor least of all from one emotional state to the next — for God and his thirst for us are "the same, yesterday, today, and forever" (cf. Heb 13:8).

———

The call to "come higher" (cf. Lk 14:10) sounds incessantly in our soul, for God will never lessen his dream of union with us. Mother Teresa's life is a reminder that it is *never too late* to heed this universal call. She shows us that each moment of our life (and not only our youth) presents us with a choice; and that our present choices still have the power to determine the remainder, and the legacy, of our life. We are all called to live an *extraordinary life through ordinary means* — or in Mother Teresa's words, to do "*small things with great love, ordinary things with extraordinary love.*"[85]

No matter who we are or what has gone before, no matter the chances squandered or time lost, we are still called by the God for whom nothing is impossible. He invites us to do things even Mother Teresa could never do, things that will go undone throughout history if we do not do them. A legacy awaits us that will never be, unless we choose to accept our higher call in the present moment, even at the eleventh hour. *"Yesterday is gone; tomorrow has not yet come. We have only today. Let us begin."*

"Be so very united to Me as to radiate My love on souls." [86]

— Jesus to Mother Teresa

TWELVE

The Beauty of God Within

In the last chapter, we looked at the mix of ordinary and extraordinary in Mother Teresa's life — ordinary in her human gifts, yet extraordinary in the challenges she faced in her mid-course call. We also identified her faith convictions, born of the grace of the train, as the doorway to her transformation and light.

Before examining the spiritual practices by which she deepened her grace of encounter, practices which we can make use of as well, let us take a moment to look more closely at the fruits of her transforming grace. We not only want to understand *how* Mother Teresa arrived at being the person she was, but to consider precisely *what* God had accomplished in her. Let us stand back and observe the full flowering of her grace, the full panorama of goodness and blessing that God worked in her — and by inference, that God can work in any life surrendered to him.

If Jesus could say, without exaggeration, that his disciples would perform the "same works" as he (cf. Jn 14:12), the very works seen in his disciples through the ages, then neither is it exaggeration for

Mother Teresa to maintain that the grace she received, and the holiness it produced in her, are as much intended *for us* as for her; that we, too, can accomplish "the same works" and achieve the same transformation, in the midst of our own Calcutta. Her life paints a clear and convincing picture of just how much grace can achieve, and of the full beauty of the holiness it engenders.

"Be My Light"

Before examining more closely the phenomenon of Mother Teresa, and the light we saw in her, we need to ask whether we are unwittingly attributing to her a goodness and a light that belong only to God.

The simple answer is no; there is no contradiction, no competition between God's light and the light we saw in her. Rather than our exalting Mother Teresa, *God himself* was being exalted in her — it was *his* light we beheld in her. Like the Virgin Mary, her soul was not magnifying herself, but her Lord (cf. Lk 1:46).

The beauty of Mother Teresa's soul is all about *him*, more than her; and about *us*, as much as her. Her beauty reflects the dignity of our role as *God-bearers*, and our full potential as living temples. Could our surprise at God's work in Mother Teresa, or in the saints, be the result of our knowing "neither the Scriptures nor the power of God" (Mt 22:29)? Did Jesus not promise that those who believed in him would "do the works that I do ... and greater works than these" (Jn 14:12)? Did he not declare to the disciples that *they* were to be the light of the world (cf. Mt 5:14)? This was Jesus' mandate to Mother Teresa, that she "be his radiance" to the poor, and his light in a world of darkness. And this she did; or this *he* did in her.

———

Mother Teresa fulfilled her mandate magnificently; shining with God's light and radiance before the world. People experienced an unexpected stirring of grace in her presence, and a new sense of God's closeness. Such enlightening moments happened not only in her physical presence, but just as often by simply reading about her, or seeing her on film. Malcolm Muggeridge told the story of a man who wrote to thank him for his book on Mother Teresa, *Something Beautiful for God*. The man happened to pick up a copy left on the abandoned top floor of his office building — where he had gone to commit suicide. The unexpected impact of those pages gave a hopeless man his reason for living.

Listening to Mother Teresa speak, people would find themselves moved, often to tears. At times, this occurred even without understanding her words. I had the opportunity to translate for Mother Teresa when she spoke in some of the large parishes in Rome. Frequently, while she was still speaking, and before I could begin to translate, I noticed people already tearing up — just from hearing her voice and being in her presence.

Her message held an obvious power — one that attracted not only the poor and the pious, but the most diverse of audiences. Among those who came to hear her were the cultured, the influential, even the agnostic. An anointing seemed to rest on her words, an unseen magnetism that drew people towards God — even the most seemingly hardened.

Once, in the mid-1980s, a young man came to visit our priests' community in the South Bronx. He told us quite openly about his previous life as a courier for the Mafia, running guns and drugs up and down the West Coast. He went on to tell us about his unexpected conversion, which he ascribed entirely to Mother Teresa. He had been driving along the highway one San Francisco morning, with a supply of illegal cargo, when suddenly his favorite music station interrupted its programming. Mother Teresa was in town, they announced. She was visiting San Francisco after being awarded the Nobel Prize, and the mayor was about to present her with the key to the city. Local radio stations were broadcasting the ceremony live, including Mother Teresa's address to the people of San Francisco.

As the young man continued driving, he became increasingly upset over losing his music — and all for the sake of some nun. Unable to find a station that was not broadcasting the ceremony, he decided to simply wait it out. Sooner or later this unknown nun would stop talking, and he could enjoy his music again. So he continued driving, having no idea who Mother Teresa was, and paying no attention to what she said — only angry that, whoever she was, she was interrupting his life.

Unexpectedly, after some minutes, he began to feel a strange sensation come over him. Tears were suddenly welling up in his eyes. He kept on driving, but the sensation in his heart kept growing, and he soon found himself sobbing uncontrollably. He finally pulled off the highway, stopped the car, and cried out all the pain and darkness in his soul.

Once this intense experience was over, he sensed that something profound had taken place. He felt clean and new, and somehow changed. He went home, phoned the radio station, and asked the name of the person he had heard speaking at City Hall. When they told him it was Mother Teresa, he replied, "But who is she?" They explained as best they could and, at his request, told him where she was staying. He went to the Sisters' convent and rang the doorbell, and to his surprise he was soon ushered in to meet Mother Teresa in person. He could not have been received more royally, he told us, had he been the mayor himself. He poured out his heart to her, she sent him for confession, and he went on to change his life. All that, merely from the anointing on her voice.

———

At times, similar responses were produced by people simply hearing her name or seeing her image. For example, in an experiment reported in the national press, volunteers in a laboratory registered alpha waves merely at the mention of her name. And then there was the time I accompanied her on a flight from Calcutta to Bombay, and watched as Hindu and Muslim businessmen in three-piece suits began exiting the aircraft, only to notice at the last moment that Mother Teresa was on board, seated by the door. As surprised as they were by her presence, they seemed still more surprised by the sudden moistness in their eyes, as they fumbled for pictures of their children for her to bless.

This response was produced not only in people of faith, but often in those of no faith whatsoever. Soon after she received the Nobel Prize, *Time* magazine's cover story told of a young man, an ardent atheist, who, after reading about Mother Teresa, realized, against all his long-held convictions, that there must be a God. Up until then, all the usual arguments for the existence of God had left him unmoved; but the radiance of that face, and the love in those eyes, and the beauty of that life — that was something different. He abandoned everything — friends and career and future — and entered a monastery.

Similar stories abound; and although most will never be told, one thing remains clear. In the midst of our hurried and worried lives, in the midst of a distracted, self-indulgent, and often self-absorbed world, Mother Teresa broke through — and God and goodness with her.

Even in the Night, Joy

The presence of God within filled Mother Teresa with a contagious joy and energy, a joy that overcame the pain of her darkness (as her letters testify), a joy that kept even her closest collaborators from suspecting the existence of her inner night.

In Calcutta and elsewhere, I often had occasion to wait for Mother Teresa while she shared a meal with her Sisters, and listened to the

sounds of laughter and delight coming from their dining room —
from young women who had joined Mother Teresa in possessing
nothing but God himself, in getting up every morning at 4:40, in
spending their days washing lepers and caring for the dying, and in
giving up radio and television and the creature comforts our culture
deems essential.

It was obvious that Mother Teresa's joy was entirely from within, unbeholden to circumstance. This joy in the midst of sacrifice was
a clear sign of her rootedness in God even in the night, of her communion with the One whose joy is in loving us.

Divinization

Mother Teresa seemed to inhabit another realm,[†] God-laden, bathed
in peace. Sensing the presence of the divine in her, people crowded
around wherever she went — not so much to catch a glimpse of a
celebrity, as to bask in the goodness and love that emanated from her.

How many of us, myself included, after contemplating God's
goodness in Mother Teresa, even from afar (as I first did in a Roman
bookstore), have felt sentiments similar to those related by this professional woman, an artist and mother of six:

> I always wanted to touch Mother Teresa. Like the hemorrhag-
> ing woman in the Gospel of Luke who pushed through a suffo-
> cating crowd of people to grasp the hem of Jesus' garment, I
> wanted to latch onto Calcutta's pious saint. My body was not
> broken, but my spirit needed a divine boost. I reasoned that if

---

[†] The extraordinary qualities and special graces enumerated in this chapter are not in
opposition to Mother Teresa's "ordinariness." All her extraordinary qualities were *God-given*
(though she cooperated to the full in cultivating them, she was not their cause or origin), and
so they are neither from her nor about her. For this reason, it is not a question of whether she
is "ordinary" or "extraordinary," but rather of her ordinary humanity and God's extraordinary
grace *co-existing*, in complementary harmony. Mother Teresa proves that God's special gifts are
not the reserve or the reward of the humanly great; they are lavished preferentially upon the
"poor in spirit," to whom by precedence *belongs* the kingdom of heaven (Mt 5:3).

I could just touch Mother Teresa, somehow her holiness would rub off, penetrating my soul. This ambition became my fervent prayer by day, my dream by night.[87]

How do we explain these experiences of the ineffable that took place around Mother Teresa, this sense of the divine so close at hand, this transformation that took place not only in her, but through her? What was this power of change, this ability to bring heaven not only down to earth, but even into the hell that was Calcutta? What was the meaning of her appeal and her extraordinary transformation — what was the process of Sister Teresa becoming Mother Teresa all about?

In the end, it was about *holiness* — about the splendor and power of *God dwelling in man.*

The ongoing appeal of Mother Teresa has its roots deep in our inescapable relationship and inborn yearning for God. In its full flowering, this human capacity for God is what we call holiness. Not just man living like God, obeying his laws, but much more: *God himself living in man.* Holiness proclaims and witnesses to the supreme value of each human being as a dwelling place of the Most High. This is the very definition of man given by the great Thomas Aquinas: "*Homo capax Dei*" — Man as *capable of God.*

Mother Teresa's transformation is about God's "light and love" taking full possession of a human being — and through her (or through us), being poured out onto the world. It is almost taboo to speak of holiness today, in a society embarrassed by public references to God. Unfortunately, even in religious circles, holiness is rarely mentioned and even more rarely found. But when true godliness is seen, even in the secular realm, even among those who would scoff at religion, people take notice, people are drawn — just as they were to St. Francis, and just as they still are to Mother Teresa.

If our secular world found itself, even despite itself, running after Mother Teresa, it was for the same reason it ran after Francis centuries before. In the end, this phenomenon is about one thing — the power, the beauty, and the attraction of *God living in man*, of God's loving gaze shining through human eyes.

A New Vision of Humanity

Holiness lifts high a vision of what humanity can become — not only in theory, as politicians and philosophers might do, but in flesh and in fact. Holiness points to the ultimate dignity of our human nature, and to the heights any human can attain, even when burdened with poverty and pain. The holiness of the saints reveals the amount of beauty and good that can be woven into one short life, and the impact that life can have, even beyond one's years on earth.

Even more importantly, though, holiness lifts the veil on the undreamt-of magnitude of God's love for us, on the beauty of his plan for humanity, and on his power to transform any life — even in our modern age. The saints of our own era, like Mother Teresa, provide a chance to witness the transformative power of grace *in our own day*, "made flesh" in our own time.

The Power of Holiness

I had my own encounter with the attraction of holiness in Mother Teresa the first time I traveled with her. We had boarded a KLM flight from Rome's Fiumicino airport bound for Amsterdam and New York. Soon after takeoff, Mother Teresa began to speak of God's love for the little, the poor, and the weak — recounting some of the small miracles of God's tenderness she had witnessed firsthand.

She told me of the time in *Shishu Bhavan*, her home for orphaned children in Calcutta, when her Sisters were anxiously searching for a certain medicine made only in Switzerland. One of the children was gravely ill and urgently needed that particular medication. With no time to order it from abroad, they asked Mother Teresa what to do.

Just then, one of the Sisters brought in a parcel of donated medicines that had just arrived. Mother Teresa opened it, and there amid the jumble of bottles and small boxes, right on top where she had put her hand, was precisely the medicine the child needed.

After finishing her story, with the kind of pride a child might have in celebrating another of her father's great accomplishments, she turned to me and said: "Don't you see how God loves us? How he takes care of us?"

After landing in Amsterdam, a Pakistani-born KLM agent came to escort us through the terminal. At one point, he turned to Mother Teresa and said: "Mother Teresa, I am a Muslim gentleman, and we Muslims believe many wonderful things about Jesus. But I tell you, Mother Teresa, in two thousand years no one do what Jesus say. You, Mother Teresa, do what Jesus say. You are love in action."

However limited his knowledge of Christianity, he was sure of one thing: that he had seen Jesus in Mother Teresa. This was also the case for so many others, in so many places — some who knew much more of Christ, and some who knew him not at all. There was the time in the Home for the Dying, for instance, when Mother Teresa was tending to an emaciated man in his last moments of life. In the midst of her silent ministrations, the man looked up into her eyes and asked, "Is Jesus like you?"

In fact, Jesus was indeed like her. Or more precisely, she had become so entirely like Jesus.

Mother Teresa's life had become a transparency for God. Her person, her work, and her message allowed us to see something of *God's* heart through hers — one smile, one bandage, one word of comfort at a time.

Radiating Christ to the Secular World

Mother Teresa's lifelong ambition was to give people everywhere, especially the poor, the chance to "look up and see no longer her," but Jesus in her. It is not surprising that her favorite prayer, one she recited every day of her life, was *Radiating Christ*, by the great English churchman, John Henry Newman:

Dear Jesus, help us to spread your fragrance everywhere
    we go.
Flood our souls with your spirit and life.
Penetrate and possess our whole being so utterly,
that our lives may only be a radiance of yours.
Shine through us,
and be so in us,
that every soul we come in contact with
may feel your presence in our soul.
Let them look up and see no longer us,
but only Jesus!
Stay with us,
and then we shall begin to shine as you shine;
so to shine as to be a light to others;
the light O Jesus, will be all from you,
none of it will be ours;
it will be you, shining on others through us.
Let us thus praise you in the way you love best,
by shining on those around us.
Let us preach you without preaching,
not by words but by our example,
by the catching force,
the sympathetic influence of what we do,
the evident fullness of the love our hearts bear to you.
    Amen.

This radiance of personal holiness touches not only the religious world, but the secular world as well. Far from being a sidelight of interest only to believers, or a parallel dimension in which she moved, Mother Teresa's holiness was the very reason for her impact in the secular realm. Throughout history, those who have had the most enduring influence on our world are the saints. Politicians and celebrities come and go, but the saints remain. Who was vying for political power in the time of Francis of Assisi? Who were the mavens of high society in Teresa of Ávila's day? Who would have topped the Fortune 500 in Augustine's time? It is holiness, God as Creator working through us, that allows us to be enduringly productive, yielding an abundance of *fruit that will last* (Jn 15:16), in time and into eternity.

Mother Teresa's secular influence was recognized even by world leaders. When U.N. Secretary-General Javier Perez de Cuellar introduced Mother Teresa at the United Nations' 40th anniversary celebrations, he presented her before the assembled diplomats as "the most powerful woman on earth." Throughout the great hall, heads nodded in agreement. Though everyone sensed it was so, perhaps few could put their finger on why — on the fact that *she reminded us of God*. She mediated for our generation the chance to experience something of God beyond our common, daily lot. In some powerful, palpable way, she had succeeded in carrying God and his love into our modern world, even into the worst of our world. She had succeeded in touching us deeply and changing us for the better, even where governments and agencies had so often failed.

———

But what practical relevance, beyond the strictly spiritual, could someone like Mother Teresa, bending over the dying in impoverished lands, have for the hale and upwardly mobile of the twenty-first century? Now that she has gone from our midst, does she still have anything of practical value to teach our secular world?

Perhaps that question is best answered with others: Will we not all one day face the specter of tragedy or illness in our lives, and in

With Indira Gandhi, in background (Marilyn Silverstone/Magnum Photos)

the lives of those we are closest to? Or find ourselves one day bending over the bed of a dying loved one? How prepared will we be to face those moments with dignity and optimism, to bring light and peace, as Mother Teresa brought to so many? When pain, financial loss, or advanced age trim our flagging self-image and challenge our culture's worship of youth, beauty, and success, will we be able to find deeper meaning — and even joy — in our limited circumstances, as she did?

Even in the midst of pain and poverty, Mother Teresa showed us that virtue trumps gratification; that it engenders its own unique set of rewards; and that, when sustained by perseverance, virtue will overcome any obstacle. She had the rare ability to draw us towards what we flee, to find beauty where we would rather not look, and to deal head-on with what we would rather avoid. She taught us to embrace the unlovable wherever we find it, in ourselves and in others, in God's name. Through her, God placed a loving hand on our hidden pain and inner wounds. She brought the same light and healing to our Calcutta of the heart as she did to the dark hovels of the city whose name she bore.

The luminosity of her life broke through those dark Calcutta shadows, not only for the poor of the Third World, but for all who had eyes to see. Her ministrations demonstrated that human suffering was not a sign of abandonment by God, not proof that the Almighty did not care, but just the opposite. She showed us that the more profound our pain is, the more profound the divine compassion is — and the greater the urgency is in him who still "leaves the ninety-nine" to seek out the one most in need.

For the many who struggled with belief, for whom the experience of pain had sown seeds of doubt and the feeling of distance from God, Mother Teresa's compassion became a north star, pointing to forgotten vistas of goodness in the heart of God. She showed us a God far closer and more tender than we had dared hope. Her charity to the neediest was a thundering, if silent, pulpit. Her compassion became a doorway for the divine into our wounded world, a channel for God's light into our darkness.

———

In conclusion, the transformation we witnessed in Mother Teresa — and the pull, the attraction, the peace, and the consolation that even the secular world experienced around her — were entirely *from God*. Mother Teresa did not set out one day to transform herself. The initiative and the power to bring it about were entirely God's. We cannot change ourselves, at least not alone and by our own strength. No one can transcend himself by himself, not even a Mother Teresa. We can only be drawn higher by the One who transcends us already, and who has made us for himself.

If people were so drawn to Mother Teresa and felt moved by her to live better, more generous lives, it was because something in our depths recognized our Creator in her, some part of our soul intuited the divine presence, as the infant John the Baptist was able to recognize Jesus' presence in the womb of his mother and rejoiced (cf. Lk 1:44).

———

But how can the grace Mother Teresa received on the train change us in any meaningful way? Surely there is divine beauty here, but is there any real power in pondering the light Mother Teresa beheld? The short answer is a resounding yes.

According to Christian tradition, it is *contemplation*, prayerfully beholding the goodness of God, that unleashes the power, and sets in motion the process, of divine transformation in the soul. Recall that the grace that will transform us in the kingdom "in the twinkling of an eye" (1 Cor 15:52) is known as the *Beatific Vision*. Our faith-vision of the divine light, the divine attributes, draws us deeper and deeper into our encounter with God — and that contact, even in faith and silence and darkness, has the power to change and divinize.

The key to our transformation, and to being able to touch and transform the lives of those around us, lies in welcoming the spark of divine "light and love," as Mother Teresa did on the train, the secret inner fire whose embers we will learn to "rekindle" (2 Tim 1:6) in the chapters that follow.

"My prayer for you [is] that you may experience the thirsting love of Jesus for each one of you." [88]

"The strong grace of Divine Light and Love that Mother received on the train journey to Darjeeling on 10th September 1946 is where the MC begins — in the depths of God's infinite longing to love and to be loved. How important it is for each . . . to desire deeply to share in this same grace." [89]

— Mother Teresa

THIRTEEN

Encounter: Seeking His Face

Encounter

We are ready to make the transition from examining Mother Teresa's lights *about* God (Section Two) to entering into her actual experience *of* God. We are moving from information to transformation; from beholding the light that shone in her night, the light that reveals God's love and draws us to him, to actually meeting the Source of that light and love.

By Mother Teresa's own account, September 10 was above all *an encounter*. As she confirmed in our conversation in the Bronx in 1984, before being a message about God's thirst for us, September 10 was an *encounter with the God who thirsts* for us. Her message, essential as it is, sprang from the encounter, and leads back to it. Fundamentally, Mother Teresa's message serves as an invitation to share her encounter.

Though we can never reproduce her extraordinary grace of encounter on the train (and neither could she), its essence — the beauty and grace and power of God's thirst — is always accessible to us in faith, just as it was for Mother Teresa the rest of her days, from September 10 until her passing.

Mother Teresa had but *one* extraordinary experience of the divine thirst, one overwhelming encounter. And, it must be pointed out, that particular encounter was *not the one that transformed her* — though it did set her on a new path, armed with new light and purpose. Her transforming encounter, the encounter that imbued her with the life-changing, divinizing power of God's love, was her *daily encounter lived in faith.* Just two days after Mother Teresa's passing, Pope John Paul II pointed to her hidden, daily encounter with the divine thirst, as the source of her inner fire:

> Every day, before dawn.... In the silence of contemplation, Mother Teresa of Calcutta heard the echo of Jesus' cry on the cross: "I thirst." [90]

As we shall see, this is the same contemplative encounter, lived in faith, to which we are all invited — and, if we are faithful to it, with the same transformative results.

Renewing the Encounter

Having reviewed the effects of Mother Teresa's encounter, we can begin to explore the *means* by which she renewed that encounter and kept it alive, even in the night. From there, we can identify the steps towards living and maintaining our own encounter — allowing us to open to this mystery that still moves mountains, heals wounds, and changes lives.

For Mother Teresa, the thirst of God was more than theory, more even than good news; it was a personal, ever-deepening, face-to-face encounter with the God who yearns for us. She continued to relive her extraordinary encounter in an "ordinary" way, in the intimacy of daily prayer. Each morning, there in the quiet of her soul, she *renewed the grace of the train.* There she met, day after month after year, the same God who never ceased thirsting to love and be loved — no matter what was taking place outside of her, and no matter the darkness within.

For Mother Teresa, everything depended on this encounter. It was the source of grace, and the sacred path to her tryst with her God: *"The most important thing is that we must encounter the thirst of Jesus...."* [91] Since she was convinced that her encounter was not given for her alone, she repeatedly assured her Sisters that the same Jesus who had revealed this mystery to her would reveal it to them as well. She bid each of her Sisters to ask herself this question:

> *Have I heard Jesus directly say this word to me personally... "I Thirst," "I want your love?"* [92]

But this grace was given for more than just her Sisters. It was meant to be shared by all — and the poor and the needy were to be the first to receive it. Since ours is a God of mercy, the least and the lost will always have first claim to his gifts. The poor to whom Mother Teresa was sent had first claim not only to her goodness, but to her grace. We can include ourselves in their ranks, but only inasmuch as we *accept* our well-hidden poverty. Mother Teresa never hesitated to encourage us to believe in, and to seek, that same grace — in whatever way God would give it:

> *Try to hear that "I Thirst, I Thirst." Try to hear Jesus in your heart."* [93]

Mother Teresa insisted that the core reality of our encounter would be the same as hers — only the modality would differ.

Respecting our uniqueness, God would use different means, at different times, to bring about the same encounter. The encounter given extraordinarily to Mother Teresa would be given to us in other, more ordinary ways — just as the same God who came to Moses, in thunder and lightning, would come to Elijah in the whisper of a gentle breeze (cf. 1 Kgs 19:12-13). The same God who first came to Mother Teresa overwhelmingly, to convince her of the reality of her message, would later come to her in quiet darkness. He will normally come to us in the quiet intimacy of our heart, in faith, in an inner "gentle breeze." If we but have "eyes to see and ears to hear" (cf. Ezek 12:2) we, too, will perceive his longing in our moments of inner silence, and be transformed.

Approaching the Encounter

In order to share in Mother Teresa's encounter, we need to open ourselves enough to do so — to suspend critical judgment long enough to welcome this grace that gently knocks (cf. Rev 3:20). As we do so, we will begin to feel the inner tug, the first stirrings of the "light and love" that drew Mother Teresa so entirely out of herself.

Her grace is already there awaiting us, ready to begin working its transformation. The seed of grace that proved so fruitful in Mother Teresa's soul can be sown just as productively in ours. The soil of our soul may not be special in any way; but Mother Teresa's transformation came not from her own soul, but from the power of the seed. In the realm of grace, just as in nature, the *same seed always produces the same fruit*. The same grace of encounter lived in our life will produce the same fruits of transformation — "thirtyfold and sixtyfold and a hundredfold" (Mk 4:20).

Our ongoing encounter with God's yearning to love and be loved will produce new energy and light, and a new enthusiasm for living — equipping us to face whatever may come. Our growing taste of the "light and love" Mother Teresa experienced will be as leaven cast into every area of our lives, leaving our previous existence divinized, revitalized, and set free.

"Prayer makes your heart grow bigger, until it is capable of containing the gift of God himself." [94]

— Mother Teresa

FOURTEEN

Secret Fire

The Mystery of Prayer

Mother Teresa's extraordinary encounter on the train and our ordinary encounter in daily life have something essential in common — they are both *experiences of prayer*.

It was precisely the practice of personal prayer that allowed Mother Teresa to renew her encounter with God's longing, day after day. Prayer was the flame that rekindled the secret fire she carried within.

The power of divine love and the practice of prayer became so united in Mother Teresa's experience that she could refer to them as one mystery, one "secret," explaining how she attained and achieved all she did:

My secret is simple. . . I pray.[95]

She knew that everything stands or falls depending on the depth of one's prayer. Our transformation depends entirely on God and, therefore, on our conscious contact with him — and so, *"What can be more important than prayer?"*[96]

Faith

If prayer unlocks the door to our encounter, then the key that unlocks the door to prayer is *faith* — the sum of our freely chosen, actively applied convictions about God. But faith is more than the sum content of belief — it is above all the *act* of belief. It is the act of clinging in the night to an unseen sun, and by that simple act, bringing the fullness of that sun within us; as St. Paul writes, "[May] Christ ... *dwell in your hearts by faith*" (Eph 3:17). Faith is a virtue; it is the God-given, beyond-human *power* ("virtue," from the Latin *virtus*, meaning "power") to place ourselves, with or without feeling, in direct and intimate contact with the very God in whom we believe:

> *Prayer is the fruit of faith. If we have faith, we will want to pray.*[97]

Faith is a compass that infallibly points to true north, illuminating the presence, and the personality of God — even in the darkest night:

> *... Love [is the] fruit of union with God through faith.*[98]

Mother Teresa's deep faith was perhaps her most impressive quality, more so than even her charity. Her uncommonly deep faith cut through every difficulty, opening the door for God's power to pass through all experiences and events, and in all things bringing her face-to-face with him whom her heart sought.

Examples of her unwavering childlike faith abound. One day a young novice came to inform Mother Teresa that there was no more food in the pantry of the Sisters' kitchen in Calcutta. It was mid-morning, and in a few hours more than three hundred nuns would be returning home from all over Calcutta, and finding nothing to eat. Mother Teresa turned to the novice and said, "*Sister, you are in charge of the kitchen?*" "Yes, Mother," came the reply. With utter calm, Mother Teresa told her, "*Then go into the chapel and tell Jesus we have no food.*"

Mother Teresa felt no need to go herself, convinced that in his goodness God would hear this little novice as much as he would her. She went about her business that morning as if all was resolved, never thinking to pick up the phone and call around the city asking for help. In the meantime, the novice went nervously to the chapel, as Mother Teresa had instructed her. After some time, the front doorbell rang, and Mother Teresa went down to answer. There at the door was a man with clipboard in hand, a truck driver for the city, announcing that the city schools had gone on strike and had sent the students home early. The authorities were left with thousands of extra packages of bread. Could Mother Teresa make use of them?

Faith Contact

At least in part, the robustness of Mother Teresa's faith was the result, and the composite, of her convictions of September 10. She knew that what she came to understand of God that day would never change, even when events changed, even when her inner sky darkened. Faith became her way of seeing in the dark, of seeing a divine reality ever present and unchangeable, though beyond the grasp of the senses. Her faith glimpsed the glory of the unseen God, in good times and bad, hidden but never absent, under each "distressing disguise."

Despite setbacks and even tragedies, she was never shocked, her faith never shaken, never derailed from her vision of God in all things. And this, by the sheer free choice of belief — as one holds to belief in the sun, even at night. Once, while she visited her Sisters in Tanzania, the small plane that was carrying her swerved off the runway after landing and tragically ran into the crowd. The propellers cut down some of the villagers who had come to welcome her, as well as two of her Sisters. Mother Teresa knew that she was indirectly responsible, yet despite her immense pain, despite her being heartsick at the inadvertent tragedy and burdened by the pain all around her, as she left the plane and surveyed the agonizing scene, she simply whispered, *"God's will."*

As Thomas Aquinas points out, the act of faith involves more than just belief in what we do not see. As one of the theological[†] virtues, the exercise of faith becomes a means of direct, *immediate contact* with God. Every act of faith places the soul in touch with the fullness of the Godhead. Faith is not just the choice to believe; it is the portal through which we approach and touch God, clinging to him whole and entire.

Faith determines the boundaries and the horizon of our entire spiritual life. We do not need more information *about* our faith, as much as we need more actual faith — more conscious faith-contact in our daily prayer-encounters with God. The dimensions of our faith become the exact dimensions, large or small, through which God and his love must pass in order to reach us. God's gifts are not a reward for our faith; they are instead the direct *consequence* of our faith, the result of opening wide the faith-portal between our soul and the Almighty.

The Divine Indwelling

Mother Teresa's faith vision revealed God's presence not only around her, but above all within her. God does not abide in some distant, inaccessible realm — we must not seek him outside of us, for he dwells in our inmost depths: "Behold, the kingdom of God *is in your midst*" (Lk 17:21). To find God, Mother Teresa invited us to look no further than our own heart, convinced that he and his love await us there:

Jesus in my heart, I believe in your tender love for me....[99]

Because God dwells in our depths, conscious communion with him is more than a possibility; it is our baptismal birthright. We are

---

† Called *theological* (from the Greek *Theos*, meaning "God") because these virtues bring about direct contact with the Godhead.

never more authentically human, never more living our dignity as temples of the Almighty, than when communing with the God within. This conviction, this awareness of God's indwelling is the *starting point for prayer*, and the first step towards our encounter with his thirst for us (since his presence within us is proof of his longing). In the words of the great Spanish mystic St. Teresa of Ávila:

> All our difficulties in prayer can be traced to one cause: praying as if God were absent.[100]

And in the words of her contemporary, St. John of the Cross:

> When it is in dryness, darkness, and desolation, [the soul] must not on that account suppose that God is far from it.... O you soul, most beautiful of creatures, who so long to know the place where your Beloved is, that you may seek Him and be united to Him, you know now that *you are yourself* that very tabernacle where He dwells, the secret chamber of His retreat where He is hidden.[101]

Love Alone

Mother Teresa is an example of the transformation that takes place when someone lives fully open to God's love. Once a love of this magnitude enters our life, it enables us to radiate that love everywhere, to step beyond our human weakness, and to bring solace and healing to others. Since the source of that divine love is not outside of us, our transformation begins by *going within*, entering the presence of God's radiant love, by "closing the door" to pray to our God in secret (cf. Mt 6:6).

> God's presence is within us, bursting with creative energy and life. If we can only tap this inner source of uncreated love, then it will radically change our whole personality.[102]

We cannot change ourselves, no matter how long or hard we try. Love alone changes us. We can only be *loved* into a new life — and most powerfully, by the One who is love. The source of all love, source of all the goodness we saw in Mother Teresa, abides within each one of us. Were we able to interrupt our hurried lives and take the time to go within, we would gradually find ourselves caught up in this tide of divinizing, transforming love.[103] But this process can only be started through prayer. It is only in prayer that we access God's unlimited love, and unleash its transforming effects in our lives.

Lost in prayer (Raghu Rai/Magnum Photos)

This transformative process begins in the innermost recesses of the soul and moves outward — to embrace thoughts, emotions, activities, and the whole of one's being. That Mother Teresa's transformation *came about through prayer* was confirmed in her own words: "*My secret is simple* — I pray." [104] While Mother Teresa was alive, one of the most common sights in Mother House was of her, sitting on the floor at the back of the chapel, alone and lost in God. She was there to renew her encounter with God's thirst, something she not only did daily, but throughout the day, through this simple practice of interior prayer.

No one can experience being loved in the way Mother Teresa was on the train, or in the way she loved others, and remain the same. But this is true of her because it was first true of Jesus himself. What became Mother Teresa's secret inner fire was first the secret of Jesus of Nazareth, who, the gospels tell us, spent entire nights in prayer to the Father, the ultimate Source of all love:

> The Gospel ... shows us again and again the effects of unlimited Love, as it progressively invades a human nature, the human nature of Jesus. ... No man had ever experienced such depth or intensity of love before; nor been so absolutely sure of its continued and lasting presence. To follow [Jesus] does not mean that we should merely imitate the outward manifestation of the inner light that burned in Him; it means that we must expose ourselves to that self-same light that it may set us afire too. [105]

Resolution: Touching the Hem of His Robe

No amount of casual contact with God can change us. No amount of routine contact with God can equal the efficacy of the briefest moments of faith-filled prayer. Recall the gospel story of the woman with the hemorrhage (Lk 8:42-48). As Jesus walked along, the crowd jostled him on every side — thousands of people touching the source of Life, but without effect. One woman in the crowd reached out and touched only the hem of his cloak, but in deep faith, and was instantly healed. Jesus immediately turned and said, "Who was it that touched me?" (Lk 8:45). He was not asking who had touched him physically, but rather who had touched him *in faith* — since at that simple touch Jesus *felt power go out from him* (Lk 8:46).

Even today, that same power is communicated, that same divine energy "goes out from him" whenever he is touched in faith. Jesus wanted this woman to know that the reason she was healed was not because she was more deserving than the others, but simply as the result of her faith — because while touching the hem of his robe, she touched his divinity with her soul.

There is a simple key to fruitful prayer. It is to first take the time to *touch God in faith* before we engage in prayer, to be in a state of contact with him before "saying" prayers. Simply put, it is to "pray before you pray."

This simple practice can change our experience of prayer. This may seem like a small adjustment, but it opens us onto a reality as large and powerful as God himself. Without conscious faith, our prayer is not true contact, not prayer at all, but simply cogitation. Transformation is God's free gift, but it is only our free act of contact in faith that makes that gift possible. We will still encounter struggles and distractions — but we will at least be touching the hem of his robe, however briefly, every day of our lives.

The Mystery of Grace

Mother Teresa knew that her daily encounter in prayer was entirely God's gift. It was not the fruit of her efforts, nor a reward for her serving the poor. It was and is pure grace:

> *The most important thing is that we must encounter the Thirst of Jesus, but the encounter with Jesus' Thirst is a grace.*[106]

Our source of transformation is not some unnamed cosmic energy to be tapped at will, and it is surely not "the universe" (as popular post-Christian literature would suggest). Instead, it is the *dynamic love of a personal God*. Therefore, its bestowal is not something mechanical or automatic, like taking a product from a vending machine, but only given in a state of *relationship* with him. Because God is love, he is more than some anonymous force whose principles, once discovered, can be bent to our will, or simply used to "manifest" our desires — God is, rather, an infinite, eternal, and autonomous *Person*.

The gift of God's love is the fruit of a free and personal decision; one that cannot be coerced or manipulated, but only requested, yearned for, and waited on in prayer. Since, as Mother Teresa insists, this encounter "is a grace," it can only be received, not earned, and surely not achieved by our artifice or efforts. To receive it, to replicate her encounter, requires but one thing — *a spirit of humility* as we enter into prayer to meet the Lord, an acceptance of our own poverty and emptiness. God will always turn this to our favor, making of our inescapable poverty the blessed terrain, the sacred space in which to pour his love, his gifts, and his very Self:

> *Love to pray, feel often during the day the need for prayer and take the trouble to pray. If you want to pray better you must pray more. Prayer enlarges the heart until it is capable of containing God's gift of Himself. Ask and seek and your heart will grow big enough to receive Him and keep Him as your own.*[107]

"He has created us to love and to be loved, and this is the beginning of prayer — to know that He loves me, that I have been created for greater things." [108]

— Mother Teresa

FIFTEEN

Drawn Into the Light

The genius of the symbol of divine thirst, given to Mother Teresa on the train, lies in its ability to engage mind *and* heart, the totality of man. Because of this ability to engage, Mother Teresa's message draws the soul towards God by its own beauty. As the prophet Jeremiah remarked, in words that Mother Teresa could have made her own: "O LORD, you have enticed me, and I was enticed" (Jer 20:7 — NRSV). Once we have met the living God, and been attracted by his goodness (described in Section Two), we find ourselves increasingly *drawn into prayer*. What before was simply duty, now becomes delight.

"Teach Us to Pray"

Jesus introduced his disciples to prayer by example and attraction, as much as by teaching. He, who has been drawn by the beauty and goodness of the Father from all eternity, communicated to the disciples that same *experience of being drawn*. On waking in Peter's house, the apostles would find that Jesus had slipped out in the night and gone into the hills to pray (Lk 6:12). In the morning, they would find Jesus still there, lost in prayer, enfolded in the presence of the Father. This so impressed them that on one such occasion they implored, "Lord, teach *us* to pray" (Lk 11:1).

In prayer at Mother House, Calcutta (Raghu Rai/Magnum Photos)

Like her Lord, Mother Teresa taught prayer as much by attraction as by exhortation. An atmosphere of prayer enveloped her wherever she went, even outside formal times of prayer. The palpable presence of God was so pronounced around her, and she turned to him so naturally, that even in a crowd it seemed as if she were alone in the chapel. She desired that her followers acquire this ease and taste for prayer as well, inviting them to seek deeper levels of prayer, even in the midst of their demanding ministry to the poor, becoming *"contemplatives in the heart of the world."* [109]

Mother Teresa herself had become a living prayer, and people felt instinctively drawn to prayer in her presence. Contemplative by nature, always sensitive to the presence of God, she was in a constant state of devotion and contact with him. Despite the struggles her darkness brought, to watch her in prayer was to witness a soul in surrender, a soul at rest, a soul in love, wrapped in God.

Every morning and evening, people of all faiths, or none, crowded into the Missionaries of Charity chapel in Calcutta, simply to pray with Mother Teresa. The reverence of her spirit evoked a longing in others, a memory of contact with God long forgotten, and a hunger for the divine, drawing them to join her in the journey of prayer. The quieting, the incense wafting in the warm air, the Rosary beads passing silently through her fingers, seeing her spend so much of her day communing with God — all these evoked in those around her an atmosphere of reverence and a growing desire for prayer.

Because Mother Teresa lived her life in a state of prayer, those who drew near her experienced not only her goodness, but God's goodness and presence through her. A young professional woman who had been away from her faith for many years came to our community in Tijuana, hoping to meet Mother Teresa for the first time. She had expected to meet a Nobel laureate, but instead was surprised to find herself suddenly in the presence of God. Reflecting on her experience, she wrote:

> I saw that when I met her; I saw Him. It changed me forever. I saw in her what I might be — a place in creation where God lives freely, free to move and express His being. She made that place for God within herself, and made it evident to others. She showed us what we might be. When she spoke, people grew quiet. They came anxious and curious, suffering and weary, and they were quieted in her prayerful presence. They saw God in her. She saw God in them.

How many people around the world has Mother Teresa led, both in life and after her death, to the threshold of intimacy with God, and a new life: "*When I met her, I saw Him. It changed me forever.*" Mother Teresa was convinced that prayer was something simple, easily accessible, and life-giving, and that it transformed us, as no amount of effort at self-improvement ever could. In her experience, the only requirement for succeeding at prayer was to take the time, to take *more* time, to actually pray. Just as one learns to swim or to ride a bicycle by doing, by practice more than study, so too with prayer:

> *If you want to pray better, you must pray more.*[110]

The mystery of Mother Teresa is nothing else than the mystery of our God-given ability to access the depths of divinity, to come face-to-face with God, simply by entering the depths of our own soul. It is there that we behold the light she beheld on the train, and follow her into the divine embrace — for each time we enter prayer, "His Hands are extended to embrace us. His Heart is wide open to receive us."[111]

The "Silence of the Heart"

Mother Teresa did not teach any particular method of prayer. Though she offered her Sisters much encouragement in prayer, she neither practiced nor recommended any specific technique. How did she pray herself? This we can surmise both from observing her at prayer and from the recurring themes she touched on in her talks on prayer:

> *We need to find God and He cannot be found in noise nor in restlessness. See how [in] nature, trees, flowers, grass, grow in perfect silence; see the stars, the moon and the sun, how they move in silence. . . .*[112]

Two themes stand out in her teaching, and were reflected in her example: *praying with the heart* and *inner silence*. Those who came to pray with her were struck by Mother Teresa's demeanor in prayer, especially by the profound stillness of her spirit, and the obvious depth of her prayer. This kind of inner depth and stillness were at the core of her teaching: *"In the silence of the heart, God speaks."* [113] This became her formula for prayer — a formula we will examine in its two components, prayer of the *heart* and inner *silence*, which together produce the depth and interior quietude wherein God can communicate and give himself to the soul.

Prayer of the Heart

Let us look first at *praying with the heart*. For Mother Teresa, prayer, and indeed all of life, was an affair of the heart. References to the heart of both God and man appear throughout her letters and talks, especially where she describes the nature of God and our relation to him.

Since God is love, the way to him is *the way of love*, the way of the "heart" — not in the sense of emotion, but of the depth of love arising from the center of our being. Conscious relating to God in prayer becomes essentially *a return of love* and, hence, an exercise of the heart.

Mother Teresa's use of the term "heart," beyond signifying the realm of the affective, pointed to its broader, biblical sense. Since the heart symbolizes what is deepest in the human person, true prayer, as an exercise of the inner man, takes place in the heart. Biblically, the heart represents our inner temple, the seat of human interiority and intimacy, the proper terrain of the spirit — and therefore, the place of our encounter with God.

Praying Deeply

If we are to follow Mother Teresa's example of praying with the heart, and placing ourselves in silence before the God who thirsts to love us, we will first need to understand what Christian tradition means by prayer of the heart.

Praying "with the heart" is principally about depth in prayer. Praying at *the level of the heart* requires the effort to go beneath the surface of our awareness, where we spend the majority of our conscious lives, to find the God who abides within, at the center of our being.

In her classic work *The Interior Castle*, St. Teresa of Ávila describes the soul's pilgrimage to its depths, to the inner sanctuary where God resides, as a king in the interior of his castle — with beasts and brigands and every kind of distraction inhabiting the outer rings of the soul, on the surface. The journey of life, and the daily journey of prayer, involves leaving behind the distractions that roam on the surface, and then seeking our depths, where God and his love can alone be found and experienced.

Our first task is to learn to *go beneath the surface* in prayer, to "find the place of the heart," as the Eastern Fathers of the Church admonished. In coming into prayer, we "come as we are," which means we come with the center of our awareness at the "head" level. And this is how things should be; we need to be centered in the faculties of the head, focused on the sights and sounds around us, in order to interact with the world. But this self-conscious activity is of little use in prayer, where our goal becomes precisely the opposite.

Ever since fleeing the Garden, a part of us still retains a deep nostalgia for God, while another part of us still flees him. A kind of centrifugal force pulls us away from our center, even as we are engaged in seeking after God. As children of Adam and Eve, original sin has left us fleeing the empty place within — where God awaits with healing and salvation in hand, gently calling our name.

Here on the surface of the soul, where we can more easily be distracted, abides not only *forgetfulness of God* (which the early Fathers considered the root of all sin), but also the commotion of our selfishness, jealousy, anger, and all that moves us to resist him. The Lord has to call us back, like Adam, inviting us to undertake this pilgrimage of return to our depths. But even as we avoid him, he is there at our center, waiting to pour himself out in love.

We seek for something or someone else to slake our inner thirst, to fill the void God created as a sacred space for himself, a void large enough that only he can fill — but we find none. Or rather, we find too many things — things that neither satisfy nor fill us, but only titillate and distract. All the while, in the depths, our "soul thirsts for God, for the living God" (Ps 42:2) — even as we pitch our tent on the surface, dying of thirst.

But God has already prepared a banquet for us, already set a wellspring within to sustain us through this life, and draw us into the next. "The water that I shall give . . . will become . . . a spring of water welling up to eternal life." (Jn 4:14). Or in the sublime words of St. Ignatius of Antioch, "There is a living water within me saying, 'Come to the Father.'"

Going Inward

All deep prayer is anchored in *interior silence*. By its very nature, silent prayer goes deep — it brings us beyond petition, beyond praise, beyond our own activity, into the deep wordless communion in which Jesus rested his soul each night. We stand silent and still before God, whose divine initiative is paramount in prayer, as in life. Before him we are but beggars, trembling at his word — a word that can re-create our soul, even as it created the heavens. The secret is silence:

> *The first means to use is silence. Souls of prayer are souls of great silence. We cannot put ourselves directly in the presence of God if we do not practice internal and external silence.*[114]

Engaging in deep prayer is much like diving for pearls. Some minimal effort is required for a pearl diver to overcome his natural

In prayer (Raghu Rai/Magnum Photos)

buoyancy, to arrive at the depths where the treasure lies — and to remain there for the duration. In prayer as well, there is a kind of natural buoyancy at work, drawing us back to the surface. Like the diver, we need some simple, persevering effort to remain there in the depths, where all is quiet and peace in God's presence.

A storm of thoughts and distractions may go on above us, but as long as we provide that minimal inner movement that allows us to stay below, the storms of distraction cannot touch us; they do not affect or interrupt our prayer. Whenever we experience turbulence, whenever we find ourselves buffeted by thoughts, it is a sign that we have been imperceptibly returning to the surface. We need only that small effort once again to return below, like the small kick of the diver's fins, and again we are at peace in an inward Eden. What this means for prayer, and our perennial battle with distractions, is that thoughts and distractions are *no longer an obstacle* — we merely stay beneath them, consistently seeking this deeper "place of the heart."

As we all know from experience, *superficial prayer cannot satisfy us*, nor satisfy the God who thirsts for us. In fact, limiting ourselves to surface prayer, to prayer that goes no deeper than the mind, inevitably leads to inner dryness, and often to abandoning prayer altogether. Little comes of it, so we invest in it less and less.

Though our transformation begins with the mind, with faith, in pondering divine light, it is the *heart* that is the true seat of change. It is the heart that opens to the divine love pointed to by faith, in the encounter of deep prayer. While the content of our thoughts is vitally important (as we have seen in studying Mother Teresa's faith convictions), and acts as a compass in the heart's search for God, *once deeper, more contemplative prayer begins, thoughts have done their job* and are no longer of service.

Thoughts and images in prayer are like signposts along the road, pointing to the destination — useful as they are, they can become surrogates and idols, if they are treated as the goal. No matter how beautiful and useful, postcards and road signs pointing to Rome *are not Rome*; and stopping our journey, being caught up with admiring them and going no further, brings us no closer to the goal. As St. John of the Cross insists, no matter how pious, "our thoughts about God are not God." God dwells beyond them and beneath them, in the center of the soul. For this reason, Mother Teresa would invite her Sisters to "*endeavor to live alone with Jesus in the sanctuary of our inmost heart.*" [115]

We need to create our own inner hermitage, an inner sanctum where nothing and no one but God can enter — where God can abide alone, "face-to-face" with the soul. This is the motive behind Jesus' teaching: "When you pray, go into your room and shut the door and pray to your Father . . . in secret" (Mt 6:6).

Finding the "place of the heart" builds on the practice of establishing faith-contact with God at the outset of prayer. Before engaging in prayer, we first take a brief moment to enter into conscious and deliberate contact — not with a God hidden above the clouds, nor floating on the mind's ruminations, but with the living God abiding in the depths of our soul.

Once we have taken this first step and consciously established faith-contact with God, we simply begin to *move the focus of our awareness* away from the surface, towards the center of the soul. We shift our attention from the level of the head to the level of the heart. There is nothing difficult or mysterious about this at all. Though the "heart" referred to here is not the physical heart per se, there is such an intimate, God-made connection between soul and body that by shifting our focus inward, to a level corresponding to the area of the heart, we find ourselves moving towards a deeper level of the soul as well.

Quieting the Heart

What do we do, once we have focused our attention inwards? Here our encounter begins in earnest, as we are drawn by the power of God's "infinite longing to love and be loved." This is where we begin to see Mother Teresa's faith convictions become "flesh" in our own experience; this is the inner soil in which the seeds of faith bear fruit in deep prayer.

Unlike Mother Teresa's illumination, which came about in an instant on the train, her *transformation* was produced over time, in deep prayer, even in the "darkness" of naked faith. But, even though this kind of deep contact is not based on feelings, this does not mean there is nothing to experience. Quite the opposite is true.

Just as the visually impaired develop their remaining senses to the maximum, so the more we spend time at this deeper level in faith, beyond our outer senses, the more we develop our inner, *spiritual* senses. As we follow Mother Teresa's path, our prayer experience is not one of ennui or "nothingness," but of a dark fullness that bathes us in a love and blessedness beyond all we have known, or could ever know with our bodily senses.

Beneath our outer awareness, in silence and peaceful night, with only inklings of God's deep and gentle touch, something is happening. "Through deep prayer, the inspirational power and healing required for positive daily living can be discovered in the depths of the soul, wherein resides God."[116] We can detect his presence, his activity, and his infusion of love, even without our senses. This is entirely real, and becomes something we are more sure of than the sun in the noonday sky; and yet we can neither describe it nor control it. But it is always there, free for the taking:

> "Every one who thirsts,
>   come to the waters;
> and he who has no money,
>   come...." (Is 55:1)

We come away from this kind of deep prayer with our entire being quieted and at peace, knowing beyond doubt that we have been with God, and that he has touched us in our inmost being.

This prayer is fundamentally God's work, God's doing. While the Incarnate Word is "speaking" his love into the soul, our part, our response, is a loving and attentive inner silence and quietude — gently focused on God, yet not interfering with his sublime work. At this level, silence is not of thought and memory alone, but of will, and of our whole being:

*Silence of the heart, not only of the mouth — that too is necessary —
but more that silence of the mind, silence of the eyes, silence of the
touch. Then you can hear Him everywhere: in the closing of the door,
in the person who needs you, in the birds that sing, in the flowers, the
animals — that silence which is wonder and praise. Why? Because
God is everywhere and you can see and hear Him. That crow is prais-
ing God. I can hear its sound well. . . . We can see Him and hear Him
in that crow, and pray. . . .*[117]

Through the practice of holding ourselves open in silence before
God's presence in the depths, resisting the stirrings of curiosity and
ego-appetites and self-will, we are continually handing the reins of
control back to God during prayer. Once we are focused on God in
the depths, we seek to say our "yes," like the Virgin Mary before the
angel, consciously consenting to the working of God's grace and the
infilling of his love. It is not enough to place ourselves in God's presence by faith; we need to actively *consent* to his work of love in the
soul — and to go on renewing that consent whenever we find ourselves distracted, whenever we turn our desire towards the thoughts
coming and going on the surface.

The goal is not to suppress thoughts during prayer, but only to
ignore them, to let them be and to let them go — and to *prefer God*,
to choose him anew whenever we wander. Our objective is not a
forced emptiness of the mind, nor inner silence for its own sake, but
for the sake of the divine voice, and the divine fullness — for the sake
of being "*filled with all the fullness of God*" (Eph 3:19). While attention,
awareness, and mindfulness are important in Christian prayer, they
are a means and not an end. The absolute primacy of love in Christian life (since God is love) means that — unlike our Buddhist brothers, whose focus is mindfulness — the attention we practice in
Christian prayer is for the sake of *intention* — for the sake of love, for
the sake of communion with the God of Love.

The aim of Christian prayer, therefore, is not emptying the
mind, but emptying the heart of all that is not God.

Consent

What form does our consent to God's action take? Let us look at some simple images, taken from the lives of the saints — images that aid in describing and practicing inner consent in prayer. Though these are not from Mother Teresa, they help to clarify and illustrate her approach to prayer.

The first is from the life of St. Margaret Mary Alacoque.[†] During a period of difficulty in prayer, she heard Jesus say interiorly: "Open your soul before me like an empty canvas before the painter, and hold it there, while I trace my image in your soul." The analogy of the canvas points to the importance of being *receptive* before God, and reminds us that God's divinizing work takes place when we are still enough, and desirous enough, to allow it. St. John of the Cross describes this attitude as "loving attentiveness to God" and to his loving work in the soul.

Finally, there is the example of the great Florentine mystic St. Mary Magdalen de' Pazzi.[††] One day, one of her Carmelite novices came to complain of her struggles in prayer. This celebrated guide of the spiritual life, consulted by churchmen from all over Europe, responded with her down-to-earth wisdom. "For the next week," she counseled, "instead of spending prayer time in your cell, go into the garden and *learn from the flowers how to pray*." Just as a flower turns it petals towards the sun in silent receptivity, no matter the temperature or the hour, despite wind or rain, cloud or shine, so too must the soul in prayer turn receptively towards the divine sun, patiently, peacefully, and perseveringly — though without strain, without agitation. "*Learn from the flowers. . . .*"

In prayer, we have only to descend to the level of the heart, and to open the great bronze doors of our inner temple to welcome the Lord,

---

[†] St. Margaret Mary Alacoque (1647-1690) was a member of the Visitation Order and apostle of the devotion to the Heart of Jesus.

[††] St. Mary Magdalen de' Pazzi (1566-1607) was the novice mistress of the Carmelite convent of Florence.

and to keep them open in welcome when tempted to wander. He does all the rest. This simple practice may at times prove difficult (when beset with dryness or distraction), but it is, nonetheless, always simple, accessible to all and deeply satisfying — simple enough to admit the newcomer, yet profound enough to captivate the proficient. This is the utter simplicity and profound power of the encounter communicated to Mother Teresa "in the silence of the heart," that she might share it with the poor and needy, among whom God numbers us all.

Abiding in the Encounter

Whenever we perceive ourselves becoming distracted, we need but gently return our awareness to God's presence in the depths, to *his* activity (rather than ours) in the soul. Even the act of observing ourselves while we pray, of asking "how we are doing" and commenting on our progress, brings us back to the surface.

When such distractions occur, there are a number of ways of returning our focus to God and re-establishing ourselves at that deeper level. The first and simplest is merely to *intend* it — since the power of intention immediately refocuses our attention on God.

For some, recalling an image that represents our desired prayer stance is helpful — such as the image of the empty canvas held open for the touch of the Master, or the image of inner doors opened in welcome.

Another means of refocusing the soul, drawn from the early desert fathers, is that of interiorly repeating a *prayer word* that represents our desire for God, whenever we feel the tug of thoughts or distractions. Once it has served its purpose of refocusing the soul on God's presence, on his activity in the depths, we simply let it go and return to rest in him. This practice has been taken up again and popularized under different forms, and while Mother Teresa never taught any specific method, she did teach the practice of using short phrases to focus the soul on God.

This kind of deeper prayer became Mother Teresa's daily means of encountering God's longing — of renewing and keeping alive the grace of the train. However, her approach to prayer drew not only on her September grace, but also on the millennial roots of all Christian prayer. In its essence, whether Mother Teresa realized it or not, *all prayer* is the soul's encounter with God's longing. In the words of the *Catechism of the Catholic Church*:

Prayer is [. . .] a response of love to the thirst of the only Son of God.[118]

Whether we realize it or not, prayer is the encounter of God's thirst with ours.[119]

Prayer is not only our response to God's thirst, but the expression of the soul's *own* thirst for God — an encounter, as the *Catechism* states, between our thirst and God's. The soul assumes a receptive, consenting, desiring attitude — affirming its "yes" to the God within, who, in his boundless humility, constantly *asks our permission* to embrace us, to fill us with himself. The soul in prayer says in response to the God who thirsts to love and be loved: *"Come, Lord Jesus. Take me and my love; love me, fill me, change me."* It is the silent voice of the canvas before the painter, the voice of the flower before the sun, the voice of the beloved before the God who loves.

This simple practice of finding the depths, opening in receptive consent, and renewing our intention when distracted brings us infallibly back to God when we wander, setting our inner compass towards God's presence for the duration of our prayer — and for the task of living that comes, freshly anointed, after our prayer and beyond.

Summing Up

At this deeper level, there is no such thing as good or bad prayer — there is only prayer. No matter how often we need to refocus during a particular prayer period, we gain immeasurably. In fact, the more we are assailed by thoughts, the more opportunity we are given to choose God above other things (represented by our thoughts); the more chance we have for preferring God to all else, and freely choosing to focus our inner thirst on him — which is the essence of prayer.

Learning to inhabit our depths in prayer, and refocusing our awareness there when need arises, actually becomes quite easy, restful, and eminently desirable — and with only a minimum of practice. With time, the whole process becomes second nature, like a camera set to auto-focus, needing only the slightest touch to bring the objective back into view. These peaceful, God-dwelt depths become our habitual inner milieu, where we find ourselves not only in prayer, but more and more, like Mother Teresa, even in the midst of daily life.

We begin to forge an inner channel, a passageway between the surface and the depths of our soul, so that even our surface living in the workaday world keeps its roots bathed and fed by the divinity within. Whenever we are given a stray moment for prayer, as brief as sitting through a red light on the way home, those great bronze doors to the interior castle that once squeaked and strained to open, now swing inward at the slightest touch, well oiled by the practice of deeper prayer.

The life effects of this simple discipline are profound, as Mother Teresa's legacy is proof. God's light and peace begin to occupy more of our waking moments. Things that once bothered us, filling us with anger or worry, now pass by barely noticed. Impatience and resentment begin to fall away. God himself becomes the companion of our days and nights, the true and conscious center of our existence. As Mother Teresa invites us to believe:

> *In silence we will find new energy and true unity. The energy of God will be ours to do all things well. The unity of our thoughts with His thoughts, the unity of our prayers with His prayers; the unity of our actions with His actions; of our life with His life.*[120]

The kind of graced transformation that gave the world Mother Teresa begins to become a reality in our own life — not that we are called to do *what* she did, but to live *as* she did, to live our own particular call as gracefully and generously as she.

The key is now in our hand, we need only begin to use it:

Yesterday is gone; tomorrow has not yet come. We have only today. Let us begin.

"The devil is the father of lies . . . he will not come as a lion but as an angel of light."[121]

— Mother Teresa

SIXTEEN

Naming the Darkness, Choosing the Light

Light and Dark

Opening to the light of Christ brings about life-changing discoveries, but it can also stir up the darkness — for the dark elements within us, and the powers of darkness around us, are threatened by the light. In the parable of the Sower (cf. Mt 13:4, 19), as soon as the seed of the Word is sown and God's light is given to man, the evil one comes and tries to take it away. We need to be prepared for the struggle, then, and to continue choosing the light we have beheld, especially in times of weakness and doubt.

This Satan-spun darkness is very different from the "night" that Mother Teresa experienced. Her darkness was neither the absence nor the antithesis of light, but the result of an *overabundance* of light — of a brilliance too great for the human spirit to behold unaided, at least in this life. This extreme of divine radiance temporarily blinds the faculties of soul — so that even while filling the spirit with grace and good works, the senses are left bereft.

In Her Darkness, Light

Not a few commentators, secular and religious, have struggled with understanding Mother Teresa's "dark night," seeing it as a crisis of faith, or worse. But a careful reading of her correspondence with her spiritual directors[122] shows that, while her darkness was indeed a challenge to her faith (and to hope and love as well) — though a challenge she navigated with grace and courage — her faith was never remotely in crisis; just the opposite. Through it all, her already robust faith was only deepened and strengthened, like a mighty tree in a storm that, rather than falling, only puts down deeper roots.

That her experience of darkness came from an *excess of* light, rather than its lack, was evident from the unmistakable effects that the light produced in her soul — her peace, her love of her enemies, her intense longing for God, her constant and contagious joy, and the sense of the presence of God that surrounded her. All these were more reliable signs that God was powerfully present in her soul than any awareness or consolation in her senses.

Mother Teresa's dark night, like our own trials of faith, would serve to carve out more space in her soul for God, for the One whom she served without seeing: "Blessed are those who have not seen and yet believe" (Jn 20:29). This kind of heaven-dwelt darkness is not a tomb, but rather a sacred womb from which new life emerges. Her darkness was the blessed crucible in which Mother Teresa became *Saint* Teresa. Far from being a stumbling block, her unflagging faith in the dark night became a stepping stone to the heights. Just as for Jesus on Calvary, rather than leaving Mother Teresa alone or far from God, darkness became her path to ultimate generosity, and to heaven itself. Pope John Paul II comments on Jesus' own experience of dark night on Calvary, which Mother Teresa would mirror and share:

> Jesus had the clear vision of God and the certainty of his union with the Father dominant in his mind. But in the sphere bordering on the senses, and therefore more subject to the impres-

Pursuing ministry with joy (Raghu Rai/Magnum Photos)

sions, emotions and influences of the internal and external experiences of pain, Jesus' human soul was reduced to a wasteland. He no longer felt the presence of the Father, but he underwent the tragic experience of the most complete desolation.[123]

Even as he cried out, "My God, my God, why have you forsaken me" (Mt 27:46), Jesus refused to bring himself down from the night of the cross, until he was raised up by the same Father whose presence he could no more feel. Likewise, despite the expressions of pain we find in her letters, Mother Teresa never sought respite or escape — only the means to continue. Her perseverance, over fifty long and fruitful years, shows us that there is meaning to the crosses we bear, and a God who watches over all, even when he is neither seen nor felt. Even in the depths of our darkness, as he has promised, he will bring the dawn:

"The day shall dawn upon us from on high
to give light to those who sit in darkness and in the shadow of
    death." (Lk 1:78-79)

Interior darkness became for Mother Teresa a *laboratory of greater love*, just as the external darkness of Calcutta's slums had been, once she left the convent. Her dark night was a school of spirit, where she learned to cling to God, even in her pain — all the while serving the pain of others, rather than being lost in her own. Even as coal is darkly forged into diamond, so also the rigors of her inner night transformed her fragile human love into something robust and divine.

Centuries before her, St. John of the Cross described this inner darkness that carves out the ego and scours the soul to become God's temple, free of the clutches of self. In surveying the wonders of grace and transformation worked in his own soul in the dark womb of the night, he could only exclaim, "*O noche dichosa!*" — "O blessed night"[124] that brings in its silent wake such blessings. Every year at

Easter, the entire Church sings of the "blessed night" in which Israel came forth from Egypt, and the still more blessed night which it prefigured, when Jesus came forth triumphant from the tomb. This biblical night, pregnant with new life, is one that all must pass through on the way to the Father's house. In the end, it is all blessing, for God's light infallibly shines through the darkness, a darkness that will never overcome it (cf. Jn 1:5).

God's mastery and triumph over darkness is seen throughout Scripture: from the Spirit hovering over the darkness of the abyss at Creation, to Jesus, Lord of the new creation, walking on the stormy sea at night. The risen Jesus, victor over darkness, shared his victory with Mother Teresa, as he does with us — a victory gained by confronting the darkness, embracing it, and turning it inside out. In keeping with Mother Teresa's mission to be, and to carry, God's light, what emerged from her trial of faith was not darkness at all, but a *new and brighter light* — a light supernal, beyond the clutches of darkness. As Scripture declares of God, and of all who belong to him: "Even the darkness is not dark to you, the night is bright as the day" (Ps 139:12).

A Beacon in Our Night

A reading of Mother Teresa's letters reveals that her victory over darkness was not taken on primarily for her sake, but for ours — for a humanity still dwelling in the "shadow of death" (Mt 4:16), for whom she promised to come down from her place in heaven, to help light our way home:

> *If I ever become a saint — I will surely be one of "darkness." I will continually be absent from Heaven — to light the light of those in darkness on earth.*[125]

In order that Mother Teresa might illumine our own dark journey, God led her through it ahead of us. He filled her with the light of faith, and made her his beacon. Even for a modern age hankering like Israel for the "flesh and onions" of Egypt (cf. Num 11:5), with little taste for manna and little patience for the journey, Mother Teresa succeeded in holding our attention. She has gone before us to light the way, as the "pillar of fire by night" (Num 14:14) that led Israel, marking out the way to the Promised Land. Thanks to God's work in her, not only the poor of Calcutta but the rest of us around the world can say:

> "The people who sat in darkness
> have seen a great light,
> and for those who sat in the region and shadow of death
> light has dawned." (Mt 4:16)

Mother Teresa is a saint of darkness as well as of light, for the two are inseparable here below; in fact, the one is at the service of the other. Mother Teresa's struggle has shown us that human darkness serves to *draw our eyes to a higher light*, a divine light which illumines every night, making every Calcutta a Jerusalem, and every dark and empty place God's temple.

Gift of Light

The treasures of light contained in Mother Teresa's path through darkness tend to escape first glance — like rough diamonds, hidden and waiting to be mined. Her letters do not only speak of her struggles — they speak of her love and devotion, her longing for God, her willingness to suffer for him and for the poor, and of the joy she found welling up within her, despite her darkness.

Darkness was not the last word, nor by far the only word, defining her relationship and experience of God. Her writings and public conferences reflect the uncommon light that inhabited her soul, a light that Calcutta's poor, though surrounded by the worst kind of darkness, could plainly see. The beauty of her spiritual vision is itself proof that she was never bereft of God's light. In fact, her lights on the Godhead (as we saw in Section Two) are so profound that some have suggested that Mother Teresa may one day take her place among the Doctors of the Church.[†]

Her light, at its core, is the mystery of God's longing to love and be loved, the radiance of his infinite thirst for man. This light was of such importance to God, so close to his heart, and so reflective of the essence of his being, that he could lament our ignorance of the light to Mother Teresa: *"They don't know Me — so they don't want Me...."* For that reason, he purposely sent Mother Teresa into the darkest reaches of our world so that the light of his longing might shine where it was least known, and most needed. She shed this light on those whose darkness she accepted to share, that we who wander in darkness might also share her light.

Toxic Darkness

By shining with God's light before the world, Mother Teresa has indirectly pointed out the darkness that is its opposite; she has helped us to *name the darkness*, to unmask the great lie.

Each time she spoke in public, after making the Sign of the Cross over her lips, Mother Teresa would repeat this line from St. John's gospel: "For God so loved the world..." (Jn 3:16). She would remind her audience that each of us is precious to God, chosen out of countless others who could have existed in our place. She would go on to say that each of us is cherished, prized as "the apple of his eye" (Dt 32:10), and that as long as we have breath, this love will never leave us. This was the light she held up before the world, reflected in her

---

[†] *Doctor*, in Latin, signifies teacher (from *docere*, to teach). "Doctor of the Church" is a title given to those saints whose teachings are recognized as having particular importance for understanding the faith. Other Doctors of the Church include Origen, St. Thomas Aquinas, and St. Augustine. More modern examples include women such as St. Teresa of Ávila, St. Catherine of Siena, and St. Thérèse of Lisieux.

words and works. This is the truth that frees us to get up when we fall, to hope in a love we cannot earn, and to become what we were made to be.

While those who heard Mother Teresa speak might have forgotten or ignored this truth, or even doubted it, Satan knows it all too well, "and trembles" before its implications (cf. Jas 2:19). God's faithful love, his undying thirst for us, represents the undoing of Satan's kingdom. It buckles the very foundations and shakes the underpinnings of Satan's empire. Since Satan cannot bring God to stop loving us — though he tries, accusing us "day and night before our God" (Rev 12:10) — he resorts to the next best thing. Since this "enemy of our human nature"[126] cannot change the heart of God, he does all in his power to change the heart of man — the focus of his strategy since the Garden. Because he cannot stop God from loving, he tries to *stop man from believing*. In the end, the result is the same. As far as we are concerned, by our unbelief in his love, it becomes as if God did not love us — and either way, we are equally lost.

Using every twist of logic, every un-redressed injustice unearthed from our past, every broken dream and unhealed wound in a pantheon of hurt, Satan gnaws away at our belief in God's love and care. While there is a "blessed night," a sacred darkness that hides a light too bright to behold, there is also an unholy night, a darkness that is the *absence of all light* — and worse, the opposite of all light, a kind of demonic anti-light. If all true light is the breath of the Holy Spirit, there is, on the other hand, a toxic darkness that is the breath of the evil one. His one desire is to nullify the light and power of God's love, to distance us from that love, to neutralize its impact on our conscious lives. He knows that the less we are aware of God's love, the less we are in touch with it, the more likely it is that we will forget or doubt it — and all the easier it will be to entice us to sin, to live instead for ego.

The Tactics of the Garden

Satan's ploy with humanity, which has not changed from the Garden until today, is to bring us to question God's intentions. He suggests that in dealing with us, God acts as self–interestedly as we do; that his commandments exist only to keep us under the divine thumb, subdued and servile. If he tells Adam not to eat of the tree, it is for the basest of reasons: God is afraid that you "will be like God . . ." (Gen 3:5). The God of Satan's packaging is a miserly giver, changeable and untrustworthy, a master who gives only in order to get, only looking to exact our worship and servitude.

Once we start to question God's intentions, though, once we doubt that he cares for our needs or listens to our prayer, what source of provision and protection is left to us beyond our own self-reliance? We are left with no other option than *taking for ourselves* whatever we lack, since God, or so we are convinced, is not looking out for anyone but himself. Satan persuades us that we have no other choice but to take whatever we want, and by whatever means, regardless of the moral implications. The enemy leads us to sin, not so much because he enjoys its perversion, but in order to distance us from the Almighty. By separating Creator from creature, he keeps God's love for us at bay, impeded from reaching us in the only way possible — through our own free choice, and by our own hand.

Satan's appeal plays to the basest of our ego-drives. By stimulating our selfish and superficial desires, he hopes to drown out our deepest God-given and God-fulfilled longing. He offers us, in exchange for the deeper gifts God has promised, only excitation and distraction: fool's gold, pacifiers, surrogates dangled before us like baubles. These are poor substitutes for the gift of divine love, impostors that deprive us of our true and lasting happiness — in God.

By making an idol of the self, and by ego run amok through sin, we pay a steep price in loss of relationship with God, with others, and ultimately with ourselves. Rather than climbing the heights to rival the Creator, to "be like God" (Gen 3:5), as we have attempted from Eden to Babel and down through history, we end up not only *not* like God, but unlike ourselves — living more basely than the animals beneath us. These are the new lows humanity has reached; this is the new poverty; these are the depths we have carved out for ourselves alone.

Shame

After accusing God of duplicity, Satan goes on to justify man's disobedience by suggesting to Adam (and his children) that *sin does not exist* — that there are no moral absolutes, no ethical standards beyond whatever suits us in the moment. God's warnings are but posturing and propaganda, he says, for there are no real consequences to sin: "You will not die," the serpent said to the woman (Gen 3:4).

But Satan knows that once we are enticed into sin, its bitterness and its bite will begin to take their toll. Sin may satisfy the senses, but it is always sour and unsettling to the soul. By the simple process of elimination, we will discover that the experience of grace and virtue trumps the sour aftertaste of sin every time, at every level. But once we begin to suspect the deception, once we realize that sin and its pain are real, and once we experience the first stirrings of repentance — Satan changes tactics.

Instead of tempting us to sin the more, instead of minimizing sin's gravity, Satan does just the opposite — he begins to fill us with shame over our fall from grace. Once he sees that our "eyes are opened" (cf. Gen. 3:7) after tasting the bitter forbidden fruit, Satan mocks the emptiness that our choices have wrought. He holds up to us the mirror of our self-induced disfigurement so that we can see that we are naked (cf. Gen 3:7). Having stretched out our hand to partake of unlawfulness, the bitter "fruit" of the tree" (Gen 3:6), Satan buries us under the unbearable weight of law, guilt, and shame.

As his end strategy to prevent us from returning to God, Satan wields the weight of shame to crush our spirit, and to block our escape into God's mercy. Though God's heart is never closed, his incessant and gentle pleas to return are drowned out by the voice of shame and doubt. And these Satan will gladly supply — taunting us with the very sins he himself had instigated, insinuating that we have forever forfeited God's gifts, and lost whatever blessing we once had.

With that, Satan's battle is won.

———

We now find ourselves alone, far from the embrace of the Father; not because God has abandoned us, but because we cannot bear the nakedness that is ours. And so we hide. We hide from one another, and were it possible, from God himself: "I was naked; and I hid myself" (Gen 3:10). We run from our one healer and only hope, and craft excuses to deflect our shame before him: "The woman whom you gave to be with me, she gave me fruit" . . . "The serpent beguiled me, and I ate" (Gen 3:12, 13). We weave a mask of fig leaves to hide our disgrace from one another. But deep in our core, we fear that our shame is without remedy, that it cannot be overturned, only held at bay by denial and distraction.

With Satan in control, God becomes an object of fear — a judge and no more. How removed this caricature is from the God who delighted walking with Adam "in the garden in the cool of the day" (Gen 3:8). Rather than living secure "in the shadow of [God's] wings" (Ps 17:8), free of self-concern and self-reference — free to fulfill our vocation to "love and be loved" — we turn our attention on ourselves, convinced that God no longer cares.

Once faith is lost, there is little to hold us back from a headlong flight into gratification, into distraction from the gaping inner void. We crown *ourselves* as the gods of our own existence — but end up becoming merely false gods who "cannot save" (Is 45:20) from death, or emptiness, or pain.

The Trap of Self-sufficiency

In either form of toxic darkness — either doubting God's goodness, or not believing in any god but ourselves — our life project becomes one of getting rather than giving, beating our rivals by any means to secure the lion's share for ourselves.

Since we presume that we have either lost God's care or that a caring God does not exist, we end up having to promote, protect, and provide for ourselves — over and against everyone else. In this scenario, sooner or later violence takes the upper hand, the law of the strongest becoming the ultimate arbiter. Adam and Eve do not have long to wait before witnessing the violence their sin has unleashed. Already in Cain, their firstborn, who slays Abel simply out of jealousy (cf. Gen 4:8), we see the inexorable consequences of giving in to Satan's lie.

Satan's grand plan for our ego's autonomy from God simply does not work, and cannot be sustained. How much energy we waste in attempting to make ourselves the focus of our existence, the center of our universe, with everything revolving around us. It is no less absurd than if Saturn or Jupiter attempted to make itself the center of the solar system, trying to drag the sun and planets around itself. The divine plan was not that we become *gods* — separate, autonomous, and self-serving — but, through his transforming love, that we become *like God*: sharing in God's life, and loving as he loves, freely and fully.

Doubting the existence of God and the reality of sin on the one hand, or fearing that we can no longer be loved on the other: this is Satan's double-edged sword, the serpent's two-pronged lie. Either way, we end up strangers, restless wanderers on the earth (Gen 4:12), bearing the unbearable mark of Cain (Gen 4:15). In this we "*all* have sinned and fall short of the glory of God" (Rom 3:23); we have all slain our brethren out of selfishness — through anger, rivalry, and revenge. Embracing Satan's message, we have all lost our way.

"Come, Be My Light"

But the story does not end with fig leaves and forsakenness. God seeks us out, and he calls us forth from our hopelessness: "Where are you?" (Gen 3:9). He promises a way out of our darkness, and delivers on his promise with the gift of his light. The narrow doorway (cf. Mt 7:13) through which we must pass into new life, however, is *framed by our belief* — by our core convictions about who and how God is, and by the attitudes and choices that flow from our convictions.

Jesus, who came to "destroy the works of the devil" (1 Jn 3:8), to heal our brokenness and undo our plight, does so by first *undoing the great lie* by his light. By illumining the face of the Father, and our true dignity as his wounded but cherished children, Jesus has lighted our path back to the Garden.

Our convictions about who God is and how he loves (not just in general, but how he loves *me*) needs to be constantly stretched and expanded by the light. Each measure of growth in belief brings us closer to the reality, the beauty, and the blessings of God. The more accurate our image, and the closer we come to grasping his "infinite desire to love and be loved," the more we will be drawn into God's "light and love" — and the closer we will come to experiencing Mother Teresa's same inner fire.

This is the importance of beholding even the refracted light given to Mother Teresa on the train, shining through her words and works of love. She has shared with us a light that outshines every darkness, a faith that "overcomes the world" (1 Jn 5:4), and a gospel vision of God and man that transforms us and sets us free. Her light was the message of God's infinite longing, her lampstand the love poured out on the unlovable on the streets of Calcutta and the world.

With this twin reflection of God's goodness in word and deed, she has offered a new understanding of the heart of God for generations to come, and opened wider the pathway from our heart to his.

"'I thirst.' What does it mean in your life, in your heart?"[127]

— Mother Teresa

SEVENTEEN

Conversion: Thirsting for God

Our God Is a Consuming Fire

Even as it consoles us, opening to God's light and love is a grace that will slowly but inevitably reshape our lives, a grace capable of shaking and transforming the very foundations of our existence.

The breath of the Spirit unleashes tectonic shifts within the soul — as when God breathed over the abyss on the first day of creation. After beholding the goodness of God, and experiencing this love like no other, we cannot remain the same.

This inner fire not only illumines, it consumes and transforms — wielding a divine power that will, one day, bring about the transfiguration of all creation. The power of this love will continue restructuring our life, as it did for Mother Teresa, unless we pull away from its divine advances. Once we have beheld this light, *we become responsible for its continued presence* in our life. We cannot excuse ourselves from making the choices necessary for living in harmony with the light, saying our ongoing "yes" to what we have seen, and to its implications for our life.

As the pillar of fire that led Israel through the desert, we are called to move in harmony with this light's leading: "For all who are *led by the Spirit of God* are sons of God" (Rom 8:14). Light is not only for knowing, but for *living*, for walking. God's self-revelation is "a lamp to my feet and a light to my path" (Ps 119:105). The knowledge produced by the light is not an idle, theoretical knowing; it is what Scripture calls *Wisdom* — knowledge that informs the art of living.

All our choices need to be held up to the light, and adjusted or discarded accordingly. As everything of value needs care, so too this inner flame. It requires tending, protecting, and nourishing — not only through the time we spend in prayer, but also in the *daily choices* we make. The life we lived before, like Mother Teresa when she was still Sister Teresa, will not contain the expansive dimensions of this new grace, this "new wine." That is why, as Jesus insists, "new wine is for fresh skins" (Mk 2:22). God is inviting us to live an entirely new life, lost in his, transformed entirely into him. He longs for much more than just the scraps of our life, for sixty minutes each Sunday and little more. He longs to take all of our life — our work, our suffering, our hopes, even our sins.

The Mystery of Pain

Our culture runs from suffering, as we devise sophisticated ways to avoid or buffer every form of pain. This flight from suffering is the fruit of our false vision of a world that insists that no good can come from suffering. We associate this flight from pain with modernity and progress, while the health of our spirits and the degree of our happiness decline.

We have all discovered, however, that *we cannot* root out pain from human experience. And though we have proven this to ourselves repeatedly, still we try. The pain we chase through the front door comes in through the back, bringing more in its train in the guise of unhappiness, anxiety, and despair. Rather than asking ourselves how to eradicate pain, the real question must become, "*What are we going to do with our suffering?* [128] What do we do with the pain we cannot avoid?"

Will we waste it, and lose grace and peace and the chance for growth, the chance to meet a God who wraps himself in our pain? Will we miss the God who shares our suffering, who makes use of a suffering he did not create to draw us to himself?

Mother Teresa taught us to use the unavoidable pain of life as a *means to focus our longing for God*, a God who is the only answer, the only true source of peace and inner comfort.

As contrary to the ego's logic as it is, the unavoidable pain of life becomes a portal to the divine — one that cannot be rejected without consequences and even greater long-term loss. For, as pain is rejected, God is rejected. God requires that we are completely his. This necessitates the relinquishment of old habits, behaviors, and attitudes that may feel quite comfortable. A lack of willingness to permit detachment from all else save God impedes the full absorption of God's presence. Without the pain of letting go, we are literally left without God. Great suffering paves the way for a heartfelt surrender to God:

> With the embrace of pain comes surrender to the Divine. Suffering where it hurts most, in our sensitive and emotional nature, motivates us to turn to God unconditionally. Such interior suffering propels the individual to God in search of consolation and relief. Life's pains and hurts are quite providential, in that they cause the soul to run quickly to the Father who is the divine comforter. If this pain is ignored or deadened, as happens during intoxication, the opportunity for union with God may be missed. Suffering, especially when it hurts most, is the great enabler, motivating union with the God of all tenderness and compassion. [129]

The very suffering and poverty we flee, Mother Teresa (in the name of her God) *sought out*, joyfully, and transformed. And, it must be added, she herself was *transformed by it* — part of the grace of September 10 as meant to blossom, and did, precisely in the rude soil of unavoidable suffering. Suffering seems to be his preferred way of blessing us with the grace of rising beyond ego and its self-occupied demands:

> Thus, Jesus works in and through interior suffering. Spiritual and emotional pain need not be considered demonic. In fact, pain may superficially be regarded as the dark evil only to be later recognized as an angel of light. This light shines in our heart only when darkness has been endured.... We see him most clearly after times of great pain. As with all communication from God, so with pain, "You will do well to pay attention to this as to a lamp shining in a dark place, until the day dawns and the morning star rises in your hearts" (2 Pt 1:19).[130]

The fact that suffering is such a large and ubiquitous part of the human condition need *not discourage or frighten us.* This small, simple woman showed us this abundantly. And what is more, we *recognized* it. We responded. Even the faithless saw her light. Her works of charity proved to us that, thanks to the redeeming power of love, *we need not reject what we cannot fix.* We need not flee from suffering, failure, and human weakness, for it is above all there that we are called to love.

No matter what pain or privation we or those around us face, in it and through it we can choose to love. Mother Teresa saw everything — every slum, every wound, every sigh — as a chance to love, a place to love. Where there was no love, she put love. And with it came light, and God — since God is love, and his light is the light of love. That is why true light, divine light, *can shine in any darkness* and can fill it completely, just as the light filled Mother Teresa and all she touched. She reminded a self-absorbed generation that, even in midst of suffering, we can be both blessed and a blessing.

While most of us wake with thoughts of what we can get today, or where we might shop, or how we can advance our careers or personal goals, Mother Teresa's waking thought was always about *how she could give.* She invites us all to at least take baby steps to move in that direction; to examine *why and for what* we live. *Why* we live becomes how we live, and how we live determines all the rest: our happiness in this life and the next, and to a large extent, the happiness of those around us.

We are created "to love and be loved." Do we know this? Do we know yet that the peace and joy we seek cannot be found in material things, nor in freedom from pain and suffering? Have we begun to open to God's invitation to live for others, echoed in our sufferings and failures, his invitation to live for *the* Other? Or might we need the inner jostling of a Calcutta slum to awaken us? Or will the Lord make use of our common, everyday reversals to jar us loose from our idols that "cannot save" (Is 45:20)? As in the gospel story of Peter in the storm at sea (Mt 14:22-33), with the apostle reaching out to Jesus to be saved, God uses the storms of life to shake us loose from solutions that do not save, from idols that betray us in the battles.

No matter what our faith, the one God is honored, more than by pilgrimages to Mecca or Varanasi or the Vatican, by the most consequential pilgrimage of all: by our personal exodus from *getting to giving*, from dominance to service, from living for self to living for others. As the apostle John points out, our neighbor "whom we can see" stands in the place of the divine Other "whom we cannot see," and is our path to him (cf. 1 Jn 4:20-21). As the great Florentine mystic St. Mary Magdalen de' Pazzi affirmed: "Whoever touches his neighbor touches God." If God is love, there can be no other path to him save that which most respects and reflects his nature — the path of love, a love given even and especially in the midst of suffering.

Turning Towards the Light

Mother Teresa was shown early on, in her dialogues with Jesus in the months after her grace of the train, that the mystery of God's thirst contained not only a message of consolation, but a call to *conversion*. In this spirit, Jesus continued inviting her to an increasing generosity:

*You have become My spouse for my Love — you have come to India for
Me. The thirst you had for souls brought you so far. — Are you afraid
to take one more step for your Spouse — for Me — for souls? — Is
your generosity grown cold — am I a second to you?*[131]

In the original Greek, the gospel term for "conversion" is
metanoia, meaning literally "change of attitude," since our behavior
is but the outer reflection of our inner attitudes. And so conversion,
changing behavior, begins by *changing our basic attitudes* — toward
God, life, others, and self. When mind and heart are formed anew by
the light, our life, and our choices, begin to change apace, cast in the
likeness of the light we behold.

In its Latin root, "conversion" comes from *convertire*, meaning
literally to "turn." Conversion implies turning away from the darkness, and towards this new light, even in the night. This daily turning towards the light allowed Mother Teresa to continue drawing
from the grace of the train, day after week after year, empowering her
to overcome, and even turn to advantage, the trials she would face.
From that September day forward, she lived her life "turned"
towards the God she had met on the train, face-to-face with the
light and love of God. In the same way, our own transformation
begins by choosing and turning towards the light in daily life, especially in times of difficulty or failure.

Power of the Word

Just as the apostle Peter, discouraged after fishing all night without
a catch, was ready to put down the nets again on the strength of Jesus'
word, we, too, need the courage and confidence to begin again, to
take up the task once more, despite past failures: "Master, . . . at your
word I will let down the nets" (Lk 5:5). Since Jesus' cry of thirst in
the gospel is a divine word, imbued with the same creative power that
framed the universe — "By the word of God heavens existed long

In conversation (Raghu Rai/Magnum Photos)

ago" (2 Pt 3:5) — our efforts at conversion and transformation are not fueled so much by our own strength as by his, as we respond to his word of thirst and invitation that draws us. In the end, doubting that we can change becomes a denial of God's creative power, and our only insurmountable obstacle.

Jesus' thirst is not sentiment, but divine *power*. Once lifted up on the cross from which he would proclaim his thirst, Jesus promised that he would "*draw all men to myself*" (Jn 12:32). Our first encounter with the energy and dynamism contained in Jesus' cry of thirst will be precisely in its *power to draw*, the same power that drew Mother

Teresa beyond herself and the comforts of her classroom. This drawing, this power to bring us beyond the boundaries of self, becomes our one great hope.

Choices and Consequences

Our choices do make a difference, as Adam and Eve and every generation thereafter can testify. Our choices reflect our convictions regarding what is true, and what will bring us happiness — but the soundness of those convictions will already be borne out in our own experience, here and now.

Any choices rooted in the illusion that serving the ego can produce happiness end up betraying us; they do not satisfy. Ego-gratification can never fill our inner longing. The light or the darkness underlying our choices will be reflected in the peace and satisfaction they bring — or in its lack: "For no good tree bears bad fruit, nor again does a bad tree bear good fruit; for each tree is known by its own fruit" (Lk 6:43-44). Just as light cannot produce bitterness, so our dark ego choices cannot produce joy. Our inner states, be they peace of soul or restlessness, testify to the quality of our choices.

The thirst of the human soul, placed there by the Creator, obeys its own laws, and so it cannot be slaked by anything but God's own living waters. The prophet Isaiah speaks eloquently of the same lesson Mother Teresa sought to teach us:

"Every one who thirsts,
come to the waters. . . .
Why do you spend your money for that which is not bread,
and your labor for that which does not satisfy? . . .
Incline your ear, and come to me;
hear, that your soul may live. (Is 55:1, 2, 3)

This is Mother Teresa's other great lesson, a complementary truth just as important as the revelation of God's thirst. Every human person is *created to desire God*; man is by nature an incarnate thirst. As Mother Teresa affirms, "*Every human being has a longing for God.*"[132]

Centuries earlier, St. Augustine had eloquently expressed this same truth: "You have made us for yourself, O Lord, and our hearts are restless until they rest in thee." Nothing but God can fill us, or ever fulfill us. The whole world cannot fill the human heart — for the only thing greater than the human heart is the One who made it.

These are the endowments and implications of being created in the image of a God who *yearns for union*. It is supremely important to our ultimate happiness to remember that we, too, are made to thirst, to long for the divine, to focus the full power of our desire on God. Scripture reminds us of this again and again:

> O God, you are my God, I seek you,
>   my soul thirsts for you;
> my flesh faints for you,
>   as in a dry and weary land where no water is. (Ps 63:1)

> My soul thirsts for God,
>   for the living God.
> When shall I come and behold
>   the face of God? (Ps 42:2)

Conversion and Desire

But we will drink of God's living waters only *in proportion to our desire*. We cannot yearn for what we do not know, and we will never know what we have seen only in passing, but never pondered. Without turning towards the light, again and again, our desire for the blessings it reveals will weaken and scatter. Our inborn power of desire will settle for things less than God, our intended object, turning instead to substitutes that "do not satisfy," as Isaiah warned.

Our transformation and divinization depends on ardently desiring it — depends on the strength of *our* longing, not just God's. Our transformation cannot begin in earnest until we are captivated, as was Mother Teresa, by the sheer beauty of God's "light and love" — until we are captivated by the God who is already captivated by us; until we thirst for the One who thirsts for us.

The Role of Desire

We are essentially *beings of desire*, created to thirst for what lies beyond us, whether we recognize our inner inquietude as a thirst for God or mistakenly scatter and squander our power of desire for created things. When made the object of our desires, created things unwittingly become our masters. Whatever we desire most becomes "Lord" of our life — master of our waking moments, our thoughts, choices, and energies. Whenever we set the sights of our soul outside of God, lower than God, we sow seeds of disappointment and malaise within.

What is this strange power of desire that defines our humanity? From where do our deepest unnamed desires come, and where do they lead? God's desire for us has left its spark in our own soul:

> When we experience the desire for "I know not what," it is God's Holy Spirit drawing us.... This deepest desire of our hearts is for God.[133]

Mother Teresa understood that this thirst for God is the foundation of our human happiness and dignity. When this desire for the divine is not recognized or heeded, its neglect becomes our deepest poverty, played out in a parade of false thirsts and deep disappointments of every kind.

Her recognition of this deeper poverty moved Mother Teresa to want to give the poor more than just a plate of rice. She sought to awaken and answer their inborn longing for God, to satisfy their thirst for a fulfillment that the vicissitudes of life cannot take away, awaiting us in the kingdom, "where neither moth nor rust consumes and where thieves do not break in and steal" (Mt 6:20).

Mother Teresa discovered this same deeper poverty in the developed world, and wished to bring this same ultimate fulfillment to those in the West. The inner hunger present in the developed nations is often overlooked and forgotten, free of the physical hunger that acts painfully and powerfully as its metaphor and reminder. In the developed world, the only echo of deeper desire is a persistent inner restlessness, a voice that, thankfully, no amount of material goods can quiet. Even as we acquire the objects of our desire, including the most legitimate, their inability to fill our deepest yearning subtly points us towards God:

> Most likely you first discover a person, you visit a place, you savor something of life . . . and it may be very, very good . . . but it won't be enough to satisfy this deepest longing in your soul. Saint John of the Cross calls this "questioning the creatures." You ask this experience, you ask this person, "Are you the one?" But they say to you, "No. What you are looking for is not here, but has passed by, scattering beauty as he went." What attracts us in creatures is the reflection of God's beauty. The creatures are honest: they tell us plainly (because they do not completely satisfy our desire) that they are not enough to fill that hole in our hearts.
>
> God is using this potent, sometimes gnawing gift of desire — which springs from God's own heart — to lead us, as with bread crumbs, to a door which we might not have otherwise chosen or even recognized in this life. Inside that door is home.[134]

"Stir into Flame"

Once we begin actively desiring the goodness Mother Teresa beheld, especially in deep prayer, the results can be profound. A peace that "passes all understanding" (Phil 4:7) begins to fill our waking hours, as we experience the stirrings of a new joy, the fruit of God's presence within. The divine presence begins to envelop even the mundane in our life, and to fill our hearts with more love than we can contain.

The secret of Mother Teresa's energy in outreach to the poor was precisely the uncontainable love with which God had filled her soul, overflowing onto those around her.

But how do we transform our desires? It is enough to begin stirring up and exercising whatever degree of desire for God we already have. Even if seemingly dormant, it is there within us, part of us since the day of our birth. Our unsatisfying ego-desires are proof and echo of our deepest desire — as a constant reminder that we are not whole in ourselves. As such, they can actually help to connect us, at a deeper level, to our forgotten desire for God.

While our conscience may parade before us our flaws and past failures, these do not define our true nature. Our sins and flaws are not the truest thing about us. Our failings hamper, but do not define us. The *truest* thing, that which does define us and which will last forever, is our inborn desire for God. Our God-given and God-directed longing runs deeper than our selfishness, deeper than our failings, deeper than our weaknesses, deeper than everything else in us. All these are passing; they were never part of God's original plan for us; they will not be there in the kingdom, nor need they govern us now.

What do we do with our weaknesses, mistakes, and wandering desires? How do we turn these toward God? Our rogue desires produce the accumulated debris of our inner lives, and they clog and clutter the inner temple, mocking our good resolutions and attempts to change. Try as we might, we will not rid ourselves, by ourselves, of our ego-driven longing.

But there in the depths of our soul, forgotten beneath the distractions on the surface, is a *divine spark*. There the embers of our thirst for God await, even if at a conscious level the divine fire seems to have gone out, smothered by surrogates. Thankfully, however, we need not spend our lives trying to remove the ruins of our broken idols. All we need is to reach down through the surface distractions and the levels of ego, to where those embers still lie, and stir them into flame once again. Simply by conscious contact with the divine desire placed within us long ago, our thirst for God will again begin to "spring . . . up to eternal life" (Jn 4:14).

This is not something difficult, and takes but an instant. In fact, it can be tried even while reading these lines. Stop for a moment to be aware of your interior; then reach into your depths and simply *be in touch with your desire for God*. It is always there, waiting to be awakened. Despite desiring a thousand things outside of God, beneath our louder and more flashy ego-desires, we do desire him, deeply. And that is enough to begin, from precisely where we are. Contrary to the tempter's telling us that we no longer know how to pray, *desiring God is already prayer*, a prayer always in reach. The more we are consciously in touch with that desire, the more it will expand in our consciousness, and in power. As those God-given embers catch fire, this one deepest desire will gradually displace our false thirsts and desires. And there's more: by its own dynamism, our newly discovered flame of desire for God will begin consuming everything else, including those areas we have long wanted to change in ourselves.

By repeating this simple exercise, by reaching down to reignite the inkling of desire within, our renewed desire for the living God will begin to cast the soul in its original beauty.

Principles of Transformation

But even with this newly awakened desire growing within, still, the pull of ego will require a constantly renewed turning towards the light — lest we fall again into forgetfulness of God, and the fire of desire once more burn out. Here again we come to the necessity of biblical wisdom: the art of choosing the light.

Summing up what we have seen, there are two governing principles that guided Mother Teresa's choices, applicable in our lives as well. She invites us to be convinced that:

- **All self-seeking is empty — and ultimately futile.** Recognize that whenever we serve our ego-demands, we are left emptier still. The Holy Spirit's purpose is to gather our scattered desires *and re-focus them on God.* Desire for God integrates us, as our life becomes focused on the only One who can fill us.

- **Only God can satisfy us.** At some level, though (as a consequence of our wrong choices since the Garden), there is a part of us still not fully convinced of this. The tempter's doubts echo and linger, and unsettle the soul. Since we have lost the gift of direct vision of God, we are left to make critical choices without seeing or feeling. And choose we must — knowing, however, that our choices and their consequences bear out Mother Teresa's lesson: that God alone satiates us fully. But as long as we fear that the ocean cannot fill our cup, we will still go about begging drops of muddied water from the created things around us, while we go from hope to disappointment in an unending cycle.

Steps to Conversion

Even after reawakening our God-given desire, we still need to be aware of the signs of our old way of being, what Scripture calls "the old man" (Eph 4:22), and to be ready to root them out when they come into awareness, as young weeds in a newly sown garden. And so:

- **We seek to discover the seeds and patterns of self-seeking in our past.** There are tendencies of self-promotion present in us since childhood, never recognized or confronted. These patterns are carried into adult life, as our false thirsts crystallize and dictate choices and behavior.

- **We unmask present manifestations of self-seeking, redirecting and subsuming them into our desire for God.**

Here we need blunt honesty with ourselves. We cannot overcome our ways of self-seeking until we begin *naming* them — as Adam gave names to the wild beasts. From there begins the task of taming and even transforming them into reminders of our desire for the Almighty.

- **We resolve to forgive all past injuries fully, and all present injuries promptly.** If a past offense still bothers us, it is a sign that we have yet to release or forgive it fully. Every time the memory returns, we can choose to see it in the light of God's power to turn all into blessing — we can come to peace with it, and move on. We need to reject any spirit of revenge and lingering ill-will, and come back into the light.

- **We are ready to accept whatever means God will use to change us.** We choose to believe, as did Mother Teresa, that nothing happens within us or outside of us that cannot be woven into God's loving providence, if we but hand it over to him, convinced that "in everything God works for good with those who love him" (Rom 8:28).

Mother Teresa's teaching on man's thirst for God casts light on the inner inquietude and stirrings we have all experienced. The presence of this God-instilled desire means that we need not battle alone, seeking transformation by our own efforts. This God-given and God-directed desire is itself *the power and the promise* behind the secret fire Mother Teresa invites us to share:

> *My children, once you have experienced the thirst, the love of Jesus for you, you will never need, you will never thirst for these things which can only lead you away from Jesus the true and living Fountain. Only the thirst of Jesus, feeling it, hearing it, answering it with all your heart will keep your love ... alive.*[135]

"God . . . thirsts for us to thirst for Him."[136]

— Mother Teresa

EIGHTEEN

Joining the Thirst of God and Man

From the Fall onwards, God's longing for man and man's wayward thirst for God had gone unanswered and un-satiated. For the first time since the tree of Eden, the thirst of God and man were united at the tree of Calvary, in the person of Jesus. The mystery and message revealed on Calvary became Mother Teresa's life mission, proclaiming and reuniting the divine-human thirst. The primary poverty she addressed was spiritual, that of a humanity hopelessly and perpetually poor apart from God — but a humanity that could now be satiated and immeasurably enriched, simply by opening our emptiness to the Creator, whose infinite riches now lay open before us at the cross.

But is there something missing as we open to this reality? Jesus' words, "I thirst," remain ever present, ever active — powerful enough to transform hearts and change lives. Why, then, have we not experienced the same effects as Mother Teresa? Why have our lives not changed, if we are focusing on the same light and love as she? Surely there is no lack of power in the divine longing. Might there be something lacking in us, then, that prevents a deeper level of encounter, the kind of encounter to which she invites us? What is it in us, what was it in her, that opens the soul more fully to this grace?

Speaking as Son of God, Jesus on the cross revealed God's thirst for man; but because he was speaking at the same time as "Son of Man," his words also reveal our human thirst for God. In the same utterance from the cross, Jesus' cry of thirst reveals the true depths of both God *and* man.

Miracles of Resurrection

Even as God thirsts for us, he longs for us to thirst for him in return. This is why he so wants us to know him, in order that we might desire him as he desires us (recall Jesus' poignant complaint to Mother Teresa, "*They don't know Me — so they don't want Me*"). By "wanting" God, we at last reconnect our desire with his, in a dynamic of mutual drawing — as two magnets irresistibly drawn one to the other. This is why God wants us to want him, why he thirsts for us to thirst for him — that we might be drawn together. Two of the great Fathers of the Church, St. Augustine in the West and St. Gregory Nazianzen in the East, proclaimed this same mystery in similar words, stating unequivocally that "*God thirsts to be thirsted for.*" [137]

All prayer is the coming together of God's desire and ours. As Pope Benedict XVI writes, prayer is the "encounter of God's thirst with our thirst." [138] And, as Mother Teresa has shown through the thousands of lives touched by her message, when the thirst of God and man are reunited, there are miracles of transformation. As Jesus assured the dying thief, who in those last moments turned his desire heavenward: "Today you will be with me in Paradise" (Lk 23:43). Each time we turn to him with our nothingness, with our sin and selfish desires and the havoc they have wrought, everything is transformed; our inner torment is changed into the threshold of "new heavens" (2 Pt 3:13).

Bringing God's longing and ours into contact is comparable to reconnecting separated power lines — once they touch, there is an immediate outpouring of energy. The key to our personal transformation becomes as simple as uniting these two thirsts in our own heart. Since God already thirsts for us, the missing element needed to complete our union is *our own conscious thirst for God*. We see this dynamic borne out in Mother Teresa — one of her most striking characteristics, together with her heroic faith and charity, was her constant, intense longing for God:

> *Night after night . . . sleep would disappear — and only to spend those hours in longing for His coming. This began in Asansol*[139] *in February — and . . . I have noticed it is from 11 to 1, the same longing breaks into the sleep.*[140]

> *Such deep longing for God . . .*[141]

> *When alone in the streets — I talk to You for hours — of my longing for You.*[142]

> *I long for God. I long to love Him with every drop of life in me.*[143]

These early expressions of her soul's longing do not wane, they will not diminish in frequency or intensity, even when night begins to fall within her soul. This divine-human desire was the true fire that would burn and consume her, even in the night. Her deep yearning, her thirsting for the God who longed for her, would continue unchanged until the last.

I witnessed many signs and expressions of her deep longing, although one in particular stands out in memory. I had returned to Calcutta, in 1996, to be with her as she began the downward spiral into her final illness. No one expected that it would still be a year before her passing, as she was already being shuttled back and forth to local hospitals in serious condition. Very early one morning, with tubes that prevented her from speaking and IV's attached to both arms, she motioned for a piece of paper from Sister Gertrude, who was attending her. Without a word, Mother Teresa struggled to take a pen and began to scrawl in a weak hand (so unlike her usually strong script) whose lines still reflect her pain and effort. In her longing to have someone bring her Holy Communion from the Mother House chapel, she simply scrawled the phone number, and these telling words: "*I want Jesus.*"

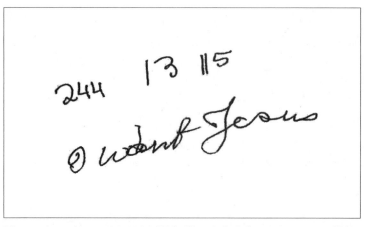

Note written August 26, 1996, Birla Hospital, Calcutta (courtesy of Missionaries of Charity)

For us as well, this dynamic of desire is the *one doorway* to deepening and maintaining our encounter with the divine thirst. This involves a daily renewing of our own thirst for God, while believing in and opening to his thirst for us, convinced that:

Right [now], today, and everyday [Jesus] is thirsting for my love. He is longing for me in my soul.[144]

Jesus makes our own explicit longing a condition for being drawn into encounter: "If any one *thirst*, let him come to me and drink" (Jn 7:37). To paraphrase the classic expression of St. John of the Cross, "Love is repaid by love," we can similarly affirm with Mother Teresa that "Thirst is repaid by thirst," longing is repaid by longing. In fact, *our thirst for God satiates his thirst for us.*

God's thirst can only be repaid by ours. Is this not what any lover desires from the beloved, to be wanted in return? Our desire for God fills us with the very God for whom we long. In the end, since God already thirsts for man, the completion of this circle depends entirely on us — on our freely chosen longing for God (not just in sentiment, but in faith and in choices), satiating both his desire and ours.

The Samaritan Woman

From the beginning, Mother Teresa seems to have understood the importance not only of our encounter with the thirst of Jesus, but of answering his thirst with our own. One of Mother Teresa's original pupils in St. Mary's School tells the story of Mother Teresa's return to Calcutta after her retreat in Darjeeling, and after her still unknown grace of September 10.

Even without openly sharing her discovery of the thirst of Jesus, Mother Teresa found a way of indirectly touching on this mystery, and of sharing its lessons with her class. As soon as she returned to Calcutta, she led her students in a meditation on the gospel story of the *Samaritan woman* (Jn 4:1-42). From the obvious parallels between this gospel and Mother Teresa's own experience, the reason for proposing this particular meditation to her pupils seems more than evident. It should be enough to recall that, two thousand years earlier, the Samaritan woman had lived her own life-changing encounter with the thirst of Jesus.

If Mother Teresa recognized a connection between this gospel and her grace of the train, and used it to communicate the mystery she had discovered, we can do no better than to follow her lead. Like her first pupils, we, too, can profit from opening this gospel and seeing it afresh, seeking the same light that Mother Teresa imparted to her pupils almost as her farewell legacy, before leaving them to launch her work in the slums.

The impact of this gospel in her life is borne out in the many references she makes to it in talks to her Sisters over the years. On one occasion, she took a calendar page depicting the Samaritan woman standing before Jesus, and inscribed at the bottom, *"Give me to drink."* Mother Teresa was so struck by the commentary on this gospel by her patron saint, Thérèse of Lisieux, that she often quoted her:

> This same God is not afraid to beg a bit of water from the Samaritan. He thirsted ... but in saying "Give Me to drink," it was the love of His poor creature that the Creator of the universe was asking. He thirsted for love.[145]

We know the initial shame of the Samaritan woman, before meeting the thirst of Jesus, and the saint she became afterwards. The following meditation, based on St. John's gospel, allows us to follow the entire process of personal conversion and transformation step-by-step — as lived by the woman in the gospel, by Mother Teresa millennia later, and as offered to us today.

Meditation on the Samaritan Woman

"If you but knew the gift of God!" (Jn 4:10). The wonder of prayer is revealed beside the well where we come seeking water: there, Christ comes to meet every human being. It is he who first seeks us and asks us for a drink. Jesus thirsts; his asking arises from the depths of God's desire for us.... God thirsts that we may thirst for him.[146]

— Catechism of the Catholic Church

STEP 1

"So he came to a city of Samaria, called Sychar.... Jacob's well was there, and so Jesus, wearied as he was with his journey, sat down beside the well. It was about the sixth hour" (Jn 4:5-6).

As Mother Teresa reminds us, we were created "to love and be loved," created for the lasting love that every human being longs for. This longing is represented in Scripture as *thirst* (see Appendix One). In this particular episode from John's gospel, the Samaritan woman represents us all. In keeping with biblical thirst imagery, Sychar's village well is used as the centerpiece and backdrop, as the symbol of the quenching of our thirst, and the fulfillment of our search.

Note that this gospel scene takes place in Israel's neighboring country of *Samaria* — a land whose people lived cut off from Israel.

The prophets often pointed to Samaria as a symbol of humanity's infidelity (e.g., "Samaria and her images [idols]"),[147] and a symbol of our distance from God. Yet even before the Samaritan woman begins her search for the God she has lost, even in the midst of her ego-driven pursuits, *Jesus is already there*, awaiting her.

He comes, the Good Shepherd, not only following after those who stray, but always ahead of them. The amazing thing is that he awaits us at the very place and in the very act of our wandering, and without a word of condemnation — only invitation. He comes not to denounce, but to lift up and transform, and he begins the process of our restoration by first *drawing us into dialogue*. Despite our repeated infidelities, he remains unwavering in his search for us, no matter how long the process may take (in this scene, Jesus comes to the well tired from the journey).

STEP 2

"There came a woman of Samaria to draw water. Jesus said to her, 'Give me a drink.' For his disciples had gone away into the city to buy food. The Samaritan woman said to him, 'How is it that you, a Jew, ask a drink of me, a woman of Samaria?' For Jews have no dealings with Samaritans" (Jn 4:7-9).

The Samaritan woman symbolizes our human poverty at its maximum. As a Samaritan, a reprobate and a heretic cut off from the chosen people, she had lost all religious dignity; as a woman, she enjoyed precious little civil dignity; and as a public sinner, she had lost her dignity as a person. She represents mankind's state of loss, having abdicated our God-given gifts.

She comes to *"draw water"* — that is, she comes seeking to satisfy her unfulfilled longing — *"at the sixth hour,"* at high noon, when thirst is greatest. At that moment, and at the place that represents her misdirected search, Jesus is there, waiting.

"Give me a drink," Jesus asks. Rather than railing against the woman's heretical state or her public sin, as the prophets of old, Jesus is deeply moved by her poverty and her ignorance of the true God,

and takes the initiative to remedy her condition. He cannot resist unveiling to her, well ahead of the "hour" of its public proclamation on Calvary, the mystery of his divine yearning — fulfilling his promise that "the last shall be first" to receive the blessings of the kingdom.

The disciples are not there when Jesus speaks to her, since this encounter can only occur *alone*, at the well of our heart.

"How is it that you, a Jew, ask a drink of me, a woman of Samaria?" She is unwittingly giving voice to our own hesitations and doubts before God's invitation. Can he really mean me? Mother Teresa, perhaps, but me? *You are a Jew and I am a Samaritan.* You are the Son of God, and I am no one, a sinner. *How can you ask of me to drink?* How can *I* ever satiate you? Among those Jesus met on his travels, no one could have been more outwardly "unworthy" than this woman of Samaria, outcast and five-time adulteress, and yet here he is revealing to her the most intimate secrets of God's heart — so yes, I *can* believe that he wishes to reveal the same to me. He comes in search of us, precisely where we sin and fail; not condemning, only promising a better, living water; only asking *"Give me a drink"* of the love we have.

STEP 3

"Jesus answered her, 'If you knew the gift of God, and who it is that is saying to you, "Give me a drink," you would have asked him and he would have given you living water' " (Jn 4:10).

Giving him a drink is not as much our gift to God, as his to us: *"If you knew the gift of God."* His thirst for us is indeed a gift, for it is only the grace of encounter with his longing that can satiate to the full our need to be loved, and to love in return. *". . . And who it is that is saying to you, 'Give me a drink.' "* He *who asks for a drink* is in fact the One who satiates, who fills our emptiness and slakes the deepest yearning of the human soul.

Had she understood that the one who asks is in fact the Giver, she *"would have asked him"* first. With these words, Jesus is seeking to awaken her longing for the One she has forgotten. This is where the entire conversation has been leading; this is Jesus' purpose in revealing his thirst to her, and to us: to awaken our own yearning for him.

Had we understood *"the gift of God,"* and who it is, present beside us even in our wandering, we would be the ones to ask. Infallibly, the experience of God's thirst for us *awakens and revives our own thirst for him.*

STEP 4

" 'Sir, you have nothing to draw with, and the well is deep.... Are you greater than our father Jacob, who gave us the well?' " (Jn 4:11, 12).

The Samaritan woman again gives voice to our doubts. She has long been searching for love and fulfillment, and though her present state is far from satisfactory, she is wary of Jesus' promises without some reassurance that he can deliver.

"The well is deep." The void in my heart is boundless. Are you able to fill it? Can a God I cannot see satisfy me entirely?

And what is more, *"You have nothing to draw with."* I don't understand how you can accomplish this. You offer none of the ways of "drawing water" — of finding love and meaning in life — that I have relied on until now. How do you propose to do it?

"Are you greater than our father Jacob, who gave us the well?" Can you give me more and greater love than I have found until now; more than what I have obtained in my own way, drawing for myself?

STEP 5

" 'Every one who drinks of this water will thirst again, but whoever drinks of the water that I shall give him will never thirst; the water that I shall give him will become in him a spring of water welling up to eternal life' " (Jn 4:13-14).

"Everyone who drinks of this water will thirst again." Jesus is declaring that everyone who relies on human means to quench their inner thirst will yet be thirsty, not only "again," but always; for nothing created can satisfy a thirst made by and meant for the Creator.

But *"whoever drinks of the water that I shall give him will never thirst."* Whoever seeks that love in God will never lack, will never go empty, and will never thirst in vain. In fact, the more we stir up our God-directed thirst, the *more* we are filled.

"The water that I shall give him will become in him a spring of water welling up to eternal life." God does not need exterior means to communicate his love. He does not depend on other persons or external events to convey it. His love, through the gift of his indwelling Spirit, will become *a living source within us*; always there, always growing, overflowing unto eternal life:

> *On the last day of the feast, the great day, Jesus stood up and proclaimed, "If any one thirst, let him come to me and drink. He who believes in me, as the Scripture has said, 'Out of his heart shall flow rivers of living water.'" Now this he said about the Spirit, which those who believed in him were to receive.* (Jn 7:37-39)

> *Then he showed me the river of the water of life, bright as crystal, flowing from the throne of God and of the Lamb.... "Come." And let him who is thirsty come, let him who desires take the water of life without price.* (Rev 22:1, 17)

STEP 6

"Sir, give me this water, that I may not thirst, nor come here to draw" (Jn 4:15).

"Give me this water. ..." Jesus' tactic is beginning to work. For the first time, the Samaritan expresses her desire for what Jesus has promised. This represents a turning point, not only in her conversion, but in ours. Even though she has discovered the divine thirst at the beginning of the scene, nothing in her will change until she allows God's thirst to awaken *her own longing for him* — for a better, living water, for the better love he offers. Once the thirst of God has touched and awakened the thirst of man, miracles of transformation and new life begin.

"That I may not thirst." This is already a step forward in the working of grace. She is not only turning her thirst towards God, but beginning to consider him superior to all that she had tried before,

and to all that had left her thirsting still — and so she begins to focus on this *one* unifying desire. She hopes, as we do, to thirst no more in vain, to be finally free of the emptiness of the past. Conversion is this gradual passage from thirsting for what is not God, to thirsting for other things *along with* God, to finally having but one abiding and overarching thirst, satisfied in God alone. "For God alone my soul waits in silence; from him comes my salvation" (Ps 62:1).

"*. . . Nor come here to draw.*" She has begun to realize another great truth. All our other thirsts not only fail to satisfy, but they also fatigue the soul. To thirst for God, on the other hand, *gives energy*, filling the soul with vitality and new life.

STEP 7

"*Jesus said to her, 'Go, call your husband, and come here.' The woman answered him, 'I have no husband.' Jesus said to her, 'You are right in saying, "I have no husband"; for you have had five husbands, and he whom you now have is not your husband. . . .' The woman said to him, 'Sir, I perceive that you are a prophet. Our fathers worshiped on this mountain. . . .'*" (Jn 4: 16-18, 19-20)

Jesus stresses the *singleness of desire* he seeks from us, and the covenant bond this creates, by casting our relationship with God in spousal terms, as the prophets before him. This is the depth of union God seeks to establish with each human soul.

"*Go, call your husband.*" Jesus is not condemning her; instead, he is inviting her to examine and name her false thirsts. At first she only acknowledges her general state ("*I have no husband*"), but Jesus wants her to uncover the specific nature of her false thirsts, naming them one by one ("*You have had five*"). Until they are each seen and admitted for what they are, as surrogate desires, they remain what they are. Until we go beyond admitting our general state of self-centered desiring, and actually begin to name our ego-desires, we make little progress.

"*. . . And he whom you now have is not your husband.*" The things we are presently longing for outside of God are not merely "mistakes," not just moral or legal infractions, they are *infidelities in love* to the One who has made himself Bridegroom of the human soul:

> *For as a young man marries a virgin,*
> *so shall your sons marry you,*
> *and as the bridegroom rejoices over the bride,*
> *so shall your God rejoice over you. (Is 62:5)*

> *"Can the wedding guests mourn as long as the bridegroom is with them?"* (Mt 9:15)

> *The Spirit and the Bride say, "Come."* . . . *Come, Lord Jesus!* (Rev 22:17, 20)

By pining after our human attachments and selfish ambitions, we *espouse* them — "Where your treasure is, there will your heart be also" (Mt 6:21). And of each of these, Jesus reminds us: *"This is not your spouse."* Whichever false thirst we have embraced, it is not our rightful spouse. The Lord himself will prompt us in this, as he did for the Samaritan. We need to avoid distracting ourselves from this examination with other, merely speculative (even if spiritual) considerations that fail to cut across the fabric of our life and our choices: *"Our fathers worshiped on this mountain; and you say that in Jerusalem is the place where men ought to worship"* (Jn 4:20).

STEP 8

"The woman said to him, 'I know that Messiah is coming (he who is called Christ); when he comes, he will show us all things.' Jesus said to her, 'I who speak to you am he' " (Jn 4:25-26).

She knows the Messiah is coming, the one who will fulfill the ancient promises. She is deeply moved by what Jesus has told her, but she is still looking beyond, elsewhere in the future for her fulfillment, when the answer to her quest is right in front of her, in the present moment of a present Jesus.

She knows that the Messiah will *explain everything*, that he will reveal all there is to know about God. "*I who speak to you am he.*" The God of the now, the God who *thirsts for us in the present moment*, is already our fulfillment. We need not look beyond the horizon, for he is *speaking to us now*. There is no need to wait, to wait for a different situation or for better conditions, to hope for some future time when we will be better able to feel God's presence. God's time, and our time to encounter him, is now.

The revelation of Jesus' thirst fulfills our desire both for love and for knowledge. "*He will show us all things.*" His thirst for us sheds light on who he is, on who we are in our full dignity, and on our relationship to him.

STEP 9

"So the woman left her water jar, and went away into the city, and said to the people, 'Come, see . . .' "(Jn 4:28-29).

"*So the woman left her water jar. . . .*" Grace has triumphed. She no longer has need of her old means of drawing water, symbolized by the jar she carried each day. She trusts Jesus now and surrenders all that made up her old life, while she goes to joyfully share his invitation with others — "*The woman . . . went away into the city.*"

"*Come, see. . . .*" Her invitation, like Mother Teresa's, is not to just hear the good news, but to *experience it for ourselves*. In turn, as we share this message, we will invite others to our same experience, to "*Come, see*" what has touched us so profoundly, as we invite them to their own encounter.

STEP 10

"Many Samaritans from that city believed in him because of the woman's testimony. . . . So when the Samaritans came to him, they asked him to stay with them; and he stayed there. . . . They said to the woman, 'It is no longer because of your words that we believe, for we have heard for ourselves. . . .' "
(Jn 4:39, 40, 42).

Encounter leads to mission, to sharing what we have received; and mission leads back to encounter, in an expanding cycle of grace. We, too, are called and equipped to pass on this light of God's love — just as the Samaritan's example became an invitation for Mother Teresa, and as Mother Teresa has become an example for us.

———

What has this gospel story shown us? We have seen that by revealing his thirst for us, Jesus hopes to awaken our own thirst for him, for God. And once we begin to express our longing for him, once we bring these two thirsts into contact and communion, the process of true conversion and transformation begins.

How do we thirst for God? Mother Teresa would tell us that it is not a feeling, but a desire, a decision, a *direction of the will* — and, therefore, it is always possible, whether we find ourselves in consolation or aridity. Our being is already an incarnate thirst for God, so our inborn thirst needs only to be redirected to him. Our inherent poverty, our human weakness itself is an expression of that thirst, a crying out for what we lack. The power of desire is already at work within us. It needs only be purified, unified, and focused again on God.

Mother Teresa spent her life raising up Jesus' words, "*I thirst*" — not only on the wall of her chapels, but in her every utterance and action. All around the world, she has brought us, and especially the neediest among us, to hear these words, and to be healed and filled. The words "*I thirst*," which already describe the heart of Jesus, are to describe our heart and inmost being as well. Only when God's thirst is answered by our own in return will the words Mother Teresa placed on the chapel wall be complete. As we have seen at the well of Sychar, and seen once again two thousand years later on the train to Darjeeling, the wedding of these two thirsts produces transformation and resurrection, even here below.

"If any one thirst, let him come to me and drink."

"'You are precious to Me, I love you.' These are not human words, Sisters. This is how God speaks [to us in the Scriptures]: 'You are precious to me.'" [148]

— Mother Teresa

Light Bearer to Our Calcutta

Living as God's Beloved

As we come to the end of our journey with Mother Teresa, a journey that brings us to the threshold of our own divine encounter, let us stand back for a moment to see in overview this saint who has blessed our world, and our own Calcutta, with new light. Now that we have learned her secret, and have found answers to the questions posed at the beginning of this book, we can attempt to sum up what she means for our world.

Mother Teresa was sent among us to echo Jesus' words "I thirst" to the poor and the downtrodden, and to pierce our darkness with God's all-powerful "light and love." She did this, in God's name and in his power, by mediating to all who approached her the life-changing experience of *knowing oneself loved*, of experiencing oneself as cherished by the Almighty:

> *"Even if a mother forgets her child, I will not forget you. I have carved you in the palm of my hand. You are precious to me! I love you."* [149]

The most important thing for us to remember is that Christ called each of us by name and that He said, "You are precious to Me, I love you." If you remember that, it makes all the difference.[150]

Foundational Experience

Beyond the human comfort this brings, the experience of being loved and cherished by God is important at a yet deeper, spiritual level. Knowing that we are freely and immensely loved becomes *the* foundational Christian experience. If this is true for us, it is because it was first true for Jesus — of whom the Father proclaimed at the Jordan, *"You are my beloved Son"* (Mk 1:11). This cherishing love, which Mother Teresa spoke of and modeled, is the ground on which our entire relationship with God is built.

The gospels hint at this *awareness of being beloved* as the daily bread that sustained Jesus throughout his life, and particularly during his passion. This was his baseline, the fabric of all his days, and of every night spent in the divine embrace, alone in the hills of Galilee. These are the deep gospel roots that underlie Mother Teresa's own awareness of being loved, an awareness she held to, "solid in her faith" (cf. 1 Pt 5:9), throughout her dark night.

Mission and Message

Mother Teresa's whole desire was to bring the poor, forgotten by society, and seemingly forgotten by God, to see themselves as God sees them — *as beloved.* Having someone mediate for us the experience of being divinely beloved, as Mother Teresa did for so many, prepares the soul for believing in and opening to God's thirst for us.

In the smallest, most ordinary ways, Mother Teresa showed us the same belovedness she had known so extraordinarily on the train. She did this with a smile, a look, a gentle hand on the brow of a dying man, a word of comfort — each gesture eloquently echoing the divine words, "You are my beloved" (Mk 1:11).

In the face of our poverty and weakness, Mother Teresa realized that our greatest suffering is not our need or weakness itself, but the feeling of uselessness, of being worthless, unappreciated, and unloved. This is the ego's anti-gospel, the voice in our culture that insists that *only the beautiful are lovable*. Add to this the murmurs of our conscience with its burden of guilt, and the tempter has an easy time convincing us that we are lost to God's love.

Sending her Sisters out (Raghu Rai/Magnum Photos)

Enter Mother Teresa, who would spend her entire life *demonstrating the opposite* — that God's love bestows beauty on all things, and inviting even the developed world to encounter the same divine thirst that her love for the poor proclaimed. She emptied herself of ego, so all that remained of her was God's message. She knew that the remedy to our sense of unlovableness was in discovering, just as she had, that we are cherished — not just accepted as we are, but beloved. Her great desire was to help God's words through Isaiah, which she so frequently repeated, reverberate in every heart:

You are precious to me! I love you. Even if a mother forgets her child, I will not forget you. I have carved you on the palm of my hands. (cf. Is 49:15-16)

Mother Teresa not only told us; she *showed* us that we are loved. She has made it easy for us to approach the mystery of God's thirst for us, and to share her inner fire; and she has invited us to do the same for one another.

Living for Love

It is not enough, however, simply to know that we are loved, and to receive God's love in prayer, nor simply to turn our desire from

Hospital patient (Chris Steele-Perkins/Magnum Photos)

worldly appetites and begin to thirst for God. This is essential, and the first step — but only the first step. We are called to return and spread abroad the love we have received — to love God with more and more of our being, in good times and bad. All that takes place in our life, in God's plan, is for the sake of love, a school of love. In the words of William Blake, "And we are put on earth a little space, / That we may learn to bear the beams of love." And as St. John of the Cross reminds us (as does Jesus, in the parable of the lambs and the goats), "In the evening of our life, we will be judged on love."

The cycle of grace Mother Teresa invites us to is not complete until our desire for the God of love becomes love for the God we desire — until we *love the Lord our God with all our heart, and with all our soul, and with all our strength* (cf. Dt 6:5).

This is the final goal of our conversion and our transformation, this alone the full flowering of our longing for God. In this lies our highest dignity — in loving as God loves, for "love is of God, and he who loves is born of God . . ." (1 Jn 4:7). Remember that God not only thirsts to love us, but that he thirsts as well to *be loved by us* — as Mother Teresa reminds us, God's desire is "to love *and to be loved.*"

Loving the God who is love unifies and elevates all the operations of the soul, and every aspect of our lives. As St. John of the Cross explains in his *Spiritual Canticle*:

All my occupation now is the practice of the love of God, all the powers of soul and body, memory, understanding, and will, interior and exterior senses, the desires of spirit and of sense, all work in and by love. All I do is done in love; all I suffer, I suffer in the sweetness of love.[151]

Love is not only the end and goal of our process of transformation; it is our path and door of access. Love *is itself* the process — for the path to the God of love is only love. Love is an enterprise always at hand, always but a choice away. As Mother Teresa assures us, love's

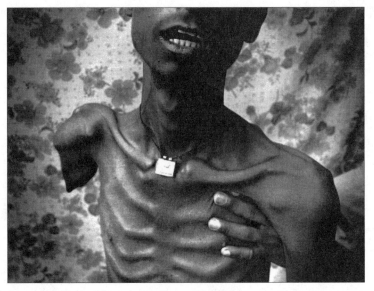

Starving train-accident victim (Larry Towell/Magnum Photos)

fruit is always in season, always awaiting and inviting us — calling out from the depths of our souls where his glory dwells, and from the wounds and needs of our neighbor, where his crucified thirst for love is most touching and urgent:

> *Love is a fruit in season at all times and within the reach of every hand. Anyone may gather it and no limit is set.*[152]

What this means is that there is no need to wait, no need to better ourselves before making some return of the immense love we have received — and continue receiving in prayer. Nothing stands in the way of our experiencing the full *"joy of loving,"*[153] and completing the circle of divine love received and given. As an anonymous author unknowingly echoed Mother Teresa's message, giving voice to the Almighty's thirst for our love no matter our condition:

Love Me as you are. I know your misery, the inner struggle of your heart and the tribulations of your soul, the weakness and infirmities of your body. I know your sins, your failings; and I tell you just the same, give Me your heart. Love Me AS YOU ARE.

If you wait to become an angel to deliver yourself to Love, you will never love Me. Even if you fail often in those sins that you would rather never know, even if you are lazy in the practice of virtue, I do not permit you to not love Me. Love Me as you are, at every instant and in every disposition you may find yourself, whether you be in fervor, in dryness, or in tepidity; whether you be in fidelity or infidelity, love Me just AS YOU ARE.

I want the love of your poor heart, your indigent heart. If you decide to wait until you are perfect to love Me, you will never love Me.... I definitely intend to form you, but in the meantime, I love you as YOU are. You ... love Me as YOU are. I desire to see this love that you have rise and increase from the bottom of your misery. I love in you even your weakness, I love the love of the poor.[154]

Love's Word

As we draw to the end of our journey, we can do no better than to honor him who "loves the love of the poor," by holding up his words "I thirst," as Mother Teresa did — simply as "*love's word.*"[155] Mother Teresa has focused our attention anew on this mystery overlooked for generations — but one that God has raised up again through her, in these days when the world's love has grown cold.

We may ask why God waited two thousand years to lift up these words before the world. If there is any discernible answer, it may be because these words have never been as urgent as they are today. If, as Pope John Paul II observed, *never in history has man so systematically and totally rejected God*, then never in history has the thirst of God for man, nor man's wayward thirst for God, been more urgent or acute. Perhaps this is why Mother Teresa had such a sense of urgency about her mission and message, and wanted to carry it "with haste," like Mary of Nazareth (Lk 1:39), to the poor and the world.

While there have been saints and spiritual writers throughout history who have had some inkling of this mystery (a brief anthology of their references to the divine thirst is presented in Appendix Three, showing that the Holy Spirit has been preparing this message over time), there is no one else in Christian history who has taken these words as the foundation of an entire spirituality, and an entire mission, as has Mother Teresa.

Mother Teresa's Witness

In the end, if we want to understand God's thirst, if we want to comprehend the divine longing, we need only look to Mother Teresa herself.

As many commentaries as can be made on this message, it remains in a special way God's gift to her, and God's gift to us *through* her. She herself remains the best of commentaries, her life the brightest light reflecting the thirst of God.

As we have seen throughout these pages, her message is something infinitely rich, yet infinitely simple. She has shown us that, as the burning desert yearns for water, God yearns for us. And the God who thirsts for us is not hard to find, since he dwells in our soul as his temple, and comes in the palpable disguise of our suffering neighbor, making it easy for us to find the unsearchable God, and to come face-to-face with Christ. For whatever we do in love, we know that "we do it to him." Our smallest acts of love reveal, *for all the world to see*, the mystery, the reality of God's thirst for man, and of man's thirst for God. Jesus' words from the cross are written gently in the wounds of every human heart; whispered in every human cry. Mother Teresa has heard, believed, and loved — and taught us to "go and to do the same."

And so what does Jesus' thirst mean in the reality of our daily lives, in a practical, livable way? God is waiting for us; God is longing for us; God is "lonely" for us. But remember: God waits for us in those who are helpless; God longs for us in those who seek for comfort; God is lonely for us in every lonely human heart.

God — whose love is infinitely humble, infinitely gentle — hides his power in pain and poverty, that we may find him ONLY THROUGH LOVE, ONLY THROUGH COMPASSION. . . .

Jesus is crucified on the cross of the world, the cross planted in every heart, especially the poorest. May Mother Teresa obtain for us the light and the grace to hear and to heed his cry of thirst; to hear him say to us as to the Samaritan, even in our own sinfulness, "*Give me to drink . . . I thirst for you.*"

As that invitation, that "gift of God," changed the Samaritan woman's life, and as it changed Mother Teresa's life, may it also change and mold our own, until that day when we will hear with our own ears what Jesus has already spoken to Mother Teresa as she entered the kingdom: "Come, beloved of my Father. . . . I was in pain and in need, and *you did it to me* . . ." — as if he were saying to us, "I drank from your heart on earth; come drink from mine in eternity. . . ."

Indeed, because of Mother Teresa and her message, because of this inner fire entrusted to her, countless generations will come to know God better. Because of her, the *painful thirst* of the One who lamented to Mother Teresa, "*They don't know Me — so they don't want Me*" is being assuaged — for she has brought us all to know him better. By knowing the "infinite thirst in the heart of God to love and be loved," how many thousands will come to not only want him, but to love him and be transformed by him.

Through her encounter, received on the train to Darjeeling, lived in the slums of Calcutta, and shared with all who would hear, she has given the world her greatest gift — for in a new and unique way, she has opened for us a window on the heart of God.[156]

In Memoriam

Mother Teresa lying in state in St. Thomas Church, Calcutta, September 10, 1997
(Raghu Rai/Magnum Photos)

For Mother Teresa: *A Psalm of Ascents*
(1910-1997)

A star of ancient Macedon,
risen over Kali's city,
sixty turns of winter sky illumined.

And mounting upward,
and towards another Jerusalem,
this day has left

Less brightly to shine,
the vault that lights
the many-teared evening.

APPENDIX ONE

"I Thirst": The Voice of Scripture

In this appendix, we will consider Mother Teresa's intuitions anew, and more deeply, by placing them against the backdrop of Revelation history — for her insights lose their full beauty and stature outside this context; just as a mosaic stone loses its true significance outside of the mosaic.

Mother Teresa's understanding of Jesus' cry of thirst on the cross (cf. Jn 19:28) was profoundly deep, but as we have seen, utterly simple. She was convinced that beyond his human, physical thirst, Jesus crucified was expressing a deeper, divine "thirst" for union with us:

When He was dying on the Cross, Jesus said, "I thirst." [157]

He was not thirsting for water but for souls, for love. [158]

Is this only religious piety, mere devotion, or is there some biblical foundation to Mother Teresa's interpretation of these words, beyond her own lights and intuition? Does the gospel back up her unusual affirmations, or does the Word of God point only to Jesus' *physical* thirst on the cross?

The evangelists provide one obvious clue suggesting a deeper, spiritual meaning to Jesus' cry of thirst. It is the fact that *nowhere in the gospel does Jesus complain of his physical discomfort* — and least of all during his passion, during this "baptism" which he *longed with longing* to undergo (cf. Lk 12:50). Recall that at the beginning of the Crucifixion, when the Roman soldiers offered Jesus a mixture of wine with myrrh to lessen his pain (cf. Mt 27:34), he steadfastly refused it. Towards the end of his time on the cross, however, as the need for water increased due to loss of blood, Jesus' physical thirst reached its apex, and became the symbol of an *inner thirst that far surpassed it.*

As we shall see, there is a rich biblical history to the symbolism of thirst — as a metaphor for both man's longing for God, and God's longing for man. Knowing that we are on solid ground, that there is sufficient biblical precedent for attributing more than physical thirst to Jesus' words on the cross, we can begin drawing out the scriptural riches of Mother Teresa's insights.

Thirst in Scripture

There is a long history of scriptural foreshadowings leading up to Jesus' cry of thirst. Throughout Revelation, the Holy Spirit has chosen to portray man's longing for God in the most accessible language possible — the language of human experience. As a nomadic people constantly in search of water, Israel could easily understand thirst as a *metaphor*. Over the centuries, the symbolic connection between physical and spiritual thirst became so embedded in the Hebrew mind, and so enshrined in the language, that the same word (*nefesh*) came to stand for both "thirst" and "soul." The soul, even more than the bodily throat, was seen as the "seat of thirst,"[159] so the simple, daily experience of thirsting for water already carried with it a deeper, spiritual meaning.

It was thanks to the language of the Psalms that the mystery of man's longing for God, expressed there precisely as "thirst," offered an early scriptural key to understanding the human person. In the vision of the Psalms, man was a living thirst for God. This choice of experiential language shows how Israel's long trek through the desert marked their consciousness, producing its own vocabulary — a unique lexicon arising from Israel's experience of longing for God as one thirsts for water in a dry land:

> As a deer longs
> > for flowing streams,
> so longs my soul
> > for you, O God.
> My soul thirsts for God,
> > for the living God. (Ps 42:1-2)

> O God, you are my God, I seek you,
> > my soul thirsts for you;
> my flesh faints for you,
> > as in a dry and weary land where no water is. (Ps 63:1)

> I stretch out my hands to you;
> > My soul thirsts for you like a parched land. (Ps 143:6)

This symbolism continued to be developed in the prophets, particularly in Isaiah, who invites all those who yearn for God: "Every one who thirsts, come to the waters" (Is 55:1). In the New Testament, thirst would continue its symbolic connotation, indicating *ardent spiritual longing*, or in the language of modern biblical scholarship, as the "passionate desire for a spiritual good"[160] — such as the "thirst for righteousness" (Mt 5:6) of which Jesus speaks in the Beatitudes.

St. John's Gospel

But the symbolism of human thirst, present in both Old Testament and New, would reach its zenith in the gospel of St. John (see chapters 4, 7, and 19). In chapter 7, Jesus is presented attending the feast of Tabernacles. This ancient festival, dating back to the Exodus, celebrated the annual harvest as the fruit of God's life-giving waters. But the feast also commemorated Israel's time in the desert, when Yahweh dwelt in the midst of his people in an ordinary tent — already an important sign of his longing. The celebration of the feast, as still practiced in Jesus' time, was rich in symbolism:

> The flowing of water from the rock in the desert was celebrated by the Israelites, after their establishment in Canaan, with demonstrations of great rejoicing. . . . On each of the seven days of the feast the priests went out with music and the choir of Levites to draw water in a golden vessel from the spring of Siloe.
>
> They were followed by multitudes of the worshipers, as many as could get near the stream to drink of it, while the jubilant strains arose, "With joy you shall draw water from the wellsprings of salvation" (Is 12:3). Then the water drawn by the priests was borne to the temple amid the sound of trumpets and the solemn chant, "And now our feet are standing within your gates, O Jerusalem" (Ps 122:2). The water was then poured out upon the altar of burnt offering, while songs of praise rang out, the multitudes joining in triumphant chorus with musical instruments and deep-toned trumpets.[161]

The symbolism associated with the feast of Tabernacles centered on water and thirst, and Jesus would apply these themes to himself, as the One who fulfills the feast's promises and foreshadowings: "On the last day of the feast, the great day," Jesus' voice was heard ringing through the temple courts. "If any one thirst, let him come to me and drink. He who believes in me, as the Scripture has said, 'Out of his heart shall flow rivers of living water' " (Jn 7:37-38).[162]

The inner thirsting of which Scripture speaks is a dynamic in *two directions* — representing both man's desire for God, and God's desire for man. Man's thirst for God, of which the Psalms speak poetically, is an inborn longing for divine life and love, without which we cannot rise above our fallen state.

God's thirst for us, on the other hand, is entirely different. His thirst is for *our sake*, and is a free gift, indicating neither need nor lack on his part, but only pure abundance. As pointed out above, though nothing in God needs us, everything in God wants us.

Particularly in the fourth gospel, Jesus is presented as the one who not only reveals but unites these two dimensions of biblical thirst, both human and divine — thirst as God's great gift (Jn 4:10) and as man's great need (Jn 7:37).

To be fully understood, then, Jesus' cry of thirst on Calvary — and Mother Teresa's insights — need to be seen in the light of St. John's gospel. It is significant that only on Calvary does Jesus speak these revealing words publicly, since, as St. John makes clear, Jesus' crucifixion is above all God's hour of *glory*, not of defeat.

Since God's glory is nothing less than the shining forth, the clear revelation of his nature, and since God's nature is love, then the maximum of divine love manifest on the cross becomes *the* moment of divine glory. As such, what Jesus does and says on the cross becomes not only a part of revelation, but stands as revelation's summit and crowning moment.

In the Name of the Father

While admitting the symbolic nature of Jesus' thirst on the cross, some have speculated that his words of thirst are addressed only to the Father, rather than to mankind. How can we know that Jesus' cry is not expressing but his own longing for the Father (which is at the core of his being), or of broken humanity's longing for God, which he had purposely taken on himself (cf. Phil 2:6ff.)?

Surely, Jesus on the cross *is* revealing himself as a living "thirst" for the Father. At the same time, he is revealing our human poverty

— not only as creatures, but as sinners — revealing his total solidarity with that poverty, "even unto death." Both of these are important truths.

But Jesus' main purpose throughout his life, and especially here on Calvary, was to *reveal the Father* — to "[make] the Father present as love and mercy."[163] Even while revealing his own love for us ("As the Father loves me, I have loved you"), Jesus is still revealing the Father, whose perfect image he is.

Jesus' every gesture was a reflection of the Father, his every word the Father's echo. Jesus declares that he has not come to speak in his own name, but in the name of the One who sent him (cf. Jn 7:16), and insists that "I declare to the world what I have heard from him" (Jn 8:26). But sadly, throughout his life, and especially here on the cross, this higher source of his words was not understood. As St. John laments, "They did not understand that he spoke to them of the Father" (Jn 8:27). Jesus on the cross would proclaim the Father's longing for man, speaking the "word" of thirst he had heard from the One who sent him: "The word which you hear is not mine but the Father's who sent me" (Jn 14:24). But the world did not understand. Jesus did not say the words, "I thirst," in his own name alone. Above all, he spoke them in the name of the One whom he came to reveal.

In that moment of limitless love on Calvary, Jesus was revealing the infinite love of the entire Trinity. Especially here on the cross, Jesus became the image, the expression, the "Word" of the Father's love — a love beyond our understanding, for which, in that supreme hour, *thirst* became the divinely chosen symbol.

If every word Jesus spoke was given him by the Father, and revealed the Father, "making the Father present as love and mercy," how much more so *these* words spoken on the cross, spoken in this greatest moment of revelation — the only moment Jesus refers to as the "Father's hour" (Jn 12:27), and the only hour St. John labels as "glory" (Jn 17:1).

Jesus insists that "He who has seen me has seen the Father. . . . The words that I say to you I do not speak on my own authority" (Jn 14:9, 10). In his humanity, Jesus was revealing our thirst for God. But in his divinity, as the eternal Word, he was accomplishing his paramount task of revealing the Father, and through this symbolic word of thirst, the Father's longing for us, his children.

Double Preface

While the context of St. John's gospel as a whole would suggest that Jesus' thirst is spoken in the name of the Father, and addressed to mankind, does the evangelist offer any more direct clues? Does the text confirm specifically that *we* are the focus of the divine thirst revealed on Calvary, as Mother Teresa believed?

From a careful examination of the gospel text (cf. Jn 19:28-30), it appears that Mother Teresa's interpretation is not only one among others all equally valid, but reflects the principal message that both Jesus and St. John wished to convey.

To assure that future generations would not misinterpret Jesus' cry of thirst on the cross, St. John has placed two invaluable clues in the gospel text, in the form of a double preface. Of all Jesus' words on Calvary, these are the only ones so carefully set off, as the evangelist's way of underlining their true intent and importance:

> *Jesus, knowing that all was now finished, said (to [fulfill] the Scripture), "I thirst."* (Jn 19:28)

Let us look more closely at this two-part preface. The first phrase, "*knowing that all was now finished,*" shows that Jesus' words are an expression of completion, that they represent a kind of compendium, a summary, even a crowning statement. The second phrase, "*to fulfill the Scripture,*" gives us an insight into the Holy Spirit's intention in using the words, "I thirst."

"Knowing That All Was Now Finished"

Even before hearing Jesus' words from the cross, the evangelist wants us to know that he is speaking them deliberately, and with a specific purpose. It was as if he had long awaited the proper hour to proclaim these words. We know that Jesus had intentionally waited for this time, not allowing himself to be arrested before — as John reminds us, "No one laid hands on him, because his hour had not yet come" (Jn 7:30). He had likewise waited and longed to finally mount the cross, for which he had come into the world: "I have a baptism to be baptized with; and how I am constrained until it is accomplished!" (Lk 12:50). And now, having mounted the cross for our salvation, he has painfully awaited the end of his "hour," finally *"knowing that all was now finished"* (Jn 19:28), to utter his cry of thirst. As soon as he does so, and receives the vinegar, Jesus "[bows] his head and [gives] up his spirit" (Jn 19:30).

He has accomplished all that the Father had sent him to do; he has revealed the love of God, saved the world from its sin, and is about to breathe his last and release the gift of the Spirit (in John's gospel, Pentecost already begins in this hour of glory on the cross). Like an artist who waits until he has finished his masterpiece before affixing a title to his work, Jesus offers his words of thirst almost as a title, a label for the great finished mosaic of his life. By uttering these closing words, the mystery of his thirst will shed a unifying light on all Jesus has said and done, so that the entire gospel becomes an expression of the Father's longing for union with sinful man.

"To Fulfill the Scripture"

The words "I thirst" were spoken not only in view of all having been accomplished, but also *"to fulfill the Scripture"* (Jn 19:28). St. John's expression seems ambiguous — and perhaps deliberately so, as there are lessons and light in both ways of understanding "the Scripture." To fulfill the Scripture can mean "the Scriptures in general." In this sense, the evangelist's expression would mean that everything God wished to reveal about himself in the Scriptures, from Genesis on, is in some way summed up in Jesus' cry of thirst. Indeed, in Jesus, God's "infinite longing to love and be loved" is revealed, and man's misdirected thirst is finally redeemed and redirected towards God. God and man are again made one. In that sense, in fact, all the Scriptures *are* summed up in Jesus' cry, and their purpose fulfilled, so that indeed, *"all is now finished."*

At the same time, "to fulfill the Scripture" may indicate a *particular* biblical passage. But which one?

Throughout his passion, from the close of the Last Supper onwards, as pious Israelite and especially as Messiah, Jesus will be praying the Psalms. Biblical scholars agree that, after being lifted up on the cross, Jesus was quoting from Psalm 22 ("My God, my God, why have you forsaken me" — Mt 27:46) as well as from Psalm 69. This latter, which St. John focuses on, is one of the "Messianic Psalms" foretelling the future glory, but also the future sufferings, of the Messiah. More than simply citing it, Jesus fulfills this Psalm — i.e., *"fulfills (this particular) Scripture"* — by living out its message: "I looked for pity, but there was none. . . . [In] my thirst they gave me vinegar to drink" (Ps 69:20, 21).

The first part of this Psalm couplet (Ps 69:20) tells of the Messiah's longing for the love of his people — a selfless love, a love for his own sake, expressed as *"pity"* or *"compassion."* The second part of the couplet compares the rejection the Messiah would endure to the act of denying water to a thirsty man, and the even greater cruelty of offering him vinegar in its place: *"[In] my thirst they gave me vinegar to drink"* (Ps 69:21).

Word and Gesture

At major moments in their mission of communicating God's word to Israel, the prophets (particularly Jeremiah) would both speak God's message and act it out symbolically. This wedding of word and gesture is so embedded in the mentality of Israel that the Hebrew sense of "word" has a double meaning, though reflected in a single term, *dabar* — meaning both word *and* deed, since deeds are equally as revealing as words. In this greatest moment of revelation, Jesus, the greatest of the prophets, does the same. The first part of this "word" Jesus speaks, as he proclaims the divine thirst; the second part he acts out, as he receives the vinegar.

Let us return to the scene described by John in chapter 19. After Jesus says "I thirst," the soldiers mockingly raise a sponge to his lips, soaked not in the water they presumed he wanted, but in a pail of dirty vinegar, used to wash blood and grime from the soldiers' tools. Even though the vinegar would bring intense pain to his already parched lips, and only aggravate his thirst, Jesus deliberately acts out the second part of this word (Ps 69:21). He chooses to *drink the vinegar* (cf. Jn 19:30), to more clearly portray the poignancy and urgency of divine thirst he has just proclaimed. The Son of God has painfully accepted the vinegar of our rejection, symbol of humanity's sin — he has succeeded at redeeming our rejection by embracing it.

We can conclude this brief examination by stating that, while Jesus was clearly longing for the Father as well, this was not the main thrust of the psalm-verse he has cited and applied to himself — nor, therefore, of his cry of thirst. This psalm that Jesus has evoked by his words and fulfilled by drinking the vinegar, speaks of the Messiah's *longing for the love of his people*, and demonstrates that Jesus' thirst on the cross is, indeed, addressed to us.

Cameo of Salvation History

In Jesus' cry of thirst and our answering him with vinegar, we see the divine initiative throughout history, and mankind's response, acted out in symbol. What takes place on Calvary becomes a cameo of all salvation history. On the cross, God's love for man reaches its maximum expression; and at the same cross, humanity's rejection of God finds its own maximum expression. In Jesus crucified, the extremity of God's love and the extremity of man's rejection meet and merge in the same event.

In this brief vignette of word and gesture, the history of God's thirst in the world is portrayed, and by the same actors who have played it out since creation — a faithful God and an unfaithful humanity. Here everything is revealed; God's unfathomable love, from Creation to Calvary, is met by man's equally unfathomable rejection: "He came to his own home, and his own people received him not" (Jn 1:11).

But the amazing thing is that, in his thirst for us, God *does not pull away* from man's rejection. Jesus does not "come down from the cross" we have prepared for him (cf. Mk 15:30), nor does he refuse the vinegar we still bring to his lips. His drinking of the vinegar was no inadvertent act — it was proof that the Son of God does not pull away, does not reject us, when we reject him. Rather, he gives yet more of himself in response to our rejection. Such is the imponderable nature of divine love, underscored by the twin symbol of Jesus' thirst and mankind's vinegar. We can only be overwhelmed by this, by a love that is constant and free and unconditional, in no way a reward for man's good behavior. Ironically, this "greater love" given to such an extreme on the cross is, in a certain sense, the "reward" of our *rejecting him*. Throughout history, God has shown us his love most when we have deserved it least.

"It Is Finished"

The conclusion of this scene, and of the symbolism St. John has carefully built around Jesus' cry of thirst, ends with the piercing of Jesus' side, long seen by Christian tradition as filled with deeper meaning: "One of the soldiers pierced his side with a spear, and at once there came out blood and water" (Jn 19:34).

Our rejection of God's love has pierced through, literally and fig-uratively, to the source of divine love — revealing what Mother Teresa described as *the thirst of his heart* — a heart pierced by a long-ing beyond our imagining, opening the floodgates of the promised Living Waters to satiate our own human thirst; and this too, beyond all we had hoped for. As Isaiah prophesied:

> When the poor and needy seek water,
>   and there is none,
>   and their tongue is parched with thirst,
> I the LORD will answer them,
>   I the God of Israel will not forsake them.
> I will open rivers on the bare heights,
>   and fountains in the midst of the valleys;
> I will make the wilderness a pool of water,
>   and the dry land springs of water. (Is 41:17-18)

From Jesus' pierced heart, like the rock struck by Moses in the wilderness from which streams of water flowed, there would now flow blood and water — the redeeming *blood* to remove the sin sep-arating us from God, so quenching *God's thirst for man*; and the liv-ing *water* of the Spirit, that would in turn quench *man's thirst for God*.

All is indeed "finished" (Jn 19:30), that all might once more begin. In the thirst of Jesus on the cross, all is accomplished; and in the thirst of Jesus to pour forth the living waters, all begins anew. This awareness became Mother Teresa's treasure, her message and her great hope — to bring the poor, and all who are thirsty, to "take the water of life without price" (Rev 22:17).

Overview

Nothing deeper could be said about God or man, or the relationship between us, than what is said and portrayed in this scene. All of

Scripture is reflected in Jesus' words, "I thirst," and in turn, Jesus' words, "I thirst," are a commentary on all of Scripture.

All is now complete. In revealing this drama to the full, Jesus has also redeemed it to the full. The cross, the proof of God's love in the face of our rejection, has redeemed our rejection. On the cross, Jesus' work of revealing the Father's thirst, and of opening the Savior's fountains (Is 12:3) to quench our human thirst for God, is indeed accomplished. The *hour when darkness reigns* (Lk 22:53) and the *hour of glory* have merged as one — but it is the light of glory that continues to shine victorious in the darkness, ours and Mother Teresa's, for the darkness "has not overcome it" (Jn 1:5).

Conclusion

This mystery entrusted to Mother Teresa, the mystery of God's thirst for man even at our worst, is so great that only this *"dabar,"* this triple gesture — Jesus' mounting the wood of the cross, the act of drinking the vinegar, and the piercing of his heart — could adequately convey the depth and meaning enshrined in the Savior's words, "I thirst."

"In this thirst of God is seen how much God wants our love and how much we need His love. . . . God is love and Jesus is God, so the love of Jesus and His thirst for love are infinite."

— Mother Teresa's Address to the
Bishops' Synod on Consecrated Life,
at the Vatican (October 1994)

"I Thirst": The Voice of Mother Teresa (An Anthology of Quotes)

Introduction

From the late 1940s until her death in 1997, Mother Teresa's conferences and letters repeatedly touched on the twin themes of *God's longing for us*, and *humanity's longing for God* — a longing she experienced acutely, becoming her greatest suffering in the dark night, yet her strongest anchor and her brightest light.

While hundreds of references can be found throughout her writings and talks, what follows is a hopefully representative sample of her thoughts and sayings on the divine-human thirst. Taken together, these can give a sense of the depth and development of Mother Teresa's spiritual genius, as she outlines for her Sisters (for the most part) and spiritual directors this her central insight into the heart of God.

—

"I thirst" (courtesy Mother Teresa Center/©MTC)

1947

Night after night the sleep would disappear — and only to spend those hours in longing for His coming. [. . .] the same longing breaks into the sleep.

— Mother Teresa: Come Be My Light, p. 84

1949

Jesus is God therefore His love, His thirst is infinite. . . . [We are called to] quench this infinite thirst of a God made Man. . . . The Sisters . . . ceaselessly quench the thirsting God by their love and of the love of the souls they bring to Him.

— Mother Teresa: Come Be My Light, p. 41

His burning thirst for souls and for love. . . .

— Second version of the Rule written by Mother Teresa
in the beginning of 1949

1954

We carry on our body and soul the love of an infinite, thirsty God.

— Mother Teresa: Come Be My Light, p. 155

1957

Such deep longing for God. . . .

— Mother Teresa: Come Be My Light, p. 169

1959

When alone in the streets — I talk to You for hours — of my longing for You. . . .

Jesus hear my prayer — if this pleases You — if my pain and suffering — my darkness and separation gives You a drop of consolation — my own Jesus, do with me as You wish — as long as You wish, without a single glance at my feelings and pain. I am Your own. — Imprint on my soul and life the sufferings of Your Heart. Don't mind my feelings. — Don't mind even, my pain. If my separation from You — brings others to You and in their love and company You find joy and pleasure — why Jesus, I am willing with all my heart to suffer all that I suffer — not only now — but for all eternity — if this was possible. Your happiness is all that I want. — For the rest — please do not take the trouble — even if you see me faint with pain. — All this is my will — I want to satiate Your Thirst with every single drop of blood that You can find in me.

— *Mother Teresa: Come Be My Light*, pp. 193-194

1960

I long for God. I long to love Him with every drop of life in me.

— *Mother Teresa: Come Be My Light*, p. 203

1965

Here we have real spiritual slums. Just as our people in India hunger and thirst for food of the body, our people here hunger and thirst for the Word of God.

— Mother Teresa's Letters to the M.C. Sisters
(August 6, 1965)

1973

He has a deep and personal longing to have you for Himself. Let Him do it.
— Mother Teresa to a Religious (December 22, 1973)

1974

The aim of the Co-Workers is to spread love and compassion . . . to satiate that thirst of Jesus for love in a very simple way and in a very small way.

— Remarks to the Co-Workers Meeting, Winona, Minnesota
(June 20-22, 1974)

1977

We have to quench the thirst of Jesus for others and for me — for love of others and for love of us. . . . By each action done to the sick and the dying,

I quench the thirst of Jesus for love of that person, by my giving God's love in me to that particular person.... This is how I quench the thirst of Jesus for others, by giving His love in action to them.

We also quench the thirst of Jesus for love of me.... by that personal meeting with Him face to face.

— Mother Teresa's Instructions to the M.C. Sisters
(September 29, 1977)

1980

The reason of our existence is to quench the thirst of Jesus Christ. When He asked for water, the soldier gave Him vinegar to drink.... but His thirst was for love, for souls.... We human beings are asked to satiate the thirst of God.

— Mother Teresa's Instructions to the M.C. Sisters
(April 1980)

What is the reason for our existence? We are here to satiate the thirst of Jesus, to proclaim the love of Christ — the thirst of Jesus for souls by the holiness of our lives.... We are here to satiate the thirst of Jesus ... that is why we must be holy.

— Mother Teresa's Instructions to the M.C. Sisters
(January 1980)

"I thirst" — we are so busy to think about all that. The words, "I thirst" — do they echo in our souls? ... Today, let us try to go over that word, "I thirst."

— Mother Teresa's Instructions to the M.C. Sisters
(February 1980)

1981

Every human being has a longing for God. "My soul is thirsting for God."

— Mother Teresa's Instructions to the M.C. Sisters
(April 16, 1981)

Look at the cross and see the words, "I thirst."

— Mother Teresa's Instructions to the M.C. Sisters

(June 18, 1981)

Satiate the infinite thirst of God.

— Mother Teresa's Instructions to the M.C. Sisters

(May 13, 1981)

Just like I am thirsty for water, I must feel the thirst for Jesus.

— Mother Teresa's Instructions to the M.C. Sisters

(September 18, 1981)

1982

Right today and everyday He is thirsting for my love. He is longing for me, in my soul.

— Mother Teresa's Instructions to the M.C. Sisters

(December 7, 1982)

1983

[Our aim is] to satiate the infinite thirst of God. . . .

— Mother Teresa's Instructions to the M.C. Sisters

(January 16, 1983)

The reason of our existence is to quench the thirst of God. I don't say even "Jesus" or "on the cross," but "of God." Try to deepen your understanding of these two words, "Thirst of God."

— Mother Teresa's Instructions to the M.C. Sisters

(January 16, 1983)

It is very important for us to know that Jesus is thirsting for our love, for the love of the whole world. . . . Ask yourself. Have I heard Jesus directly say

this word to me personally? Did I ever hear that word personally? "I thirst."
"I want your love"... If not, examine yourself: why could I not hear?

> — Mother Teresa's Instructions to the M.C. Sisters
> (December 1, 1983)

1985

That word, "I thirst," has it penetrated into my heart?... We are called to
quench the thirst of God.

> — Mother Teresa's Instructions to the M.C. Sisters
> (September 23, 1985)

1986

Who will bring those souls to Him to satiate that thirst of the infinite God
dying of love.... Can you and I continue to stand by, a mere spectator? Or
pass by and do nothing?

> — Mother Teresa's Message to the Youth of the Netherlands
> (March 14, 1986)

1992

Are we truly seeking to satiate the thirst of God, our loving Father in heav-
en for our holiness — the thirst which Jesus expressed on the cross when He
cried out, "I thirst"...

> — Mother Teresa's Letters to the M.C. Sisters
> (March 6, 1992)

Seek wholeheartedly to love God and long to find Him. In this way you sati-
ate the thirst of God who thirsts for us to thirst for Him.

> — Mother Teresa's Message for Youth 2000 in Dallas
> (May 23, 1992)

At this most difficult time He proclaimed, "I thirst." And people thought He
was thirsty in an ordinary way and they gave Him vinegar straight away;
but it was not for that thirst; it was for our love, our affection, that inti-

mate attachment to Him, and that sharing of His passion. He used, "I thirst," instead of "Give Me your love" . . .

"I thirst." Let us hear Him saying it to me and saying it to you.

— Mother Teresa's Instructions to the M.C. Sisters
(August 9, 1992)

1993

Jesus himself must be the one to say to you, "I thirst." Hear your own name. Not just once. Every day. If you listen with your heart, you will hear, you will understand.

Remember this: "I thirst" is something much deeper than just Jesus saying, "I love you." Until you know deep inside that Jesus thirsts for you, you can't begin to know who He wants to be for you. Or who He wants you to be for Him.

How approach the thirst of Jesus? Only one secret — the closer you come to Jesus, the better you will know His thirst. "Repent and believe," Jesus tells us. What are we to repent? Our indifference, our hardness of heart. What are we to believe? Jesus thirsts even now, in your heart and in the poor. He knows your weakness, He wants only your love, wants only the chance to love you. He is not bound by time. Whenever we come close to Him, we become partners of Our Lady, St. John, Magdalen. Hear Him. Hear your own name. Make my joy and yours complete.

— Mother Teresa's Letters to the M.C. Sisters
(March 25, 1993)

He longs for you. He thirsts for you . . . My children, once you have experienced the thirst, the love of Jesus for you, you will never need, you will never thirst for these things which can only lead you away from Jesus, the true and living Fountain. Only the thirst of Jesus, feeling it, hearing it, answering it with all your heart will keep your love . . . alive. The closer you come to Jesus the better you will know His thirst.

> — Mother Teresa's Letters to the M.C. Sisters
> (July 29, 1993)

This longing [for holiness] is prayer [emphasis added].

> — Mother Teresa's Letter to Co-workers
> (November 28, 1993)

1994

Jesus is thirsting for us right now . . . Do we listen to Him saying, "I thirst for your love"? Just think of His thirst. Do we really hear Him? Here in this chapel His mouth is open and we know He is saying it right now.

> — Mother Teresa's Instructions to the M.C. Sisters
> (February 1994)

Grow in that intimate love, and you will understand not only "I thirst," but everything. Humanly speaking we cannot understand "love one another as I have loved you;" "Be ye holy as I am holy." But it all comes under "I thirst." The fruit of faith is the understanding of "I thirst."

. . . Get rid of sin quickly so we can hear Jesus say, "I thirst for your love." The most important thing is that we must encounter the thirst of Jesus, but the encounter with Jesus' thirst is a grace.

> — Mother Teresa's Instructions to the M.C. Sisters
> (February 1994)

That boy and girl who fall in love with each another, that love is "I thirst." You have to experience it. Same thing — we come to that conviction . . . His love is thirst . . . Love and thirst are the same word. We are very fortunate that Jesus has disclosed His thirst to us.

> Mother Teresa's Instructions to the M.C. Sisters
> (February 1994)

Question: When was the first time you experienced Jesus' thirst?
Mother: First Communion.
Question: But as experience?
Mother: It is reality — not just an experience [that is felt], but reality.

— Mother Teresa's Instructions to the M.C. Sisters
(February 1994)

Do you feel the thirst of Jesus? Do you feel it? Do you hear His voice? Do you really hear His voice? If no, you have never known His real love for you. Put your whole heart to satiate the thirst of Jesus . . .

— Mother Teresa's Instructions to the M.C. Sisters
(February 1994)

What is that word, "I thirst," to you personally? What connection do you make in your life? . . .

— Mother Teresa's Instructions to the M.C. Sisters
(August 8, 1994)

1996

"The strong grace of Divine Light and Love that Mother received on the train journey to Darjeeling on 10th September 1946 is where the MC begins — in the depths of God's infinite longing to love and to be loved. *How important it is for each . . . to desire deeply to share in this same grace . . ." [emphasis added].*

— Mother Teresa's Letters to the M.C. Sisters
(April 24, 1996)

But we ask for the most important thing, to stand . . . under the Cross of Jesus, to hear Him say "I thirst." . . . Just take the trouble to be close to Jesus to hear Him say, "I thirst," to you, individually, to understand His Word, love it and live it. As Jesus did to Mother, He now does it to you. Try to hear properly.

— Mother Teresa's Instructions to the M.C. Sisters
(July 31, 1996)

1997

On the cross He said very clearly, "I thirst." For what was He thirsting? For love, for that tender love from all of us! To satiate the thirst of God. . . .

Let us understand this thirst of Jesus as well as we can. The better we understand it, the more close we get to Him. . . .

Have we understood this thirst? . . . Do we know it? Have we experienced His thirst? . . . Jesus came into this world to draw souls closer to His Father. . . . Just think, God is thirsting for you and me to come forward to satiate His thirst.

— Mother Teresa's Instructions to the M.C. Sisters
(February 15, 1997)

God spoke of His infinite thirst for each of us and for all His children, especially the Poorest of the Poor, through His beloved Son, Jesus Christ, dying on the Cross. . . .

I believe He said two or three times, "I thirst." Terrible suffering, to see His suffering! What is the meaning of "I thirst?" Everybody understood it was for water, not for love, for compassion. . . .

Jesus himself said, "I thirst," right on the Cross. Love's word. He did not say anything else after that. Try to deepen your knowledge of "I thirst."

— Mother Teresa's Instructions to the M.C. Sisters
(June 30, 1997)

The Voice of Christian Tradition: Saints and Spiritual Writers

Mother Teresa was not alone in finding deeper meaning in Jesus' cry of thirst. She is but the latest — though undoubtedly the most prolific — in a long line of witnesses to this mystery, reaching back through Christian history.

This third appendix contains a survey of citations on the thirst of God for man in the writings of saints and prominent spiritual writers. While none may reach the profundity we find in Mother Teresa, these writings demonstrate that her interpretation is not new in Christian tradition, even if infrequently cited. The uniqueness of Mother Teresa's contribution lies not only in the profundity of her insights, but in the unprecedented importance and focus she gives to this mystery of the thirst of God for man.

The following anthology of citations is divided into two sections. The first contains quotes from those who have been given the title of *Fathers of the Church* (the preeminent exponents of the faith of the Church's early centuries) and *Doctors* (theologians outstanding in both wisdom and holiness). The second section presents the more modern voices of those saints and spiritual writers who have contributed their commentary on the thirst of Jesus.

Section One: Fathers and Doctors of the Church

St. Augustine

God thirsts to be thirsted for.[164]

On the cross Jesus said: "I thirst!" But they didn't give him what he thirsted for. He thirsted for them, and they gave him vinegar....[165]

He asks for a drink, and he promises a drink. He is in need, as one hoping to receive, yet he is rich, as one about to satisfy the thirst of others.[166]

St. Bonaventure

In Jesus is revealed God's thirst to pour forth life. He thirsts, not out of lack, but out of overabundance. The love of God by nature is self-effusive.[167]

St. Bernard of Clairvaux

By his thirst, the Lord Jesus places before us an image of his ardent love for us....[168]

St. Thomas Aquinas

We see Jesus' ardent desire for the salvation of the human race.... Now, the vehemence of this desire is clearly expressed with his thirst....[169]

St. Robert Bellarmine

Our Lord said, "I thirst," in the same sense in which he addressed the Samaritan woman, saying, "Give me to drink." For when he unfolded the mystery contained in these words, he added, "If you but knew the gift of God, and who it is that says to you, Give me to drink, you would have asked of him, and he would have given you living water." . . . Does he not refer to himself in saying, "If any man thirst, let him come to me and drink?" (Jn 7:37). And is he not that rock of which the Apostle speaks: "And they drank of the spiritual rock which followed them, and the rock was Christ?" (1 Cor 10:4). Is it not he who addresses the Jews by the mouth of Jeremiah the Prophet: "They have forsaken me the fountain of living water, and have dug themselves cisterns, broken cisterns, that can hold no water?" (Jer 2:13). It seems to me, then, that our Lord from the Cross, as from a high throne, casts his gaze over the whole world, full of people who are athirst and fainting from exhaustion, and by reason of his parched state he pities the drought which mankind endures, and cries aloud, "I thirst" . . . The thirst that I suffer from my desire that men should know by faith that I am the true fount of living water, should come to me and drink that they may not thirst for ever. . . .[170]

St. Catherine of Siena

O sweetest, boundless, beloved charity! It was your infinite hunger and thirst for our salvation that made you cry out that you were thirsty! Though your agony caused you intense physical thirst, your thirst for our salvation was greater. There is no one to give you anything to drink except the bitterness of sin upon sin! How few there are who give you a drink freely and with pure loving affection![171]

There [on the cross] they [the saints] found in the Lamb slain such a fire of love for our salvation, seemingly insatiable. He even cries aloud that he is thirsty, as if to say: "I have more zeal, thirst, desire for your salvation than I can show you with this finite suffering."[172]

There [on the cross] we find the Lamb slain and opened up for us with such hungry desire for the Father's honor and our salvation that it seems he cannot effectively show by his bodily suffering alone all that he longs to give. It seems this is what he meant when he cried out on the cross, "I am thirsty!" as if to say, "I have so great a thirst for your salvation that I cannot satisfy it; give me to drink!" The gentle Jesus was asking to drink those he saw not sharing in the redemption purchased by his blood, but he was given nothing to drink but bitterness. Ah, not only at the time of the Crucifixion, but later and even now we continue to see him asking for this kind of drink and showing us that his thirst persists.[173]

St. Thérèse of Lisieux

The last and youngest witness among the Doctors of the Church is the one whom Mother Teresa looked to as patroness, from whom she took her name, and with whom she spiritually identified.

One Sunday, in the parish Church of St. Pierre, as St. Thérèse gazed on a picture of Jesus crucified, his cry of thirst penetrated her soul:

[Jesus' words, "I Thirst"] set aflame in me a lively and unknown ardor. . . . I wanted to satiate my Beloved, and I felt myself devoured by His same thirst for souls. . . . I seemed to hear Jesus saying to me as to the Samaritan: "Give Me to drink;" and the more I gave Him to drink, the more the thirst of my soul grew. . . ."[174]

Jesus doesn't need our work, but only our love, for this same God is not afraid to beg a bit of water from the Samaritan. He thirsted . . . but in saying, "Give Me to drink," it was the love of His poor creature that the Creator of the universe was asking. He thirsted for love. . . .[175]

Section Two: Saints and Spiritual Writers

Throughout Christian history, the witness of saints and spiritual writers to the significance of Jesus' cry of thirst has been more vast and varied than might be imagined — though too plentiful to fully investigate here.

St. Laurence Justinian

What Christ said to the Samaritan Woman, "Give me to drink," he repeats to all of us from the Cross when he says "I thirst."

This word "I thirst," which Jesus pronounced on the Cross when he was expiring, was not a thirst which proceeded from dryness, but one that arose from the ardor of love that Jesus had for us. This thirst springs from the fever of his love.

Because by this word our Redeemer intended to declare to us, more than the thirst of the body, the desire that he had of suffering for us, by showing us his love, and the immense desire that he had of being loved by us, by the many sufferings he endured for us. . . . This was his thirst — he thirsts for us, and desires to give himself to us.[176]

St. Basil of Seleucia

Jesus Christ, in saying that he thirsted, would give us to understand that he, for the love which he bore us, was dying with the desire of suffering for us even more than what he had suffered: "O that desire, greater than the Passion."

St. Alphonsus Liguori

The Scripture, which was to be fulfilled, is the text of David: "And in my thirst they gave me vinegar to drink" (Ps 69:22). But, O Lord, you are silent about the intense pains which hasten your death, and do you complain of thirst? Ah! The thirst of Jesus was very different from that which we imagine it to be. His thirst is the desire of being loved by the soul for whom he dies. Thus, my Jesus, you do thirst for me . . . and shall I not thirst after you, who are infinite good?

But, Lord, how is it that you make no complaint of those many pains which are taking away your life, but complain only of your thirst? Ah! I understand you, my Jesus; your thirst is a thirst of love; because you love us, you desire to be beloved by us, Passion and Death of Jesus Christ.[177]

St. Margaret Mary Alacoque

One of my greatest sufferings was caused by the divine Heart addressing to me these words: "I thirst with such a terrible thirst to be loved by men in the Blessed Sacrament that this thirst consumes Me. Yet I find no one trying to quench it according to my desire by some return of my love."

Sister Consolata Betrone

"Love me . . . I thirst for your love, just as a parched man thirsts for a spring of fresh water."

"Tell all souls that I prefer an act of love . . . to any other gift which they may offer Me . . . for I thirst for love."

Sister Josefa Menendez

"I love them. Nothing indeed is wanting to my heavenly beatitude, which is infinite, but I yearn for souls, I thirst for them. . . ."

"I love to hear you calling Me, I thirst for love."

"Do not cease thinking of souls, of sinners. . . . Oh, how I thirst for souls."

"Yes, give Me to drink, for I am thirsty. You know well that I am thirsting for souls, the souls I love so much. You can give me to drink. . . ."

"I was thirsty and you slaked My thirst. I shall be your reward. Yes, my one desire is to be loved. If souls but knew the excess of my love they would not disregard it ... that is why I go seeking them out, to have them come back to me. ... I will return this evening, that you may slake My devouring thirst, and I shall take My rest in you."

"Come slake my thirst to be loved by souls, especially to be loved by those I have chosen. ... Behold this Heart on fire with longing for their love. ..."

"Share with me the flames that are consuming my Heart: I thirst for the salvation of souls. If only they would come to me. My Heart gives divine worth to your small offerings, for what I want is love. What is so wounding to my Heart is that often instead of love I meet only with indifference. Give me love and give me souls, unite all your actions to my Heart. Stay with me who am with you. I am love and desire only love. Oh, if souls only realized how I wait for them in mercy."

"When you call me, I am very near to you. But when I call souls, they do not hear me. So many go away. But you at least comfort me by calling me and longing for me. Slake my thirst by your desire for me."

St. Pio of Pietrelcina (Padre Pio)

My heart feels as if it were being drawn by a superior force each morning just before uniting with him in the Blessed Sacrament. I have such a thirst and hunger before receiving him that it's a wonder I don't die of anxiety. ... When Mass ended I remained with Jesus to render him thanks. My thirst and hunger do not diminish after I have received him in the Blessed Sacrament, but rather, increase steadily. Oh, how sweet was the conversation I held with Paradise this morning. The Heart of Jesus and my own, if you will pardon my expression, fused. They were no longer two hearts beating but only one. My heart disappeared as if it were a drop in the ocean.

Sister Mary of the Trinity

"Oh, how I thirst for souls — How I long for them to surrender themselves to me so that I may transform them, for them to surrender their humanity to me so that I may work in the world! Why do you not hear my call? Have not I exhausted every means to beg for your attention and your gratitude?"[178]

Blessed Julian of Norwich

For this is Christ's spiritual thirst, his longing in love, which persists and always will . . . to gather us all into him, to our endless joy.

With all the power of his divinity, he suffered pains and passion and died for love, to bring us to bliss. He says: it is a joy, a bliss, an endless delight that ever I suffered my Passion for you. We are his bliss, we are his reward, we are his honor, we are his crown.

For he still has that same thirst and longing which he had upon the cross, which desire, longing and thirst, as I see it, were in him from without beginning. . . .

For as truly as there is in God a quality of mercy and compassion, so truly is there in God a quality of thirst and longing; and the power of this longing in Christ empowers us to respond to his longing, and without this no soul comes to heaven.

And this quality of longing and thirst comes from God's everlasting goodness. And though he may have both longing and mercy, they are different qualities, as I see them; and this is the characteristic of spiritual thirst, which will persist in him so long as we are in need, and will draw us up into his bliss.[179]

Mother Catherine Aurelie

The mysterious Thirst which the divine Crucified One breathed from the height of his cross has found an echo in my poor heart. I have meditated upon it; I have relished it; I have understood it; and, in my turn, I have cried in ardent transports: I thirst. Words fail me to express the extent of the burning desire which has gushed from the heart of my Jesus into mine. . . . Jesus is athirst for love; I crave for hearts that will return him love for love, hearts that will unite themselves in prayer, reparation, and suffering to that of the holy Victim who knew so perfectly how to love, how to obey and how to suffer in order to procure the happiness and salvation of souls . . . would that all hearts might hear his Thirst and thus become springs of living water to quench [him]. . . .[180]

Archbishop Fulton Sheen

The cry of Christ from the Cross, "I Thirst," refers not to a physical thirst, for he refused the drink they offered him. It was his soul that was burning and his Heart that was on fire. He was thirsting for the souls of men. The Shepherd was lonely without his sheep; the Creator was yearning for his creatures. . . .[181]

Catechism of the Catholic Church

2560 "If you knew the gift of God!" (Jn 4:10). The wonder of prayer is revealed beside the well where we come seeking water: there, Christ comes to meet every human being. It is he who first seeks us and asks us for a drink. Jesus thirsts; his asking arises from the depths of God's desire for us. Whether we realize it or not, prayer is the encounter of God's thirst with ours. God thirsts that we may thirst for him (cf. St. Augustine, *De diversis quaestionibus octoginta tribus* 64, 4: PL 40, 56).

2561 "You would have asked him, and he would have given you living water" (Jn 4:10). Paradoxically our prayer of petition is a response to the plea of the living God: "They have forsaken me, the fountain of living waters, and hewn out cisterns for themselves, broken cisterns that can hold no water!" (Jer 2:13). Prayer is the response of faith to the free promise of salvation and also a response of love to the thirst of the only Son of God (cf. Jn 7:37-39, 19:28; Is 12:3, 51:1; Zech 12:10, 13:1).

Pope Benedict XVI

Christ's thirst is an entranceway to the mystery of God.[182]

Meditation: "I Thirst for You"

The divine words, *"I thirst,"* first spoken on Calvary, still echo throughout every time and place. God still speaks them in the empty space, the dark and lonely place in every human heart.

> *"Jesus is thirsting for us right now. . . . Do we listen to Him saying, "I thirst for your love?". . . Do we really hear Him . . . He is saying it right now."*
>
> — Mother Teresa's Instructions to the M.C. Sisters
> (February 1994)

"Behold, I stand at the door and knock" (Rev 3:20).

It is true. I stand at the door of your heart, day and night. Even when you are not listening, even when you doubt it could be me, I am there. I await even the smallest sign of your response, even the slightest hint of invitation that will allow me to enter.

I want you to know that whenever you invite me, I come. Always, without fail. Silent and unseen I come, but with infinite power and love, bringing the many gifts of my Father. I come with my mercy, with my desire to forgive and heal you, and with a love for you beyond your comprehension — a love every bit as great as the love I myself have received from the Father. *"As the Father has loved me, so have I loved you"* (Jn 15:9). I come longing to console you and give you strength, to lift you up and bind your wounds. I bring you my light, to dispel your darkness and all your doubts. I come with my power, that I might carry you and all of your burdens; with my grace, to touch your heart and transform your life; and my peace I give to still your soul.

I know you through and through. I know everything about you. The very hairs of your head I have numbered. Nothing in your life is unimportant to me. I have followed you through the years, and I have always loved you, even in your wanderings. I know every one of your problems; I know your needs, your fears, and your worries. I hear your every whispered prayer, always. Even when it seems I am silent, I am ever at work in your life to bless you and protect you.

Every movement of your heart I follow, and your every thought. I know all your pain, your struggles and trials, your failures and heartaches. And yes, I know all your sins. But I tell you again that I love you, and not for what you have or haven't done. I love you for you; I love you because you are. I love you for the beauty and dignity my Father gave you, creating you in his own image. It is a dignity you have forgotten, a beauty you have tarnished by ego and sin. But I love you as you are, infinitely, completely, without reserve; and I have shed my blood to win you back. If you only ask me with faith, my grace will touch all that needs changing in your life, and I will give you the strength to free yourself from sin and from all that binds and burdens you, and from all that takes you away from me.

I know what is in your heart. I know your loneliness and all your hurts: the rejections, the judgments, the humiliations. I carried it all before you. And I carried it all *for* you so that you might share my strength and my victory. I know especially your need for love, how you thirst to be accepted and appreciated, loved and cherished. But how often have you thirsted in vain, seeking that love outside of me — I who am its Source — striving to fill the emptiness inside you with passing pleasures, and often with the even greater emptiness of sin. Do you thirst for love? *"If any one thirst, let him come to me . . ."* (Jn 7:37). I will satisfy your desire for love beyond your dreams. Do you thirst to be appreciated and cherished? I cherish you more than you can imagine, to the point leaving heaven for you, and of dying on a cross to make you one with me.

Don't you realize that your thirst for love is a thirst for me, I who *am* Love? I am myself the answer to your deepest desires.

I THIRST FOR YOU . . . Yes, that is the only way to describe my love for you: I thirst to love you and to be loved by you — that is how precious you are to me.

- Come to me, and I will fill your heart and heal your wounds. I will make you a new creation, and give you peace in all your trials.
- You must never doubt my mercy, my acceptance of you, my desire to forgive, my longing to bless you and live my life in you.
- If you feel unimportant in the eyes of the world, that matters not at all. For me, there is no one more important than you.
- Open to me, come to me, thirst for me, give me your life — and I will prove to you how important you are to my heart.

Don't you realize that my Father already has a perfect plan to transform your life, beginning from this moment? Trust in me. Ask me every day to enter and take charge of your life — and I will. I promise you before my Father in heaven that I will work miracles in your life. Why would I do this? Because I thirst for you. All I ask is that you entrust yourself to me completely. I will do all the rest.

Even now I behold the place my Father has prepared for you in my kingdom. Remember that you are a pilgrim in this life, on a journey home. The things of this world can never satisfy you, nor bring the peace you seek. All that you have sought outside of me has only left you more empty, so do not cling to material things. Above all, do not run from me when you fall. Come to me without delay. When you give me your sins, you give me the joy of being your Savior. There is nothing I cannot forgive and heal. So come now, and unburden your soul.

No matter how far you may wander, no matter how often you forget me, no matter how many crosses you may bear in this life, there is one thing I want you to always remember, one thing that will never change: *I thirst for you* — just as you are. You don't need to change to believe in my love, for it will be your belief in my love that will change you. You forget me, and yet I am seeking you every moment of the day, standing at the door of your heart and knocking. Do you find this hard to believe? Then look at the cross — look at my heart that was pierced for you. Have you not understood my cross? Then listen again to the words I spoke there, for they tell you clearly why I endured all this for you: "*I thirst*" (Jn 19:28). Yes, I thirst for you — as the rest of the psalm-verse I was reciting says of me: "*I looked for pity, but there was none*" (Ps 69:20). All your life I have been looking for your love — I have never stopped seeking to love you and to be loved by you. You have tried many other things in your search for happiness. Why not try opening your heart to me, right now, more than you ever have before?

Whenever you do open the door of your heart, whenever you come close enough, you will hear me say to you again and again, not in mere human words but in spirit:

No matter what you have done, I love you for your own sake. Come to me with your misery and your sins, with your troubles and needs, and with all your longing to be loved. I stand at the door of your heart and knock. Open to me, for I thirst for you.

———

"Jesus is God, therefore His love, His Thirst, is infinite. He the Creator of the universe, asked for the love of His creatures."

— Explanation of the Original Rule

"He thirsts for our love. . . ."

— Mother Teresa's Letters to the M.C. Sisters
(May 11, 1994)

"These words: 'I thirst' — do they echo in our souls?"

— Mother Teresa's Instructions to the M.C. Sisters
(February 1980)

"Today Jesus had His arms extended to embrace you. Today Jesus' Heart was opened to receive you. Were you there?"

— Excerpt from Mother Teresa's Letters to M.C. Sisters
(April 8, 1977), paraphrasing St. Alphonsus Liguori

Notes

[1] Published in an interview with ZENIT News Agency (December 21, 2002).

[2] Brian Kolodiejchuk, M.C., *"Mother Teresa: Come Be My Light"* (New York: Doubleday, 2007), p. 44.

[3] Ibid. p. 40.

[4] Much of the content of these paragraphs is adapted from an article published by the Gale Group, shortly after Mother Teresa's death. Printed in *National Catholic Reporter* (November 21, 2003).

[5] Ibid.

[6] Ibid.

[7] Dominique LaPierre, *The City of Joy* (New York: Grand Central Publishing, 1990), p. 46.

[8] Mother Teresa's letter to the M.C. Sisters (July 31, 1996).

[9] As cited in http://en.wikipedia.org/wiki/Darjeeling_Himalayan_Railway.

[10] Mother Teresa's letters to the M.C. Sisters (April 24, 1996).

[11] Ibid.

[12] As cited in www.americancatholic.org/Messenger/Oct2003/Feature1.asp#F6.

[13] Mother Teresa's letters to the M.C. Sisters (April 24, 1996).

[14] Pope Benedict XVI, Angelus meditation (February 24, 2008); emphasis added.

[15] Kolodiejchuk, *Mother Teresa: Come Be My Light*, p. 1.

[16] Mother Teresa's letters to the M.C. Sisters (April 24, 1996).

[17] Pope John Paul II (September 18, 1992).

[18] Mother Teresa's letters to the M.C. Sisters (April 24, 1996).

[19] Kolodiejchuk, *Mother Teresa: Come Be My Light*, p. 77.

[20] Ibid., p. 98.

[21] Mother Teresa's Instructions to the M.C. Sisters (June 22, 1981).

[22] Kolodiejchuk, *Mother Teresa: Come Be My Light*, p. 1.

[23] Mother Teresa's Instructions to the M.C. Sisters (January 16, 1983).

[24] Peter G. Van Breemen, *The God Who Won't Let Go* (Notre Dame, IN: Ave Maria Press, 2001).

[25] Mother Teresa's Instructions to the M.C. Sisters (January 16, 1983).

[26] Pope Paul VI, apostolic exhortation *Evangeli Nuntiandi*, n. 21; emphasis added.

[27] Father Sebastian, M.C., as cited in americancatholic.org/Messenger/Sep2004/feature2.asp.

[28] St. Augustine, *De Trinitate*, VIII, 8, 12: CCL 50, 287.

[29] Kolodiejchuk, *Mother Teresa: Come Be My Light*, p. 77.

[30] Brian Kolodiejchuk, M.C., "The Soul of Mother Teresa: Hidden Aspects of Her Interior Life" (Part 2) (ZENIT News Agency, 2002).

[31] Mother Teresa's letters to the M.C. Sisters (October 10, 1988).

[32] Kolodiejchuk, *Mother Teresa: Come Be My Light*, p. 99.

[33] Ibid. p. 99.

[34] Ibid., p. 77.

[35] St. Catherine of Siena, First Letter to Pope Gregory XI (1375).

[36] Cited in Brennan Manning, *The Relentless Tenderness of Jesus* (Grand Rapids, MI: Revell, 2004), p.12.

[37] "God's passionate love for his people," in Pope Benedict XVI, encyclical letter *Deus Caritas Est*, n. 10.

[38] Mother Teresa's Instructions to the M.C. Sisters (February 1994).

[39] Mother Teresa's letters to the M.C. Sisters (April 1, 1988).

[40] Kolodiejchuk, *Mother Teresa: Come Be My Light*, p. 41.

[41] As cited in http://aboverubiesandpearls.blogspot.com/2008/05/im-little-pencil-in-hand-of-writing-god.html.

[42] Some of the ideas in this paragraph are inspired by material in *Peter Calvay — Hermit*, by Rayner Torkington (Victoria, Australia: Spectrum Publications, 1977).

[43] Mother Teresa, *No Greater Love* (Novato, CA: New World Library, 2003), pp.59-60.

[44] Pope Benedict XVI, encyclical letter *Deus Caritas Est*, n. 10.

[45] James Burtschaell.

[46] Mother Teresa's Instructions to the M.C. Sisters (April 1980); Mother Teresa's Instructions to the M.C. Sisters (February 1994).

[47] Mother Teresa's "Varanasi Letter" (March 25, 1993).

[48] Mother Teresa's Easter message (1997).

[49] François Varillon, *L'humilite de Dieu* (Paris: Centurion, 1974).

[50] Ibid.

[51] Ibid.

[52] Literally, "Father with a womb of Tenderness."

[53] Pope Benedict XVI, Message for Lent (2007).

[54] Ibid.

[55] Origen, *Homélies sur Ezéchiel*, 6:6.

[56] Henri de Lubac, *Histoire et Esprit*, 1950, pp. 241-243.

[57] St. Augustine, *Treatise on John*, CCL 36: 154-156.

[58] Pope Benedict XVI, Message for Lent (2007).

[59] St. John of the Cross, *Spiritual Canticle*, 8.

[60] Mother Teresa's Instructions to the M.C. Sisters (January 1992).

[61] Mother Teresa's Instructions to the M.C. Sisters (December 10, 1981).

[62] Mother Teresa, *No Greater Love*, p. 93.

[63] Ibid., p.57.

[64] Brennan Manning, *The Wisdom of Tenderness* (New York: Harper Collins, 2002), p.29.

[65] Mother Teresa's letters to the M.C. Sisters (March 6, 1992)

[66] Mother Teresa, *No Greater Love*, p.24.

[67] Manning, *The Relentless Tenderness of Jesus*.

[68] Stephen Cottrell.

[69] Mother Teresa's Instructions to the M.C. Sisters (August 8, 1994).

[70] Pope Benedict XVI, Message for Lent (2007).

[71] Mother Teresa's Instructions to the M.C. Sisters (February 1994).

[72] Explanation of the Original Rule.

[73] Mother Teresa's Letters to the M.C. Sisters (May 11, 1994)

[74] Mother Teresa's Instructions to the M.C. Sisters (February 1980).

[75] Excerpt from Mother Teresa's letters to M.C. Sisters (April 8, 1977), paraphrasing St. Alphonsus Liguori.

[76] Mother Teresa's Instructions to the M.C. Sisters (May 21, 1986).

[77] As cited in http://www.ewtn.com/MotherTeresa/words.htm.

[78] Kolodiejchuk, *Mother Teresa: Come Be My Light*, p. 96.

[79] Ibid., p. 97.

[80] Ibid., p. 98.

[81] Ibid., p. 99.

[82] Ibid., pp. 99-100.

[83] As cited in EWTN.com (http://www.ewtn.com/motherteresa/words. htm).

[84] Eileen Egan, *Such a Vision of the Street* (New York: Doubleday, 1985).

[85] Mother Teresa's Instructions to the M.C. Sisters (May 21, 1982).

[86] Kolodiejchuk, *Mother Teresa: Come Be My Light*, p. 48

[87] Donna G. McMaster, "Mother Teresa's Lasting Influence," http://www.cuf.org/Laywitness/LWonline/mj08mcmaster.asp.

[88] Letter of Mother Teresa (October 3, 1990).

[89] Mother Teresa's letters to the M.C. Sisters (April 24, 1996).

[90] Pope John Paul II, Angelus meditation (September 7, 1997).

[91] Mother Teresa's Instructions to the M.C. Sisters (February 1994).

[92] Mother Teresa's Instructions to the M.C. Sisters (December 1, 1983).

[93] Mother Teresa's Instructions to the M.C. Sisters (February 1994).

[94] Mother Teresa, *Mother Teresa: In My Own Words*, compiled by José Luis González-Balado (New York: Gramercy Books, 1997), p 5.

[95] As cited in http://aboverubiesandpearls.blogspot.com/2008/05/im-little-pencil-in-hand-of-writing-god.html.

[96] Mother Teresa's Instructions to the M.C. Sisters (1994).

[97] Mother Teresa's Instructions to the M.C. Sisters (September 1, 1990).

[98] Mother Teresa's letters to the M.C. Sisters (August 6, 1970).

[99] Mother Teresa's letters to the M.C. Sisters (April 24, 1996).

[100] As cited in http://www.centeringprayer.com/fruits/fruits01.htm.

[101] St. John of the Cross, *Spiritual Canticle*; stanza 1; emphasis added.

[102] Torkington, *Peter Calvay — Hermit*, p. 41.

[103] Ideas in this section are inspired by Torkington's *Peter Calvay — Hermit*.

[104] Mother Teresa, *No Greater Love*.

[105] Torkington, *Peter Calvay — Hermit*, p 52.

[106] Mother Teresa's Instructions to the M.C. Sisters (February 1994).

[107] Mother Teresa's letters to the M.C. Sisters (February 18, 1967).

[108] Mother Teresa's speech, Prayer for Peace, London (July 7. 1981).

[109] Mother Teresa's Instructions to the M.C. Sisters (November 20, 1979).

[110] Mother Teresa's letters to the M.C. Sisters (February 18, 1967).

[111] Brother Angelo Devananda, *Mother Teresa Contemplative at the Heart of the World* (Ann Arbor, MI: Servant Publications, 1985) p. 59.

[112] Mother Teresa's letters to the M.C. Sisters (December 27, 1963).

[113] Mother Teresa's letters to the M.C. Sisters (September 29, 1981).

[114] Mother Teresa's letters to the M.C. Sisters (October 11, 1968).

[115] Spiritual Directory of the Missionaries of Charity Sisters.

[116] Paul DeBlassie III, *Deep Prayer: Healing for the Hurting Soul* (New York: Crossroad Publishing Company, 1990), p.1.

[117] Mother Teresa's Instructions to the M.C. Sisters (June 19, 1978).

[118] *Catechism of the Catholic Church*, n. 2561, with this note at the end of the text: cf. Jn 7:37-39, 19:28; Is 12:3, 51:1; Zech 12:10, 13:1.

[119] *Catechism of the Catholic Church*, n. 2560.

[120] Excerpt from Mother Teresa's letters to the M.C. Sisters (December 27, 1963), paraphrasing Abbe Gaston Courtois.

[121] Mother Teresa's Instructions to the M.C. Sisters (1984).

[122] See Kolodiejchuk, *Mother Teresa: Come Be My Light.*

[123] Pope John Paul II, General Audience (November 30, 1988).

[124] See *La Noche Oscura* in *Complete Works of John of the Cross* (Washington, DC: ICS Publications, 1979).

[125] Kolodiejchuk, *Mother Teresa: Come Be My Light*, p. 1.

[126] St. Ignatius of Loyola.

[127] Mother Teresa's Instructions to the M.C. Sisters (February 20, 1989).

[128] Suggested by Rev. Michael Keating.

[129] DeBlassie, *Deep Prayer: Healing for the Hurting Soul*, p. 9.

[130] Ibid., pp. 9-10.

[131] Kolodiejchuk, *Mother Teresa: Come Be My Light*, p. 48.

[132] Mother Teresa's Instructions to the M.C. Sisters (April 16, 1981).

[133] William A. Barry, S.J., *Finding God in All Things* (Notre Dame, IN: Ave Maria Press, 1991), pp. 40-41.

[134] Curtis Almquist, S.S.J.E., *God's Desire; Our Desire.*

[135] Mother Teresa's letters to the M.C. Sisters (July 29, 1993).

[136] Mother Teresa, Message to Youth in Dallas (May 23, 1992).

[137] St. Augustine, in *De diversis quaes*, 64, 4: PL.40, 56; and St. Gregory Nanzianzen, in *Orationes*, 40, 27: SC 358, 260.

[138] Pope Benedict XVI, General Audience (August 22, 2007).

[139] Asansol is a town, about 175 miles north of Calcutta, where a Loreto convent was located. Mother Teresa was assigned there from January to July of 1947.

[140] Kolodiejchuk, *Mother Teresa: Come Be My Light*, p. 84.

[141] Ibid., p. 169.

[142] Ibid., p. 193.

[143] Ibid., p. 203.

[144] Mother Teresa's Instructions to the M.C. Sisters (December 7, 1982).

[145] St. Thérèse of Lisieux, *Story of a Soul: The Autobiography of St. Thérèse of Lisieux*, trans. John Clarke (Washington, DC: ICS Publications, 1976), p. 99.

[146] *Catechism of the Catholic Church*, n. 2560, with this note at the end of the text: cf. St. Augustine, *De diversis quaestionibus octoginta tribus* 64, 4: PL 40, 56.

[147] Is 10:11.

[148] Mother Teresa's Instructions to the M.C. Sisters (December 9, 1981).

[149] Mother Teresa, Night of Prayer for Peace, London; the text of this speech is included in Mother Teresa's Instructions to the M.C. Sisters (October 31, 1982).

[150] Mother Teresa's Instructions to the M.C. Sisters (June 2, 1981).

[151] St. John of the Cross, Explanation of Stanza 28, part 8.

[152] Susan Conroy, *Mother Teresa's Lessons of Love & Secrets of Sanctity* (Huntington, IN: Our Sunday Visitor, 2003), p. 158.

[153] Ibid, pg 10.

[154] Excerpts are taken from http://sanmigmol.blogspot.com/2004/09/love-me-as-you-are.html and *The Book of Catholic Wisdom: 2000 Years of Spiritual Writing*, Teresa De Bertodano (Chicago: Loyola Press, 2001), p. 247.

[155] Mother Teresa's Instructions to the M.C. Sisters (June 30, 1997).

[156] Portions of the Conclusion are from a homily delivered by the author in Mother House, Calcutta, on the anniversary of Inspiration Day, September 10, 1997.

[157] Mother Teresa's speech at Synod of Bishops, October 1994, and at the National Prayer Breakfast, Washington, DC.

[158] Mother Teresa's Instructions to the M.C. Sisters (February 1994).

[159] Raymond Brown. See examples in Ps. 42, 63, 143, etc.

[160] Gerhard Kittel, *Theological Dictionary of the New Testament, Volume VI* (Grand Rapids, MI: Wm. B. Eerdmans Publishing Co., 1964), pg. 226.

[161] Ellen G. White, *The Story of Patriarchs and Prophets* (www. whiteestate.org/books/pp/pp.asp), p. 412.

[162] Ibid.

[163] Pope John Paul II, encyclical letter *Dives in Misericordia*, n.3

[164] St. Augustine, *De diversis quaes.* 64, 4: PL.40, 56.

[165] Ibid.

[166] St. Augustine, *Treatise on John*, CCL 36: 154-156.

[167] St. Bonaventure, *Breviloquium* 1, 2; *Itinerarium* 6; *De Mysterio Trinitatis* I, 2; cf. *DeV* 37.3.

[168] St. Bernard of Clairvaux, as quoted in Missionaries of Charity Fathers' *Charism Statement*, Tijuana (1990).

[169] St. Thomas Aquinas, *In Jo. xix. Lect. 5.*

[170] St. Robert Bellarmine, *The Seven Words Spoken by Christ*, ch. 9.

[171] St. Catherine of Siena, Letter 37, to Bishop Angelo Ricasoli, at Florence (1375).

[172] Ibid.

[173] St. Catherine of Siena, Letter 66, to Abbot Giovanni di Gano da Orvieto.

[174] St. Thérèse de Lisieux, *Manuscrits Autobiographiques*, MA.

[175] Ibid. MB.

[176] St. Laurence Justinian, De tr. Chr. Ag. C. 19.

[177] St. Alphonsus Liguori, "Passion and Death of Jesus Christ," p. 213.

[178] Sister Mary of the Trinity, *Writings of Sr. Mary of the Trinity*, no. 231.

[179] Blessed Julian of Norwich, *Showings*, 31.

[180] Mother Catherine Aurelie, quoted in *The Magnificat* (July 1963).

[181] Archbishop Fulton Sheen, *The Greatest Calling*, p.13.

[182] Pope Benedict XVI, Angelus meditation (February 24, 2008).

Author's Acknowledgments

This book could never have become a reality without the help and support of so many.

My heartfelt thanks go first of all to my mother for her encouragement and prayers over the many years of preparation of this manuscript. From the first scattered attempts to record Mother Teresa's insights for a broader public, she was an enthusiastic supporter. Without you, Mom, neither book nor author would have made it through the long process of gestation.

My deepest gratitude also, and obviously, to Mother Teresa herself, for much love and many lights she afforded me over the years. May these pages, my small attempt to pay forward what I have so generously received, be the beginning of my thank you.

My thanks also to the members of her community, the *Missionaries of Charity* around the world — Sisters, Brothers, and Fathers, actives and contemplatives — who have prayed for me and this project, and supported me in countless ways over these decades of following Mother Teresa in their company. A particular thanks to Father Bob Conroy, M.C., superior of the M.C. Fathers, for backing the project from its inception, and to all my community Brothers here in Tijuana, for generously affording me the time to complete this manuscript.

Thanks to Bridget Leonard, my very capable and creative literary agent, and sincere devotee of Mother Teresa's message. She has gone the extra mile from the beginning with ideas and resources for the manuscript. Thanks to Greg Erlandson, president of Our Sunday Visitor Publishing; Beth McNamara, editorial director; John Christensen, marketing director; and the entire OSV team for their belief in this project.

My gratitude to my insightful and patient editor, Rev. Michael Keating of St. Thomas University, Minnesota, especially for his structural suggestions and his help to make Mother Teresa's many-faceted message more understandable and accessible. A word of thanks, also, to professor Bill Snyder of St. Vincent's College, Latrobe, Pennsylvania, for going over the final edit page by page; and to Jim Towey, president of the college and great friend of the author and of Mother Teresa, for arranging my time at St. Vincent's to complete the final stages of the book.

Special thanks to Father Brian Kolodiejchuk, M.C., postulator of Mother Teresa's Cause of Canonization and director of the Mother Teresa Center (and my Brother in community), as well as to the Sisters of the staff, for their kind assistance in searching out the references to Mother Teresa's quotes, and for permission for their use.

Finally, my thanks to the reader — since, ultimately, this book is for you — for investing your time, and for opening your mind and heart to the message shared in these pages. There is still so much to say, so many riches in the mystery of God's longing — may this small effort be the beginning of an adventure of grace that carries through this life and into the next.

Publisher's Acknowledgments

Unless otherwise noted, the Scripture citations used in this work (with emphasis added in some passages) are taken from the *Second Catholic Edition of the Revised Standard Version of the Bible* (RSV), copyright © 1965, 1966, and 2006 by the Division of Christian Education of the National Council of the Churches of Christ in the United States of America. Used by permission. All rights reserved.

Where noted, some Scripture citations are taken from the *Catholic Edition of the New Revised Standard Version of the Bible* (NRSV), copyright © 1989 and 1993 by the Division of Christian Education of the National Council of the Churches of Christ in the United States of America. Used by permission. All rights reserved.

English translation of the *Catechism of the Catholic Church* for the United States of America copyright © 1994, United States Catholic Conference, Inc. — Libreria Editrice Vaticana. English translation of the *Catechism of the Catholic Church: Modifications from the Editio Typica* copyright © 1997, United States Catholic Conference, Inc. — Libreria Editrice Vaticana.

English translations of papal documents and other Vatican documents are from the Vatican website, www.vatican.va.

Reader's Notes